ACTIVITY METHODS
for Children Under Eight

ACTIVITY METHODS
for
Children Under Eight

by

Marion Anderson
E. R. Boyce
Margaret Bradley
N. Clarke
C. E. Cooke
Dorothy Davis
Lucy Diamond
Dorothea Fleming
A. N. Gillett
Muriel Green
Kathleen Melzi
Jean Murray
Barbara Priestman
Kathleen Rich
Phyllis Rolfe
Mary D. Sheridan
Barbara V. R. Smith
Elsa Walters
E. Yanovsky

With a
FOREWORD
by
Lillian de Lissa

EVANS BROTHERS LIMITED

Published by Evans Brothers Limited
Montague House, Russell Square, London, W.C.1

First published 1950
Tenth impression 1969

PRINTED IN GREAT BRITAIN BY
MORRISON AND GIBB LIMITED, LONDON AND EDINBURGH

237 28001 9 PR 4895

THE CONTRIBUTORS

MISS MARION ANDERSON, L.R.A.M. Formerly Music Mistress, Northgate Grammar School for Girls, Ipswich. Author of *Playtime Tunes for the Nursery School*, *Rhythmic Work from Nursery to Senior School*, etc.

MISS E. R. BOYCE. Formerly Headmistress of a London Infant School, and H.M.I. Author of *Play in the Infant School*, *Infant School Activities*, etc.

MISS MARGARET BRADLEY, N.F.F. Vice-Principal of Homerton College, Cambridge.

MISS N. CLARKE. Headmistress, Imperial Avenue Infant School, Leicester.

MISS C. E. COOKE. Senior Woman Organizer of Physical Education, Bristol Education Committee.

MISS DOROTHY DAVIS. Lecturer, Trent Park Training College; formerly Headmistress of an Ealing Infant School.

MISS LILLIAN DE LISSA. Formerly Principal, Gipsy Hill Training College. Author of *Life in the Nursery School*.

MISS LUCY DIAMOND. Formerly Headmistress of a Leicester Infant School. Author of *How the Gospel came to Britain*, *When He was just a little child*, etc.

MISS DOROTHEA FLEMING. Advisory Officer, Nursery and Infant Schools, Leicestershire County Council.

MR. A. N. GILLETT, M.A., B.SC. Vice-President, Birmingham and District Federation of Parent-Teacher Associations.

MRS. MURIEL GREEN. Formerly teacher at Oakwood Collegiate School.

MISS KATHLEEN MELZI, A.R.C.A. Lecturer in Art, Homerton College, Cambridge.

MISS JEAN MURRAY, B.SC. Lecturer, Matlock Training College.

MISS O. B. PRIESTMAN, B.A. Principal, Froebel Institute Demonstration School, Roehampton.

MISS KATHLEEN RICH, B.A.(LONDON). Formerly Headmistress, Old Road Infant and Junior School, Chesterfield.

MISS P. M. ROLFE, L.R.A.M.(ELEC.). Inspector of Primary and Nursery Schools, Somerset.

DR. MARY D. SHERIDAN, M.A., M.D., D.C.H. Lecturer in School Hygiene, Mount Pleasant Training College, Liverpool; formerly S.M.O., Manchester.

THE CONTRIBUTORS

MISS BARBARA V. R. SMITH. Formerly Headmistress of a Rural School.

MISS ELSA WALTERS, B.A., PH.D. Lecturer in Education, Froebel Educational Institute, Roehampton.

MISS E. YANOVSKY. Lecturer for The Children's Council of the C. of E. Council for Education.

Editor : CONSTANCE STURMEY, N.F.F.
Editor of *Child Education*.

EDITOR'S NOTE

THIS book has been planned to assist the many teachers of young children who are desirous of introducing freer methods into their schools and classes.

Teachers who have been using more formal methods rightly hesitate to change over to activity methods before fully understanding their underlying principles ; and even then realize the importance of careful organization and planning.

In this book the theory and practice of activity methods are described by specialists and teachers who are running their schools successfully on the new lines. Descriptions of activities in various types of schools are not, of course, intended as schemes to be copied (which would be a negation of the principles involved) but are included as helpful illustration of the working out of these methods under widely differing conditions.

For those teachers who are unable, for various reasons, to discard formal methods entirely, suggestions are made for the use of the activity approach in modified form. Here again, outline programmes of work have been included in illustration.

The final section reviews in outline the work that normally should be covered by the under-eights, and may usefully serve as a guide to teachers in Nursery and Infant Schools.

Some repetition, especially concerning fundamental principles, is inevitable in a work of this kind where, for greater facility of reference, the subject under discussion is considered independently in each section.

Grateful acknowledgment is made to Miss Lillian de Lissa for her interest in this project, to Miss Dorothea Fleming for valuable suggestions and helpful criticism, and to the many other educationists who have so willingly assisted in the preparation of this book.

ACKNOWLEDGMENTS

FOR kind permission to reproduce the photographs following pages 64 and 80 acknowledgment is made to :

Middlesex County Council and Tottenham Divisional Executive,
Ealing Education Committee,
Miss Edith Cooper, Burleigh Road Infant School,
W. Escott, Esq., Cotham Studio, Bristol.

All photographs following pages 144 and 160 are reproduced by kind permission of Dr. A. L. Smallwood and Miss C. E. Cooke.

To Mr. A. A. Milne, for kind permission to reproduce on page 161 the verse from *The House at Pooh Corner* (Messrs. Methuen).

W. Hacott, Esq., Corbian Studio, Bristol.

CONTENTS

PART THREE

THE RELIGIOUS TRAINING OF YOUNG CHILDREN

PART FOUR

THE PHYSICAL NEEDS OF YOUNG CHILDREN

PART FIVE

SUBJECTS AND SKILLS IN RELATION TO ACTIVITIES

FOREWORD

by LILLIAN DE LISSA

THE second world war and all that has emerged from it has left the nations confronted with one of the greatest tasks that ever fell to humanity. If man is to survive he must build a new world order which will be secure and free from the evils that brought the old world crumbling to earth. In planning this better order, the part played by education and the forms it should take are vital factors. A nation's system of education is the source of its power and inspiration. The contribution that men and women are able to make to the enrichment of national and international life depends upon the nature of the education they have received and on the outlook, wisdom, and character it has developed in them.

This book is concerned with early stages in this important task, which can either give strength and stability to the whole, or so weaken it that the hopes on which the nation's heart is set can never be realized. A great charge, therefore, rests upon teachers of young children. They are responsible for a stage of life in which the child is forming his ideals and his attitude towards life and his fellow men, when habits of thought and feeling are being established and the pattern of personality is taking shape. It is no longer a matter for speculation, but is known positively, that impressions gained in these early formative years have far-reaching influence for good or ill on subsequent development. The quality of education at this stage is therefore of deep significance. All teachers, and perhaps especially teachers of young children, are concerned, as Dewey has pointed out, not merely with the making of men but with the making of nations. Undoubtedly theirs is a task that should not be undertaken except with a true sense of vocation.

Old-time teaching methods in which children were taken by the teacher step by step along a set path and taught, trained, and drilled *en masse* at every move, are dying a natural death. From experiment and research, conviction has been born that, given suitable conditions and wise guidance, the child is his own best educator. As a consequence, here and there a new type of school has come into being in which the 'sit-stillery' of yesterday is replaced by active and full living in a democratic community.

The nature and purpose of education in Nursery and Infant Schools can be understood only if considered in relation to the developmental needs of the children for whom it is designed.

Therefore a brief summary of the changes that come about between two and seven years of age should serve as a useful introduction to the various chapters that follow.

The Physical Growth of the Young Child

In the years that lie between birth and childhood, the young human being grows and changes so much that the difference between the helplessness of a newborn infant and the sturdy independence of the average seven-year-old is greater than that occurring during any other seven years of life. Teachers are not directly concerned with the years under two, but these years are of such importance and throw so much light on the nature of growth that every thoughtful teacher who wants to understand her children should make a study of this important period.

After the child learns to walk and talk and to attain, as a consequence, to a degree of psychological and physical independence, development proceeds very rapidly. He is ceaselessly busy and indulges in many kinds of experimental activities: running and walking, crawling and climbing, swinging and balancing and handling everything within reach. In all these acts he is spurred by a subconscious desire to establish neuro-muscular co-ordination and to gain control over his body with all its complex movements. He is, in fact, engaged in the early stages of his education and as it proceeds he progresses from the uncertain steps of the two-year-old, clutching his toys with two hands, to the fleetness, agility, and acrobatic skill of a seven-year-old with capacity for handling tools.

At five years of age the pace of growth is intensified and, as a consequence, the need for bodily movement is as insistent as in the years before five. Left to himself the child is rarely still and is busy exercising himself and developing ever-finer muscular co-ordination and control. In fact he continues, at a higher level, the physical education commenced as a toddler, discussed in the previous paragraph. If he is denied the opportunity for bodily movement and for manual manipulation that is so characteristic a feature of it, and is kept sitting still, the consequence is a *general retardation of all aspects of development.* Not only does he suffer from emotional frustration in having to dam back the impulsive desires so strongly urging him on; he remains physically illiterate, clumsy, and unco-ordinated, to a greater or lesser extent. This causes mental retardation for there is a close connection between psychological development and physical growth. A child's power of learning is not absolute; it is limited by physical structure and neuro-muscular co-ordination. Until the areas in the brain that control physical movement are well developed it is not possible for the centres concerned with thought and mental activity in general to function well. This is one of Nature's protective devices which education must respect. It is therefore of the utmost importance for children in the Infant School to have abundant opportunity for the varied forms of activity towards which each child is urged by inner compulsive drives.

The need for attention to bodily conditions in general is as great in the Infant School as in pre-school years. Periods of rapid growth (of which five to seven is one) carry with them their own dangers. As babyhood emerges into childhood the legs grow long, feet are enlarged in length and width, and the head becomes almost as big as it will ever be. Milk teeth are replaced by second and permanent teeth and the cutting of these teeth 'is often accompanied by nervous disturbances as significant as those of the first dentition.' (*Report of the Consultative Committee on Infant and Nursery Schools, Appendix 2.*) During these years the child is particularly susceptible to acute infection and fevers, such as whooping cough, measles, chicken-pox and diphtheria. The whole five years is a period in which the closest attention to physical growth and the conditions essential to ensure it is vital. His vigour and health, valuable in themselves, also exercise influence on the quality of both mental and emotional development, as has already been discussed. The open-air school, the meals and milk service, medical inspection and treatment and training in hygienic habits are therefore essential features of education at this age. Teachers, whose task it is to nurture all-round development, must be as intelligently concerned with the education of the body in health and strength as they are in teaching reading or number and they should co-operate wholeheartedly with the health services.

The Developing Intelligence

The impulse to be active and the nature of the child's activity cease to be purely physiological at quite an early age. A rapidly developing intelligence urges him towards experimental play. All he develops in skill and in knowledge of the nature of his material world, experiments lead on to construction and the child becomes increasingly interested in making and inventing things. At first he is satisfied with the crudest attempts, but his creations grow more realistic as fantasy, which plays a prominent part at three or four, gives place to a demand for real things and actual processes at six or seven. In watching play from two years of age upwards it is possible to note that the child whose play-material is suitable becomes, as the years progress, more critical of himself and his activities and shows increased ability to imagine, think and plan, to judge and to make decisions, to exercise initiative and to concentrate, and, in fact, to use his mind in all the ways characteristic of human intelligence. It is particularly interesting to note that the child does not have to be taught such things. They come about during the process of growth as naturally as learning to walk or the eruption of teeth. The teacher who understands the significance of natural development keeps in her place. She realizes that her part is that of co-operation with the child in his spontaneous impulse towards growth, helping him to become what he subconsciously seeks to be. She sees herself as the servant of life, and her first duty is to study the life she serves and provide conditions in which it can flourish.

Social and Emotional Development

While the child's body and mind are developing thus rapidly, he is also maturing in other respects, all of which are combined in the making of personality—provided his all-round growth is being nurtured. From the days when he clings to his mother or keeps close to his teacher, showing little interest in other people and occasionally hostility towards other children, there is steady progress and a widening of social interests. Step by step he approaches other people with trust and friendliness. He begins to enjoy the company of other children, playing first near them, then with them in a spirit of give and take, and he acquires increasingly a capacity for co-operative behaviour. The seven-year-old has his special friends, plays well for short periods with groups of children, and is ready for simple though not long-sustained team games. At the same time he is making progress in emotional stability when he is handled lovingly and wisely. He passes from the frequency of uncontrolled emotional outbursts characteristic of the two-year-old, who is often timid and is apt to be obstinate and rebellious when thwarted, to the trusting seven-year-old, self-controlled and self-confident, with a courageous attitude towards difficulties and sufficient trust in adults to co-operate with them freely and to be obedient to their demands.

In noting the gradualness of development between two and seven years of age it becomes clear that the child's interests and capacities increase in scope but remain essentially the same. Broadly speaking, he appears to be busy on two main tasks. He is discovering himself and his powers, gaining skill in movement and control over his body and his mind with its complex activity, and at the same time he is learning to express his thoughts and wishes in word and deed. He is also accumulating a wealth of information about the nature of the world in which he lives, both human and material, taking adventurous steps in the discovery of both and learning adaptation. By seven or eight he should have made enough progress in these tasks to have reached 'school maturity' as Charlotte Bühler calls it, and be ready to tackle all the demands of schooling.

'Growth-Centred' Schools

To anyone who knows young children it seems but common sense to keep their education substantially the same in method and approach—though naturally widening in scope—through the rapid growth of the first seven years. The purpose throughout should be to aid the child in the attainment of optimum all-round development and the co-ordination and unifying of all aspects of his personality. This, it is believed, can best be done when he is left free to follow his innate impulses and to develop his interests in an environment that provides both stimulus and control. Such teaching as is given must be devised to follow and assist the child and seek, not to standardize attainments in specific skills by a specified age, but rather to safeguard for each individual the opportunity to grow, to learn, and to develop skill in his own way and at his own pace, thus preserving and strengthening the uniqueness of his personality. This is only possible if the teacher knows every child in her group and knows him as a whole. It is not enough for her to see him only in school. She must be aware of the influences playing upon him in his home and neighbourhood and also his reaction to these influences. To acquire all this information requires time and trouble, but is well worth while. Without it the teacher's real care and education of the child can be little more than blind fumbling. This is the principle upon which the good Nursery Schools are organized, and valuable experiments have been undertaken in carrying these principles into the schools for older children. Where this has been done it has meant making a complete break with traditional methods of class teaching. Such schools cease to be merely learning shops. They become communities in which children live fully, freely, and joyously, and where each one is helped according to his need.

In setting up these schools, though much is required from the local authority, there is a great deal that the teacher can and must do to make them all they should be. Basically there must be a new approach to school planning both in regard to buildings and daily régime, for both must provide for all the activities appertaining to human living. With the introduction of school dinners, children now spend many hours on school premises and it is of the utmost importance that the *day as a whole*, as well as every part of it, should be of educational value to the child in the Infant department as it is in the Nursery School. Thus cloak- and toilet-rooms should be suitably equipped with hot and cold water, basins, mirrors, liquid soap and clean towels and should contain lockers for individual toilet requisites. The daily régime should include time for full use of these rooms, not only for the under-fives but throughout, and should lead to the cultivation of a permanently good attitude towards personal cleanliness and a care of communal property. There should be kitchen, servery, and dining-rooms, planned and equipped to enable children to take part in the preparing and serving of meals, and in washing, scrubbing, cleaning, and polishing. There should be a good library with books attractively bound and printed (including good picture-books) and it should be well set out in a pleasing room with comfortable chairs. There should be a large hall and indoor playrooms for wet weather. This is especially important for the midday break after dinner as well as for the usual play periods. There should be workshops well supplied with all kinds of material and tools, carpenters' benches, tables, and shelves ; rest-rooms with beds for little children and comfortable chairs and rugs for the older ones who also feel the need for times of relaxation in a day of activity, times which can be spent so happily listening to music, poetry, and stories. There is need, too, for ample cupboard space, both for storage of materials and for children's personal possessions. The traditional asphalt yard, barren and ugly, must go and its place be taken by real playgrounds generously supplied with see-saws, apparatus for climbing, swinging, and jumping and the other agility exercises enjoyed by six- and seven-year-olds, in addition to the jungle gyms, balancing-boards, and movable planks for the under-fives. There must be paved surfaces and grass plots and a well-stocked garden to be a source of aesthetic delight and nature knowledge. There must also be space for children's gardens, for paddling and bathing pools.

Though it is likely to be some time before all our Primary Schools are made fully adequate for the education they have to provide, the introduction of progressive methods need not be delayed. Past experience has shown what can be achieved by ingenious teachers with the pioneering spirit, despite poor buildings and inadequate equipment. Though no one would condone these unnecessary and hampering conditions, they need never become the excuse for the persistence of outworn methods. Whatever the setting, children should be encouraged to pursue their own self-directed activity, singly or in groups, as they themselves decide. Resourcefulness and knowledge, imaginative thinking and skill, increase daily and give the teacher her cue as common interests and group play arise spontaneously. From these beginnings she will lead children to more co-ordinated activities in the many ways discussed in this book. And in doing so she will introduce new ideas, stimulate the greater use of skill, read aloud stories and poetry, and show how the use of books can enrich the children's own efforts. In these ways she can feed the children's interests and encourage them to initiate and pursue wider fields of activity. This kind of education helps the child to acquire the habit of intelligent and purposeful action, attending to all he does. It accustoms him to work with other children easily and naturally and to co-operate with adults happily and wholeheartedly. It is an excellent introduction to the work he will have to do in the Junior School and a sound foundation for life.

The above description of the general needs of children between two and seven is not intended to imply that children of this age-range should necessarily be provided for in one school. There is a strong argument for the small Nursery School with its simplicity, iuformality, and homelike character, and such Nursery Schools should be found in all areas, where they would provide excellent centres for research. Nevertheless there is widespread belief in the wisdom of extending the amenities and arrangements usually associated with Nursery Schools beyond the age of five and avoiding any break either in the nature of the child's education or place of schooling until he himself leaves babyhood behind in becoming a child. This he does between seven and eight years of age. During the next few years there is likely to be considerable variety in school planning as is desirable until more is known about the real needs of children under seven. In cases where one school combines the entire range up to seven, special care will be needed in planning building and garden, and in administration, so as to protect the youngest children from the harmful effect of large numbers and the noise and bewilderment they create. Six- and seven-year-olds are too quick-moving and vigorous for the safety and comfort of two- and three-year-olds and though there should be contact between children of all ages the rooms and gardens should be so arranged that young children are never over-run by the older ones. Nor should the older children be hampered in their activity by young children whose speed of movement and interests are so different.

The transition from the informality of the nursery years to the more organized play and learning of the six- to seven-year-old calls for research. Not enough is yet known about the nature of growth and its relation to the capacity for both general and specific learning. Obviously this transition must be made gradually and it is likely to vary from child to child. This calls for great flexibility in planning and organization and much freedom for the children. Though in very early life Nature has her safeguards for protecting children from being taught or trained before they are neurologically ready to learn (as many experiments with babies have shown) the five- to seven-year-old is more plastic. His adaptability and the skilful way in which a capable teacher can exploit it leads to the erroneous assumption that the teaching and curriculum in the traditional Infant School are suitable and enjoyable to the children. It is believed that permanent harm is done by early forcing of special skills before the child is ripe to learn, such as 'doing sums' before there is understanding gained by practical experience of the processes involved, or being taught to read when this is merely sounds or words that have neither meaning nor purpose. Observation of children playing freely shows their play interests and their way of learning to be of a very different nature. In schools that wish to be thought progressive, it sometimes happens that the newer activity methods are used not, alas, to give the children the freedom of choice and the widened experience for which they were devised, but to chain them even more slavishly to the three R's by teacher-devised projects, adult ideas of playful ways of learning reading, writing, etc. For, truth to tell, many teachers do not believe children are being educated unless they are being trained in these skills ! So schools go on being 'three-R-centred,' however this may be disguised, instead of being growth-centred.

This book should encourage bolder action, as other publications on similar lines have already succeeded in doing. It should help to make all schools for children under eight alive and delightful, places of purposeful activity, adventure, and wide experience. They should be real children's lands. It should do much also to stimulate research and experiment as to the kind of teaching and learning really related to the development needs of children between two and seven years of age. Though research calls for specialized workers and conditions, useful experiments can be undertaken by any teacher who cares to tackle the problem thoughtfully and to keep careful records. It has been teachers in their day-to-day work in schools who have evolved the activity approach, and through it have enabled children to reveal their real interests and capability. Research workers with their special contribution have followed where these pioneering teachers have led. The teacher who would make a contribution must approach the subject with an open mind, seeking not to prove a theory but to discover truth. If teachers work in teams co-operatively their diverse approaches should provide very valuable material. Opportunity for such experiments is likely to be generous in the years ahead because of the variety of provision open to Education Authorities. If it is fully explored in the coming years when so much will be in a stage of transition, it should be possible to collect much that will inspire progressive development in the education of young children.

PART ONE

ACTIVITY METHODS DESCRIBED AND ILLUSTRATED

Chapter I

ACTIVITY METHODS AND THE CHILDREN WE TEACH

THERE has been considerable research in recent years on the development of young children and conclusions have been reached which have deep significance for the teachers of children at the Nursery and Infant stage. No longer do we regard the school as a rigid institution where children are grounded in the skills of reading, writing, and arithmetic, although this grounding will take place incidentally where play-way methods are in action.

Basically, it is important to see the child as a growing individual and to appreciate that the function of the good school is to set up an environment which will provide for the satisfactory all-round growth of each child. We now recognize that a child's development is four-sided and this means that the school must provide for his physical, intellectual, social, and emotional needs.

Physical Development

Physical development is fostered by the school medical services and by the provision of school meals, milk, orange juice, cod-liver oil, and the like, but there are other requirements. Growing children need ample space and frequent opportunity for movement and spontaneous play in addition to organized physical training. In many schools, teachers are today faced with the problem of inadequate space and this fact has been borne in mind in the chapters which follow. Suggestions are made showing how, even in overcrowded conditions, judicious planning will help to solve the problem in the interests of securing all-round growth. We should remember that up to the age of seven or eight, and probably well beyond these years, children need daily play with self-chosen and creative materials, especially the crude materials such as wood, sand, clay, water, paints, and scrap material, for free construction. It is important to keep in mind the physical limitations of each stage of development so that demands are not made on the finer muscles until they have matured through exercise in play. The close inter-relatedness of each aspect of growth is seen when one notes how in acquiring washing and toilet habits, serving meals, preparing for sleep and the like, the child gradually grows in personal independence, thereby gaining poise and confidence. When he passes into the

Infant department, at the age of five, the child's physical needs do not suddenly change, even though his material environment may afford less scope for movement. Many children will come straight from home at the age of five not having had the benefits which a good Nursery School affords, and these facts should be recognized and plans made to ensure that every facility is provided for physical growth. The numerous suggestions made in the chapters on activity programmes may help many teachers who hitherto have felt that their prime concern must of necessity be the children's grounding in the basic skills. Modern experience shows that speedy development in acquiring these skills is fostered where ample provision is made for purposive play as part of the daily routine.

Intellectual Development

Intellectual development is closely linked with, and related to, physical development. As he plays the child learns how to think, first in terms of activity and later, as he acquires command of language, he learns how to reason and to solve problems in his mind without the need for concrete material. During these early years the school must give adequate opportunity for the development of the mental processes. We accept it as a truism that the child learns by doing; hence we must see to it that the school environment gives full scope for development of initiative, curiosity, experimenting, and problem solving. Rich play experiences, and learning through free choice work, centres of interest, and activity programmes are the most likely ways to ensure that the young child will grow in ability to attend, to observe, to concentrate, and to remember, primarily because they appeal to his spontaneous interests. Readers will be able to trace this development in subsequent accounts of children's thought and behaviour as described by teachers who have experimented with these ways of learning in a variety of conditions. In the past there have been too many classrooms where time-table and methods were likely to cramp rather than to stimulate thought on the part of the children. Today the teacher who is alive to the need for fostering this side of the child's growth will be amply rewarded in watching how rapidly the thought processes develop, where there is opportunity created for them to do so. Experiment in activity schools shows that this holds in the case of dull children, as well as with those who are more gifted.

Emotional Development

On the emotional side the child grows in his ability to experience feelings and to express them, and later he learns to control them. The process of learning control and stability is slow and is very dependent on the child's environment. Again there is need to emphasize the value of play as affording an excellent outlet for emotional energy and the resolving of tense experiences. Thus the small child who experiences intense fear of dogs or of the coalman overcomes his fear, perhaps, by acting the role of dog or of the coalman in his play, thereby getting on top of the situation, as it were. A very real danger is that too often children are expected to conform to standards of behaviour which are impossible in view of their emotional immaturity, resulting in frustration and anxiety on the part of the child which in turn may lead to resentful and aggressive behaviour. Mature and understanding parents and teachers who know how to exercise patience and calm guidance can do much to assist emotional growth and can often prevent the development of serious behaviour problems.

Social Development

Closely related to emotional growth, and largely dependent on it, is the child's social development. The process whereby the child learns to adapt his behaviour to meet the demands of society is a gradual one, often involving conflict with his natural impulses. The programmes of modern Nursery and Infant Schools afford excellent opportunities for helping the child to develop socially, and every encouragement should be given to foster, but not to force, co-operative activity. It must be remembered that before he can be a useful and acceptable member of the group, the child must have acquired a certain degree of self-control, he must feel that he is wanted, and that he has a contribution to make to the group. The teacher's responsibility, therefore, lies primarily in helping each child to become self-reliant and independent, as these stages are pre-requisites for later participation in group activities. Small responsibilities, such as waiting at table, keeping the classrooms tidy, helping to feed and look after the school pets, will be joyfully undertaken. Such experiences have much value in that they are real-life situations for which the child sees the need, and in this way he develops the social consciousness which is essential for good citizenship at a later stage.

Basic Needs

If the growth of the whole child on the lines suggested above is to take place, each child must be assured of (*a*) security, (*b*) affection, and (*c*) opportunity for effort affording experience of achievement and suited to his stage of development.

Security

This implies more than the provision of adequate food, sleep, shelter, and clothing. The child needs mental and emotional security, the basis of which is a loving, harmonious, home background where both parents are ready and eager to share responsibility for their children, and a happy, working relationship between home and school. A degree of discipline is necessary for security. The child must be aware of the standards expected of him and there should be complete consistency in the attitude of home and school. Quarrelsome parents, inconsistency, nagging, all detract from a sense of security, making the child anxious and irritable, and often leading to disturbing behaviour problems.

Affection

The child's environment is in large measure made up by the people who surround him, and it is they who determine whether or not his feelings grow along desirable lines.

It should also be the heritage of every child to know and feel that he is loved and wanted. Pampering and spoiling are the outcome of perverted affection and are likely to produce unhappy and uncontrolled children. Both parents and teachers carry a responsibility in this matter, for the far-reaching effects of the child's early experiences of affection or the lack of it cannot be over-emphasized. In this connection we do well to remember that where a reprimand for undesirable behaviour has to be made, words should be carefully chosen so that the disapproval is directed towards the actual behaviour rather than towards the child. The same procedure might well be extended to older children whose need of affection is equally strong, especially at times when they know they have misbehaved. It is at such times that the child's own quiet feelings (whether these are apparent or not) may give rise to disturbing fears that he may lose the love of the disapproving adult. A little calm reassurance, especially when he has been particularly naughty, will often work wonders, whereas threats or even suggestions of an opposite nature will almost certainly result in further difficult behaviour.

Effort and Achievement

All children need opportunities for activity which will call forth effort and result in the experiencing of success and achievement. To meet this need we must be aware of the potentialities of the child at each stage of development and care must be taken not to expect performances which the individual child cannot possibly achieve. Too often his parents may nurture ambitions which cannot be reached, due to the child's immature stage of growth or to his limited endowment. All such problems should be met by the closest relationship and understanding between parents and teachers, so that progress, however slow, is fostered by an encouraging attitude in the home and at school. Happiness and sound mental health are of prime importance and it is well to realize that the child who feels inferior, who is beginning to regard himself as a failure, is well on the way to a state of maladjustment and is in immediate need of understanding treatment.

Individual Differences : Measurement of Intelligence

A fundamental principle underlying all modern methods of teaching is the recognition of individual differences among children. With the majority of children we find that their stage of all-round development is in line with their chronological age. There will always, however, be a certain number in any group who are in advance of, or behind, the stage normal for their age. Some children may be advanced in one direction and lag in another. Thus a five-year-old may have a mental age of six years, while on the emotional side his behaviour may be more in keeping with that of a four-year-old. Such variations demand understanding and insight if the school is to cater for each child according to his needs.

Most teachers are now familiar with the idea of individual variations in intelligence and the problems these variations present in teaching large classes. It is for this reason that some knowledge of intelligence, and the methods of measuring it, is desirable for all teachers if serious effort is to be made to ensure that each child is to develop to his fullest capacity. A more detailed account of this topic will be found in Appendix I.

The Attitude of the Teacher in Approaching New Methods

Teachers who study this book will soon discover that a careful aim has been pursued in compiling it : namely that of preserving a harmonious balance between presentation of theory and practice. Some chapters are concerned with straightforward considerations of children's growth and their corresponding needs based on the findings of experts in the study of child development. Other chapters are given over to detailed accounts by individual teachers of their experiences in working some of these newer methods with their own children. In part the accounts are descriptive ; largely, they concentrate on how children develop in a classroom environment which is set up with the sole aim of meeting their needs at different stages. It should be remembered, however, that the working programmes described are not of mushroom growth ; the teachers who have contributed their own and their children's experiences have had to move very gradually before their ' activity ' classrooms were working realities.

Some readers who for a variety of reasons have, perhaps, clung so far to the older, more formal methods, may, after perusing these articles, find their attitude altered and feel the urge to introduce some of the newer type of programmes into their schools. The initial attitude of teachers who are thus inclined should be one of readiness to ' hasten slowly.' This is essential if the children's need for security is to be preserved. Too much in the way of sudden change can seriously upset small children; behaviour problems are likely to result, and enthusiastic teachers who rush at transforming a formal classroom may be overwhelmed and come to a hasty decision that formal methods are safest! Such an attitude would be regrettable, and a little judicious planning can avert such a situation.

Essentially, the teacher herself must feel secure and confident in her experiments and this involves from the start an understanding of underlying principles; the reason *why*, in the interests of the children, each change is made.

Changes in routine or activity should be introduced singly or a few at a time; one day the Wendy House or Play Corner with a few dressing-up clothes may be set up, and perhaps simultaneously the Book Corner, with free access to picture-books; next week a table for free construction work with scrap material: cardboard boxes, cotton reels, and glue; presently the nature table, on which exhibits must be kept fresh and living creatures carefully tended; later, water play, painting, clay, and other activities. Naturally, during the introductory stages, all the children will want to be occupied with the new activities. Quiet insistence on ' turns ' must be the rule; too many children round one activity can be disastrous, yet the imposing of sanctions, understood by the children, presents an easy solution. Only those children who co-operate and do not spoil the play of others are allowed to participate. Absolute fairness and impartiality must be the rule, and once promised, it is essential that the ' turns ' do materialize. Small children live in the present, so that long-distance promises should if possible be avoided.

It is wise to choose an auspicious day for the initial changes: the first day of the new term, the beginning of a week, or an individual child's birthday; and each new introduction can have its own little ceremony. The children may be gathered round, and behaviour rules for enjoying the new activity or routine are carefully enumerated, avoiding threats for non-co-operation, but stressing the pleasures in store for all who help to make it a success.

Knowledge of individual children's difficulties should be kept in mind and wisely catered for; for example, the strongly self-assertive child who may be given a special responsibility; the child who has not yet learned to be patient, and who should not be kept waiting too long for his turn. Gradually the new activities will be seen to help the difficult children as they not only afford release for pent-up energy and emotion, but also offer scope for giving small responsibilities, so badly needed by children who are troublesome, often because they have come to think of themselves as failures and having no contribution to make.

Once inaugurated, the wisdom of setting up and organizing the materials for the various activities before the children come in each day is no doubt self-evident, but some features, such as the setting up of the Nature Table or the new Book Corner, may very well be done ceremoniously in front of all the children, and with their help. They will no doubt treat the new materials with more care, just because of the special way in which their purpose was introduced to them. It seems unwise to lay down too many general rules, as each individual teacher must approach these newer methods in her own way, if the children are to derive real value from them, and if the harmony of the classroom community is to be preserved. Yet all have something to learn from those who are already practised in these ways of making the school child-centred; hence quiet study of the ensuing chapters, simultaneously attempting to translate them into terms of one's own school, will be well repaid.

Until the children and teacher grow used to the new methods, there will inevitably be minor difficulties. There will be more noise and happy chatter, and no doubt a less tidy classroom than in the past; perhaps odd spills, where the under-fives are experimenting in serving at table, or the older ones are watering the plants in the Nature Corner. Yet all such minor departures from the formal order of the past are actually healthy signs that the classroom is serving the children's growth needs. The mature teacher will remain calm, placid, and helpful during the experimental stages, considering any extra trouble involved as a small price to pay for the worth-while returns in the form of the children's development. In the Infant School the fuller type of activity programme may grow from the introduction, in the first place, of one period at the beginning of the day set aside for free choice work on the pattern outlined in succeeding chapters (see Chapters II, II and V, I). After such a period, it will be found that the children settle far more readily and satisfactorily to the more formal types of skill work. In time it will be found that the basic skills, especially the three R's, will often develop from the activity period. A group want to write a story about the train and railway station they are building; another group want to keep diaries of what is happening in the Nature Corner, or to do sums related to the business of the class shop or post office. Just because the children themselves see the need for it, the drill work in the tool subjects becomes more purposive and new effort and interest are given to it. Once a daily free choice period has been introduced, the teacher should be careful to keep some kind of record of each child's daily and weekly activities and achievements. She must select the right moment to invite a child to try a new activity which he has perhaps shunned for some weeks. Encouragement and patience and a readiness to wait, are necessary all the while. Care should be taken, however, to see that each child is progressing, not only in skill but in experimenting, with a variety of media. Plateau periods, as we may call the times when a child seems to make no obvious progress, are an inherent characteristic of learning, but, a richly inviting environment and the teacher's appropriate guidance at the right moment will almost certainly ensure that each child is going forward and mastering a variety of skills at his own pace.

Each teacher's own working conditions may impose limits on the reaches to which she may take the new methods. In one case the actual structure of the building may call for modification in the manner of working. In another case the teacher in a Rural School may have the demands of various age-groups to consider. To all in these categories it may be said with confidence that some experimentation, however modified, will be well repaid by the fact that the daily tasks take on a new colour when lifted out of the pedestrian groove of the old formal teaching, which makes arduous demands of the teacher and where so often the children appear to derive comparatively little from the outlay of effort. Perhaps the most helpful reassurance for the teacher about to experiment, but who is yet doubtful of how her aim is to be achieved, is to be found in Miss Boyce's book, *Play in the Infant School*. Here is the account of an experiment on freer lines which really starts from scratch. The conditions under which Miss Boyce and her team began could not well have been more difficult, yet the venture early met with success far beyond the dreams of those who tackled it. Difficulties were overcome and the experiment became an actuality to inspire all who would serve the needs of the children they teach.

Dorothea Fleming.

Chapter II

IN THE INFANT SCHOOL

I. THEORY AND PRACTICE OF ACTIVITY METHODS

In the preceding chapter we are reminded that educational research is constantly bringing fresh evidence which strengthens the belief that in action young children's natural interests cause them to grow in physical strength and control; in power to persist at a task, solve problems, and remember facts; in good feelings about themselves and towards life; in capacity to share others' interests and work.

Many teachers have for years recognized the implications of this belief and have attempted to base their work in schools more and more on natural activity. The main difficulty which confronts those who wish to adopt a more active type of programme is that no hard and fast rules of method can be laid down. Our knowledge of how to use children's impulses to self-education is still rudimentary, but the essence of successful activity work will always be the degree to which it sincerely expresses the children who engage in it. It is essentially flexible and refuses to conform in detail to any preconceived or fixed pattern of method.

It is necessary then that we should forego the comfort and security of nicely worked-out schemes, even when presented under such an acceptable name as centres of interest. We must be prepared to follow more adventurous paths and our first need is to study the broad principles from which main directions for activity work can be deduced. Then we must apply these principles faithfully and critically by sharing life and interests with the group of children for whom we are responsible.

This chapter will therefore first consider principles; then illustrate their working in an activity carried out by children, and finally give very general guiding lines for further work in schools.

The First Principle: Interest

Interest arises from the impact of what is outside upon our impulses. A sand pile in a Nursery Class will readily bring forth the curiosity of a child of three. He will handle the sand, bang it, mould it, and gradually his constructive tendency may cause him so to shape it that he recognizes what he has made. He will then name it: a cake. Next he calls for someone to pay attention to his prowess. During this period of play he will have shown what we call interest.

Similarly, a boy of eight is aroused by the gift of an aeroplane kit. Such is its effect on his inner nature that he separates its pieces, identifies them on the blue print, opens the tube of gum, weighs the balsa wood in his hands, turns to the sheet of directions and reads what he can make. There probably ensue periods of absorbed activity, continuous or erratic according to the boy's persistence, or his opportunities, or the availability of help, until he emerges successfully and his aeroplane takes the air masterfully.

A group of boys and girls between seven and eight years were recently taken to a farm not far distant from their town school. Their eager observation of the animals, their expression of protective feelings towards the young creatures, their dartings to and fro, their attempts at driving, all constituted the response of the innate urges to find out, to protect, and to master. These were spontaneous reactions to a new and provocative situation. Again, we call this response interest.

When, as teachers, we take trouble to discover or, if necessary, promote children's interests, when we join with children in working out such interests to satisfying conclusions, we may assume three main effects.

(i) *Attitude to Self*

The first effect is to be seen in the children's feelings towards themselves. On the whole, and of course varying from one child to another, where curiosity has been felt and has been satisfied in a sequence of activity, the result is a sense of fulfilment and well-being; similarly with the urges to construct, to be powerful, to protect. Hence a school programme based on activity, whose aim is the reaching of goals set by the children's interests, will help to bring about a state of happiness which includes self-confidence and a feeling of adequate power. Such feelings give rise not only to joyfulness but to restfulness. Conversely, such a programme will tend, as far as the children's school experience goes, to avoid feelings of frustration, anxiety, and inadequacy.

If we see such 'feelings about self' in the context of the external world, we shall no doubt recognize their importance. Our contemporary life fiercely challenges the individual through its dominant conflicts and inherent insecurity. Thus it forces on education the urgent responsibility for building such mental health in children that they will be armoured to meet the difficulties of such a world.

(ii) *Attitude to Life*

The second effect is observed in the children's attitude to life. If they have been encouraged to take the initiative, to experiment, to strive, and to persist until, say, the aeroplane flies, or the play is produced, then the elation born of a self-imposed task well done fosters a zest for life. Life appears worth while and this tends to increase further vigour of attack. Unconsciously, the effect of purposive activity is increased purposefulness.

Put this picture against the inertia of many children leaving school at fifteen and the lack of enterprise in many adult workers today and again, as teachers, we feel responsibility for the kind of attitudes to life our school programme sets up. We must think of this not only from the point of view of individual happiness but also of State efficiency.

(iii) *Attitude to Learning*

The third effect is on our children's learning in the more intellectual sense. As all teachers know, it is relatively easy to persuade young children to spend lengthy periods of practice in arithmetic and English for no further reasons than the appeal of gaining skill and the desire to please the teacher. It is, however, common knowledge that such motives work better for the brighter children. Even so, we must ask ourselves is there not a better way, one in which children are freed to a greater extent from the influence of the teacher, as far as the inclination to learn is concerned. When it is necessary to write a letter asking to visit a dairy, to calculate and enter bills in order to open shop, to measure accurately to make a rabbit hutch, then a new sort of willingness to learn creeps in, and with it a keener determination. This is to some extent independent of the teacher and shows learning as a reasonable means to an end. Further, with heightened determination comes heightened attention which makes for vividness and lastingness in learning.

Under the pressure of interest, children's desire for a high standard is also beneficially influenced. A teacher has many weapons with which to force her own standards on children. But how far does such external pressure really help to develop personal powers of judgment which are within the limits of the children's level of growth? The 'forcing' of standard leaves children exhausted and essentially lacking in interest when the energy of the teacher is removed. At the Infant stage, children have little ability to judge the quality of their work. The most teachers can do at this time is to allow the need for quality to come from the nature of the work itself. We must be satisfied with the standard each child can produce in answer to such demands. For example, the letter which is to bring an appeal to a real dairyman, the arithmetic which is to help us to be shopkeeper, the printing which is to produce an attractive wallpaper, the reading which tells us how to keep pets, all impose on children natural and inescapable levels of work. From striving for standards which are functional and from the inner growth of critical powers comes gradually a child's appreciation of quality as such.

Finally, when children are free to solve the problems with which purposive activity confronts them, the desire brings forth the full use of intelligence and tends, where necessary, to prolong the effort by which a solution is reached.

For example, faced by problems of making an electric milking-shed as part of a floor game showing the processes involved in preparing the milk they drank in school, children struggled experimentally until by trial and error they made a replica which in their eyes was convincing. The more real the problems tackled by young children, the more spontaneous and vigorous is the exercise of intelligence. And only by exercise can potential intelligence develop.

We see therefore some of the reasons underlying the first principle of activity work. The main justifications for basing children's work on their interests are to be found in their increased self-respect, love of life, purposefulness in learning, and application of intelligence to problems.

The Second Principle: Wholeness of Growth

Perhaps one of the most unsatisfactory things about the more formal type of Infant programme is that the children work individually and that little thought is given to their social development. During the Nursery years they have been encouraged, particularly through the natural contacts of the free choice period, very gradually to learn to control their self-seeking impulses. They have learned to relinquish physical attack as the chief means of solving social conflicts and are often heard making reasonable contracts in getting what they want; for example, "You have this pail and I will have this wheelbarrow." They have gradually adjusted and become able to share, to take turns, and even to play co-operatively in twos and threes for short periods. Also they have acquired some independence. Their free play has moreover helped them to assimilate the inevitable frustrations which such control involves. Aggression has been somewhat deflected to inanimate materials, for example, and release from the irksomeness of self-control has been obtained through the exercise of like discipline on dolls.

Normally, the five- to seven-year period is one of slowly increasing interest in one's fellows and of readiness to play together. Quite apart from the conviction of progressive educationists that school education must continuously develop all sides of personality, it is particularly imperative at this point in human history that the education of social attitudes and capacities is not neglected. It is clear that the hope of our tortured world lies in such co-operative undertakings as the United Nations, the World Food Council, and Unesco. While the social feelings and techniques which operate in the setting up and successful working of such organizations seem very far removed from the Infant School stage, yet it is an accepted fact that any gap in education will seriously retard the onset of maturity and, indeed, the ultimate level of maturity which is reached. Thus we cannot risk social immaturity in adults by failing to give social experience to children at the stages appropriate to it in their growth.

Given free opportunity, children from about six years onwards do begin to group naturally as the result of common interest. For example, Mr. and Mrs. Brown, two small dolls, called on a class of twenty-five six- to seven-year-olds and said the housing shortage was such that they could not find anywhere to live. Could the children possibly provide them with a furnished house? It was not long before most of the children wanted to do something about this, and although the strength of interest varied from child to child, each thought he would like to contribute. There followed inevitably a period of sustained planning in which the teacher acted as guide. The size of the house, the number of rooms, the furniture and decorations, the garden, had all to be considered. The question of what materials to use, and how to share the work had to be dealt with. Thus before any practical work could be started, considerable planning had to take place. Children had to put their ideas clearly, listen to each other's arguments, criticize suggestions, make decisions, foresee needs and think in terms of sharing work according to numbers and personal wishes.

The children helped in the provision of materials but relied on meticulous organization on the part of the teacher for the successful carrying out of the different kinds of group work. For example, those making furniture needed orderly placing of matchboxes, rectangles of solid wood, paper, seccotine, and paint; they also needed interesting examples of this type of furniture by way of inspiration. Those transforming a large sugar-box into the house needed floor space, tools, sand-paper, and paint. Further problems of co-operation arose in connection with relative size, uniformity of colour schemes within rooms, acceptable standard of work, which the children could not foresee. The need for instruction also arose in regard to such skills as stick-printing, potato-blocking, measuring wall and floor coverings, and using saws and planes. Other times were devoted to the types of plants to be grown in the garden and their cultivation.

When the house was ready for the Browns, a letter had to be sent. At this point, the children brought up the question of the price of the house. Their suggestions ranged from a fantastic £2,000 to a realistic 5s. which approximated to their expenditure. It was interesting to note that the children determined to find out the price of a pre-fabricated house, many of which were being assembled near the school. Even so they decided to charge 7s. 6d., which covered real costs and gave a little profit. The less mature children had clearly been influenced by the desire for reality typical of the more advanced ones. They chose that each should learn to write the business letter and the best one be sent to the Browns.

The final ceremony when a delighted and loudly appreciative Mr. and Mrs. Brown, arriving in a horse-drawn cart with personal possessions, moved into the house was one of keen joy for the children. Work will probably now develop around the Browns and the use of the 7s. 6d. provided by the teacher out of school funds.

From such an experience it can be seen that the children practised important social skills, such as group discussion, co-operative planning and work, social judgment, and leadership. The inherent satisfaction of the activity and the ultimate pleasure of result would be likely to encourage further co-operation.

The Third Principle: Experience

The first two principles of activity work are interest and wholeness. The third emerges from those two. Where the content of the school programme is governed by children's interests, there is an almost certain guarantee that it will be within their mental grasp. Under these conditions activities at the early stages of the Infant School will be mainly imitative of adult occupations, and materials used will be representative. For example, the articles in a shop will be dummy packets, fruits and vegetables made from plastic materials, and money from cardboard. The local bus will be built of chairs with paper frontage, conductor's equipment experimentally constructed or a play set, fares approximations, and journeys imaginary. At the later Infant stage, however, the intellectual need for reality will have increased, observation deepened, constructive skill improved and the capacity to see cause and effect slightly matured. Thus an interest in the market will lead to the making of realistic stalls, selling real goods such as small books made by the children, pots made from clay, fresh bunches of flowers and baskets of home-grown cress. Money will also be real or, at least, prices of goods will be realistic.

It follows, however, that little remote material, either geographical or historical, will be used, because the children will not be spontaneously interested in it nor have they the intellectual power either to interpret words apart from experience or to solve problems at the abstract level.

Thus the third principle underlying activity methods may be described as that of experience.

An Activity Based on Children's Collections

A class of thirty-five children of seven to eight years of age were invited to bring their collections to school. Things brought were shells, cigarette cards, postcards, marbles, newspaper pictures, army badges, buttons. Each child spoke about his collection and the class decided to exhibit the whole series. They also planned that each child should label his collection and write notes about it. For these notes simple folded booklets were made with a figure-of-eight stitching and a new decorative technique (paste-painting) applied to the cover. The children wrote quite freely, but the teacher offered to correct any work brought to her. Many of the children asked for spelling corrections and for this reason wrote first in rough. They also entered corrections in a spelling-book for future reference.

Labels varied in size but were all measured correctly. This led to work on plotting rectangles with the use of half-postcard set-squares. A length-measuring corner was set up. Here the children worked in groups during formal arithmetic periods on such tasks as measuring coloured paper strips pinned to the walls, lengths of coloured braids, book covers, labels, etc. Results were entered on individual work-sheets for correction. Approximations were also set, such as: "What length do you think the green ribbon is?" "Guess the length of the dog's lead in the first picture." Guesses had to be entered and checked against real measurement. The children enjoyed this practice for its own sake and some of them at least understood its relation to their need sufficiently to be able to measure accurately and fairly quickly.

While this work was proceeding, the children spent many of their free moments looking at each other's collections and even brought contributions for one another. The teacher added some interesting examples to the shells and stimulated accurate identification by the provision of F. Martin Duncan's *British Shells* (King Penguin) and Eileen Mayo's *Shells and How They Live* (Cresset Press). The children's interest in these books led to their asking to paint shells. Pictures were eventually pinned behind the shell table, descriptions copied from the books and coloured tapes taken from them to the actual shells on the table. The children were also helped in their task of identification by being given puzzle reading-sheets.

Meanwhile, the question of further ways in which to develop

a collection arose and, with encouragement from the teacher, the children decided to make a class collection of interesting buttons and to investigate what lay behind each one. A final exhibition was to be opened for the whole school. Brothers, sisters, and friends had already shown interest and had brought things for the collections and it was felt that an opportunity to see the final show would be attractive to them.

The first button dealt with was from a naval uniform. The children supplied all the information they could and then asked where they could get more. The teacher suggested bringing in a friend who had been recently demobilized from the Navy after serving in destroyers. The children received this idea enthusiastically and asked for help in writing a letter of invitation. They also had to get the head teacher's permission, make a simple road plan of the way to the school from the centre of the town and fix alternative suitable dates. The young man accepted the invitation and, having been carefully primed by the teacher, gave a lively and informative account of his ship, his life as an officer, and the adventures of the destroyer in Mediterranean waters. The result of this experience was that the children did the following things :

(i) made a wall-chart of different kinds of Navy ships from newspaper pictures, photographs, postcards, and drawings copied from such books as the *Puffin Book of Ships* and the *Wonder Book of Ships* ;
(ii) wrote stories of an officer's life on board a destroyer ;
(iii) coloured hectographed outlines of a naval officer ;
(iv) mounted yellow braids on blue cards to show naval ranks ;
(v) wrote imaginary stories of the adventures of a destroyer.

Each child chose which kind of work he would do, but work was so organized that it covered the whole range of the investigation.

The next button to be studied was brought by a child whose father had been in the Fire Service during the war. The study began by the children examining a large wall-picture of a fireman in uinform round which detailed pictures of his equipment, such as hatchet, ropes and cutters, were placed. From this observation, the children deduced a general idea of the fireman's work, which was enlarged by the teacher telling a dramatic story of a fire and ending with Belloc's cautionary tale *Matilda*.

This beginning so caught the children's imagination that they demanded a visit to the town fire station. They wrote the necessary letter, posted the best and, on receiving permission to go, organized their expedition, including the formulation and recording of questions they wished to ask and the allocation of these to selected children.

The expedition was absorbing. A most helpful fireman answered the children's questions efficiently and simply and also added much they had not known before. They saw a demonstration of fire fighting and of response to an alarm, and they climbed over the fire engine and clanged the bell.

On return to school next day, they were bursting with plans. These included making the fire station with its essential equipment, setting up an electric alarm bell, making firemen from wire dolls, and finally demonstrating the fire engine going into action. They felt a letter of thanks should be written and although they could hardly wait to start their constructive work, they wrote vivid and appreciative accounts of how they had enjoyed the expedition for which they were saying thank you. It was clear that they now had to use and spell many new 'fire-station' words. The teacher provided a series of spelling activities based on the Schonell Spelling Scheme as a result of which most children had learned to spell the words in a few weeks.

Constructive work on the floor game took some weeks and was shared according to individual choice as far as possible. A few who were willing to give up their original choice did so in order that all plans might be completed.

Finally, when experimental play with the model had given them sufficient practice to stage a demonstration, the children orally built up a running commentary. This was recorded and learned and there followed further practice periods in which volunteers were tried out to give the commentary while others worked the demonstration. These trials continued until the children were satisfied that they had chosen the best people for the various jobs.

As this show was to be part of the total exhibition, other children were chosen as guides to the collections. Finally, the class decided to charge ½d. entrance and to give the money collected to the Firemen's Fund and a child was put in charge of all money collected. Invitations were issued to the other classes in the school and posters made to advertise the exhibition.

The children stood the test of publicity well, and many were the expressions of enjoyment when the last guests had gone. The money received was checked, changed into a postal order and sent off to the fire station with a considerable sense of importance on the children's part.

It must be noted that outside this main activity the children still needed music, literature, scripture, art, formal practice in arithmetic and reading, and physical activity. These subjects found separate places on the time-table while unbroken periods of from one to two and a half hours were given to the undifferentiated programme.

Some Guiding Lines for Further Work in Schools

It may be helpful to examine here the place of the teacher in children's activities.

First, she is responsible for discovering or promoting interests. For this she must be sensitive, friendly, and watchful. One of the best ways for those inexperienced in such observation is to arrange free play or hobby periods once or twice a week and allow the natural interplay of interest to cause spontaneous grouping of the children as it inevitably does. She can help to stimulate the development of one or another of the emerging lines of activity. For example, a play-house led a group of children to play experimentally round the posting of letters. Others soon joined in, bringing parcels, telegrams, and cables from fathers in the Services. At this point the teacher would have been justified in encouraging and helping the children to plan further developments of their play.

It is probable that children in the Infant School will show interest in :

DRAMATIC ACTIVITY, such as the production of simple plays, glove puppet shows, experimental cinemas.

ACTIVITY REFLECTING ADULT OCCUPATIONS, such as in the home, shops, markets, cafés, on railways, road transport, and docks, in town schools ; in country schools, farming, river transport, locks, the life of gypsies.

SPECTACULAR ADULT ROLES, such as policeman, fireman, milkman, nurse, doctor.

LOCAL AND SEASONAL EVENTS, such as pageants, circuses, fairs, May Day, festivals, Christmas.

NATURE ACTIVITIES, such as gardening, pet-keeping, nature collections.

COLLECTIONS, such as the heterogeneous ones described.

These directions of interest are authentic in that they have been observed in large numbers of children. They may serve as a guide to teachers both in recognizing and promoting interest. But their working out cannot be preconceived and must necessarily differ with every group of children. Here the teacher's second function arises.

Secondly, she must be able to see the possibilities of development imaginatively while avoiding any arbitrary control. With keen judgment and willingness to join in play, she must contribute to the educational yield of developing activity. For example, in bringing a Navy button she turned curiosity into a productive investigation. In bringing new shells and suitable reference books she centred interest and put the children in the way of new learning. In stepping into Wendy House play she took interest forward into fresh experience.

Thirdly, the teacher must guide the children's planning so that it leads to successful work. Otherwise the path of effortful striving will not be ultimately pleasurable and the children will be disappointed with the results. For the same reason she must organize materials efficiently so that external order gives a setting in which good work can be done.

Fourthly, she must be prepared to help children to find ways of co-operating, clearly explaining the need for this, as for example when many children want to do work which absorbs only a few.

Fifthly, she must put at the children's disposal her knowledge and skill in directing them to places where they can find out by observation, to adults who will give them simple though expert explanations, and to suitable books.

Sixthly, she must teach thoroughly when the need arises, whether it is a question of skills in the three R's, constructive skills, or imparting facts. In order to make full use of the fact that the need for practice of skills is often shown up through activities, she must arrange continuous and individual practice when and as it is appropriate. This means that purposive skills can be assimilated with relatively less effort on the part of the children.

Finally, she must understand the children's need to round off certain activities and should be prepared to help them to organize exhibitions, performances and such-like culminations. In this way she will ensure that recognition of achievement so necessary to the children's growing self-regard, and their feeling of power to deal with life, both of which lie at the root of the healthy development of personality.

Margaret H. Bradley.

II. AN ACTIVITY PROGRAMME IN DETAIL

The curriculum is to be thought of in terms of activity and experience rather than of knowledge to be acquired and facts to be stored.

(Report of the Consultative Committee on the Primary School.)

Little children learn either by interest or by fear in varying degrees, and since it is obvious to the good teacher which method she should adopt, there confronts her continually the search for an approach through interest. Centres of interest should arise from the children themselves and these will best be discovered by watching their undirected activities. The children's creative forces must be released so that they can learn to use them and develop them to the full; for it is our duty as teachers to help children to become all that they might become in body, mind, and spirit.

"Whenever one finds children happily and profitably occupied, owning the mild and unobtrusive and almost unfelt sway of the teacher, but so 'keen on the job' in hand that they are hardly aware of the teacher's physical presence, there the spirit of the truest discipline breathes," says Raymont.

Centres of interest generally spring from something the children have seen: for example, a hospital, a fair, or a wedding; or from something they have experienced, in the home, a shop, or the post office; or from pure fantasy, as in a jingle, a fairy tale, or the land of Father Christmas. Few teachers who try to put these ideas into practice will have the opportunity, at present, of developing them to the full, for still from many quarters comes the demand for early results. "Our great mistake in education," said Lord Avebury, "is, as it seems to me, the worship of book-learning—the confusion of instruction and education. We strain the memory instead of cultivating the mind. . . . The important thing is not so much that every child should be taught as that every child should be given the wish to learn. . . . If we succeed in giving the love of learning, the learning itself is sure to follow."

There is a tendency in the school curriculum to separate the emotions from the intellectual life, but in reality they are closely interwoven. A child who works with his heart and his hands as well as with his head will go farther than the child whose intellectual development is forced at the expense of his emotions. Many of the troubles in which young people find themselves today can be attributed to this early intellectualizing, for their creative powers have had no legitimate outlet.

The Significance of the Nature Corner

A lively Nature Corner and frequent Nature walks will do much to remedy this, and so they form an integral part of our school activities. The children's sense of wonder is aroused and their powers of observation are stimulated by the keeping of pets. Even country children need help in following the life cycle of such simple creatures as frogs and insects.

All through the year we have some living things in the Nature Corner. Stick insects are easy to keep as they feed only on privet, and the children are continually intrigued by their powers of camouflage. Silk-worms, Puss moths, Roman snails, and tadpoles are also suitable and of great interest to the children.

On a Nature walk our children caught a dragonfly larva from

a pond. They kept it in a separate aquarium because it would have devoured the tadpoles, and fed it till it was ready to emerge. Fortunately, this metamorphosis took place in school-time and the children were thrilled as they watched the nymph climb out of the water, saw its skin split and the jewelled eyes appear. It was a wonderful experience, and one which let in the other-worldly light.

Then there are the white mice which have just had a family. The children bring cheese and crusts to feed them and see that they are kept clean and provided with water. Occasionally a child will take one home for the night, and there are always volunteers to look after them in the holidays.

All the children take an interest in the Nature Corner, but it seems to have a special value for those who are not allowed to keep pets at home. Responsibility grows and deepens in even the youngest children when they have opportunities of caring for small, living creatures, which they see to be dependent on them. In so many ways the under-sevens are themselves dependent on the adults in their environment and deep-seated psychological needs are met when they in turn find living creatures dependent on them for their well-being.

Introducing Freedom into Formal Work

An atmosphere of freedom is essential for the development of creative activities. But, even in a formal school, it will be possible to give the children a choice within a lesson as, for example, paper of different sizes and a choice of paints and crayons in an art lesson, and writing cards of various lengths to copy in a writing lesson. Then, for handwork, the children might empty the junk-box for which the class has collected tins, cotton-reels, matchboxes, bits of wire, milk-tops, etc., using these materials in their interest of the moment: a train and carriages, for instance, with the railway lines drawn in chalk, perhaps, on the floor. Not all the class would be engaged in this activity; the rest would be occupied with clay or 'busy books' in which they draw or write as they choose. In the next lesson of this kind, the 'railway' group might continue with a station while another group could be moving about making a doll's house from two orange boxes and fitting it up with matchbox furniture.

It takes some time to get the children to use their own initiative when they have been trained in formal methods. A brief outline of how this was accomplished in one school might be of general interest.

Orange boxes were nailed together by the Grammar School woodwork class who also fixed the staircase for a house. Our children painted these and made the chimneys and windows, drew pictures and made rugs and curtains. The house had four rooms : a kitchen with table, dresser, chairs and sink ; a bedroom with double bed and cot, a modern dressing-table with a mirror, and an easy chair ; a sitting-room with a low fireplace, a grandfather clock and a piano ; and a bathroom, with a sardine-tin bath, painted white, a towel-rail and a chest of drawers. We used milk-tops and 'dud' torch bulbs for the electric lights, but the more ingenious teacher might be able to rig up a battery system with the class. The house was peopled with dolls made from bits of electric wire and scraps of material. There was no 'finish' to these dolls, but when their faces were painted and their rug-wool hair sewn on, they seemed alive. This piece of co-operative work has now become a permanent toy.

Through the making of the doll's house the children began to work individually in handwork, and art and handwork soon became interchangeable. Then it was that they felt free to ask, "Can we go on with our aprons this morning ?" and, to make me understand that they were not trying to evade arithmetic, they volunteered to do sums in the afternoon. At this stage, a short free period, in which the children could choose what they would do, followed the Scripture lesson. Some read, others fetched their needlework, some drew, and it was not uncommon to see one or two enjoying their sums or their writing. "I seem to take a fancy to sums now," said Ann.

After a time the children would get out a piece of work which was occupying their minds and continue it before school began, and it soon became clear that the necessity of stopping them for a set lesson was causing an interruption in their interest. I found, too, that the children were far more receptive to a Scripture story at the end of the morning. So now, in the first period, they are quite free to choose what they would like to do, and although there are some who would hold that this is a waste of time, I am quite sure from my own observation of the children that this free play is fundamental to their natural development. "These activities are not aimless, but form the process by which children grow. They are, in a very real sense, their education." (Introduction to the *Report of the Consultative Committee on the Primary School.*)

Useful Materials for Children's Activities (6–7 years)

It might be useful here to give a list of materials which should be available for the children's activities.

Paints, chalks, crayons	Large blackboard
Paper of different sizes	Nature corner
Scissors, paste	Bricks

Property box	Clay and Plasticine
Books (stories, arithmetic, writing)	Plaster of Paris
Reading corner	Enamel paint
Hammers, nails	Pieces bag (wool, material)
Puppet theatre	Felt, dyed hessian
Shop	Large doll and bed
Movable furniture	Bowls, soap, pegs, line, travelling-iron
Junk-box (wire, matchboxes, milk-tops, tins, cotton-reels, etc.)	Sand table
	Water

Gaining Full Independence

By this time the children had become quite spontaneous and were not afraid to depend on their own initiative. Some would work in groups, one or two alone. A visit from the school doctor had prompted three little girls to ask for nurses' caps, and a hospital was their main activity. Others joined as patients or a doctor and before long they were making up beds, taking temperatures, writing charts and menus, preparing food and medicine, and even erecting an X-ray. Then came a request for the gramophone " to play some music like David did to make the King better."

The nurses' caps and aprons were made from an old white curtain and the food was made chiefly from plaster of Paris. Coloured with yellow paint it made scrambled egg ; with brown, it made cakes which were often ' iced ' with a thin layer of white. Medicines were of different-coloured powder paints : for chicken-pox, yellow, for measles, red, etc.

This centre of interest was pursued for several days. The milkman called and a specified number of pints of milk had to be taken ; so the need to learn pints and quarts arose, and the children veritably enjoyed the practice periods. Then, " It's time the patients had their dinner ! " so they learnt to tell the time. They wrote letters to tell the mothers how their babies were and made notices of visiting days which had a permanent place on the wall as long as the hospital interest lasted.

WEDNESDAYS	FRIDAYS
Mothers and Daddies	*Aunts and Uncles*
3 o'clock till 6 o'clock	4 o'clock till 7 o'clock

The children discussed the spelling among themselves but asked me for any word they could not find.

Then came the menus and here I was invited to approve the diet.

BREAKFAST	Porridge Bread and marmalade Milk
DINNER	Cabbage Potato Damsons and custard
TEA	Cakes Cup of tea
SUPPER	Scrambled egg An apple Coffee

This last activity led to the starting of a restaurant, and with the writing of more menus the cost of meals was queried. So it was that the children were introduced to £ s. d.

The girls were very anxious to do some real cooking, and even brought carrots which they cooked and served up with their elevenses. (It is a pity that there is, as yet, no stage between the mud pies of the toddlers and the cookery class of the seniors !)

A One-day Interest

As a centre of interest, the hospital is now a thing of the past, but reference is still made to it from time to time. Some centres of interest last for weeks, others, like the Harvest Festival, only for a day.

" I am going to be the vicar. You be the curate." " What can we have for a cassock ? " They dressed up in blackout curtains with their nurses' caps for surplices. " We're going to have a choir," they decided, and any likely child was asked to join. " Can we have the bell ? " they asked, and after arranging the seats, tables, books, and flowers they announced, " Hymn No. 17. ' All things bright and beautiful.' " I was asked to play and soon they said, " We are ready now." The hymn over, the congregation was told : " All kneel down, please," and then Mary said the opening words of the Lord's Prayer. The rest joined in and I have never witnessed greater reverence. At the end of the prayer she enquired : " What number's ' O come, all ye faithful ' ? " then, " Silence ! You've got to be quiet in church.

All stand up." To me she said, "Will you play the music?" and at the end of the hymn: "Who are we going to have to read? Elizabeth won't." The children looked in the Bible but said: "We can't find 'And there were in the same country'," so came for help. As soon as they had found and read it, they announced, "We've finished it. Now we're going to talk. Put your books up. We're not going to sing yet. We're going to talk." Then began the 'address.' "You know when you come to church with fruit? (Tins, etc. represented their gifts.) Where does it go?" "To the hospital," came the reply. "Yes, we're going to send it to the hospital. That's the end. Stand up." The next hymn was given out. "No. 3 at the back." This was the Carol of the Birds and I was again invited to play for them. To end the service they knelt down and said one of their short prayers, and then asked me to play, 'Now the day is over,' while the children walked out singing, but the procession came back and Marion reminded the 'congregation,' "Don't forget, we shall have a Harvest Festival tonight. Who wants to come to our Harvest Festival? Come on, then. Sit down," and they repeated the whole thing. This time, all except three children had joined in and before the end only one boy sat watching from a distance.

This activity could have been followed by a visit to a farm while harvesting was in progress, but we had already been so I believed it to be better to leave it as an isolated interest.

When the Fair came to our Village

A fair visits the recreation ground from time to time. When it came this year the children were soon making a roundabout from a see-saw with a blackboard across it. The charge was 3d. a time, and one sat on the edge while four children took hold of the corners and ran round twice. I was given a 'ten-shilling note' with which to pay for my rides. Then there was a sweet-stall with dishes of sweets and rock made from Plasticine. The shop was used for this stall with scales and weights and counterfeit money. Coconut shies were there too: tennis balls mounted on Vim tins; these were patronised at 5 for 3d. Ice creams and refreshments occupied another stall where cakes and buns from clay and plaster of Paris were offered, lemonade and orangeade from powder paint, and toffee apples from music sticks with a clay knob. Even the fortune-teller was there. The den was made from an easel covered with a blanket and Susan had dressed herself as a gypsy. She fetched me to patronize the palmist, and on taking my hand informed me that I was to have six children.

The Growth of Imagination

One of the most interesting developments in this atmosphere of freedom has been the growth of imagination which is revealed in many ways.

The children will dress puppets, make up plays and transport the whole class into fairyland. Glove puppets are the simplest ones to make, and the dialogue is invented as the children go along.

Their stories, too, are entirely original and individual. At first, they made up only a few sentences which they illustrated in their 'busy books.' Soon it was evident, however, that they needed a separate book for these stories and now each child has his own book which he covers with bright manilla paper and decorates in his own particular way. The following story was written by a seven-year-old boy of average ability:

> One day I saw a little bird and it was in the wood and it sung me a song of all the other birds.

and this one from another:

> One day I went to a Punch and Judy show and there were lots of pictures and punch made us laugh and we went home and we had dinner it was chicken and I had two plates full then we saw a squirrel it saw us and it ran away it was winter.

A little boy of five-and-a-half years asked for a story book. I thought he was too small and said so. But the next day he asked again, so I gave him one, being interested to know what he would do. He wrote a few hieroglyphics before drawing a vigorous picture of houses, people, and a loaded lorry, which he showed me with great pride. I asked him to read it to me and it went thus. "They used to live in this house and now are moving to that one." (His family had just moved house.)

In music, too, the children's imagination is fully alive. Their sense of rhythm is strong and they often ask, "Will you play some music for us to make up a dance?" They often dress up and even when they are not dramatizing they will ask: "Can we keep our long frocks on? Will you hear us read in our house today?"

Their pictures give opportunity for expression of imaginative ideas through another medium. There is the painting of "the King in his castle while the Queen goes out shopping in the rain," or the crayoned picture of a boy who says, "We're out in the forest. That's our camp up in a tree. It's a big strong dog we've got with us and here's a lion in a cage; we've captured it. I'm going to do a buffalo tied up to a tree. It's kicking up dust because it wants to get away. We've got a wolf on a big thick chain because it's a strong one. I'm going to do a banana tree and a pineapple tree. We've captured these monkeys and ostriches. That's their mother. One of the apes is throwing an Indian down because he doesn't like him."

Through these creative activities the children begin to develop their personalities and to work out unconsciously some of their deeper problems. But in order that this development may reach its fullest realization the teacher must have a sympathetic understanding of the needs of her children, she must be a friend to whom they can turn for advice and co-operation and, above all, her attitude towards them must be one of faith and trust and of unselfish love.

Barbara V. R. Smith.

III. SUMMARIES OF ACTIVITIES IN DIFFERENT TYPES OF SCHOOLS

Post Office Stores

Age of Children

Infant class in J. M. and I. school. Country district. Five- to seven-year-olds. Average-sized classroom with no corridor space.

Beginnings of Interest

Interest arose from shop-play. The equipment included a well-stocked grocer's shop in one corner of the room which the children used regularly. But they wanted to sell stamps like the real village shop. During the discussion of their ideas, it was decided to extend the shop to include the post office and to call it the Post Office Stores. The grocer's shop was to sell anything which the real shop sold, *e.g.* medicines, brooms, toys, etc.

Constructive Activity

The children made a second counter from boxes, fixed up laths and strung up knitting cotton across to represent the post office. They cut stamps from the school correspondence and brought more from home. (The stamps were kept separately, according to value.) A letter-box was made from a carton with small cards showing times of clearance; the children collected envelopes and notepaper, a small postman's bag, and a hat. Cotton-reels were found which could be used for stamping letters and pads were made from felt and paint, fixed in tin lids. A good deal of cardboard money was cut out and marked.

Dramatic Play

Each week a list of shopkeepers, their assistants (who were responsible for the P.O.), and the postman was put on the News

Board. Every child kept a supply of cardboard coins and could shop during activity periods and during individual work periods if he had finished his preparation for the day. The older children kept shopping books and recorded their transactions. They often bought paper and envelopes and wrote a letter, bought a stamp and posted it.

Practice Work

There were class discussions on the cost of stationery and stamps. Short mental arithmetic practice was taken on the cost of more than one stamp and change from 6d. or 1s. Individual practice cards were worked with similar examples for six-year-olds and more difficult ones for the older children. Lessons in measurement were given, and the instruction was applied practically to the measuring and making of stationery.

Every day, the total takings of (*a*) the stores, and (*b*) the post office were calculated and recorded on a wall account, and added up at the end of the week. The younger children listened as the piles of twelve pennies were made up.

The older children had blackboard lessons in writing letters and addressing envelopes. They also learned how to spell some commoner words needed in letter writing and recorded them in their home-made dictionaries.

Progress of Interest

The Post Office Stores remained part of the Infant room equipment and as the seven-year-olds were promoted, the interest was taken over by the younger children.

A Floor Town

Age of Children

Six- to seven-year-olds in a small town school. A small, crowded classroom, no hall, no corridors, room connected to others on each side.

Beginning of Interest

A creative handwork period had recently been introduced and the children were successfully choosing their own activities during the first part of the afternoon session. Among the material provided was a number of shoe boxes which the children were making into shops and houses. One afternoon, the teacher suggested that they should be arranged together on the floor for the rest of the class to see. "It's a little town," was the comment. "Where is the traffic?" "There ought to be lamp-posts." "And telegraph poles!" "And traffic lights!" There were volunteers to make the missing parts and the constructions were pushed away into shelves and under the teacher's desk.

Teacher's Contribution

Next day the teacher invited the children to push back the desks to allow enough floor space. " Shall we plan Floor Town ? " she suggested. They crowded on top of desks and sat on the floor, dictating where the main streets and buildings should be. Temporarily it was marked out in chalk but when the children had gone home the teacher painted the plan white.

Constructive Activity

Each day, a large section of the class worked at something for Floor Town. They made shops and houses, garages, vehicles, traffic signals, a town hall, a clock tower, a cinema, a church, pavements (from lids of boxes), poles, lamp-posts, etc. They also made people to live in the houses and some furniture. Then they began to name the people. Every day, the town was laid out for a short time so that they could see what had still to be built.

Dramatic Activity

There was no space for the children to play but those who wished played with the pipe-cleaner families they had made. Some children pretended to be landlords and collected rent.

Discussion

The children asked many questions, *e.g.* how bricks and roads were made. They were much concerned about the ownership of various public buildings. " Who paid the rent ? " they asked. Rents and landlords were discussed ; eventually every house and shop was assessed and a wall-chart showed how much they paid. The children counted out cardboard shillings and paid them to a landlord weekly. The teacher explained how fire stations and other such buildings were maintained.

Expeditions

Visits to the fire station and the town hall.

Progress of Interest

When Floor Town was finished, it was arranged on the floors of the other classrooms for the benefit of the children who asked questions and were answered by the builders. Certain children explained the work to the other classes and showed them various posters which they had made called Town News. A boat interest had arisen among another group of the same class and in a few days' time, the houses were being turned into docks and ships.

A Class Theatre

Age of Children

Seven- to seven-and-a-half-year-olds in a city school. Average-sized classroom with use of wide corridor.

Beginning of Interest

The school equipment included a dressing-up box which was kept in the corridor and used by several classes.

The acting, as it was first called, began one afternoon when group of girls pushed four K.G. tables together and called it a stage, then dressed up and began to act ' a turn.' Other children sat down in front of the ' stage ' to look on.

Teacher's Contribution

Later in the day, the teacher suggested that the group could rehearse a play suitable for their theatre. They chose Rumpelstiltskin. The whole English period was devoted to planning the play and the rehearsals were carried on in subsequent English periods and during the creative activity periods.

Constructive Activity

The girls fixed up a ' dressing-room ' by screening off a corner of the classroom with old curtains hooked on to string, near enough to the ' stage ' so that they could step straight on.

They made a ticket office from two wooden boxes and set it up in the corridors. Tickets were in two colours, and labelled 6d. or 1s. A poster announced ' Front Rows 1s., Back Rows 6d.' Meanwhile, a group of boys had arranged an orchestra of percussion instruments, a ' drum,' ' banjoes,' and ' trumpets,' and stands to hold music and instruments. Battens were fixed up by some older pupils and provided a framework for the curtains of the stage. The girls made these from sacking and fixed them on expanding rods. Some properties had to be made.

Dramatic Activities

Other plays were added and the final programme included verse-speaking, singing, and a band performance. Besides the actors, there were attendants, cashiers and cleaners.

Practice Work

Letters were practised and finally sent to the other classes, inviting their attendance. Handwriting was practised and posters displayed. Mental arithmetic and individual card practice of money sums were practised dealing with a number of tickets at 6d. or 1s. and the change from 2s. 6d., 5s., or 10s.

Programmes were written.

Books were consulted for details of costume, *e.g.* the dwarf's head-dress.

A Garage

Age of Children

Six- to six-and-half-year-olds in a town school. Me sized classroom.

Beginnings of Interest

The interest began with two children who had brought a large box to school for the purpose of making a garage. They chose an empty space on the floor by a wall and began to build petrol pumps with bricks. Other children became interested and enquired what they were doing, then went away to make cars for the garage.

Progress of Interest

During the next few days, a large number of cars of all sorts were made from waste materials and pieces of wood. Some toy cars were brought from home. They were all given numbers and named according to their make. Meanwhile, the original couple had put their names over the garage and made notices, such as *petrol, oil, car park, service.*

Dramatic Activity

There followed a great deal of play where cars were pushed along, imaginary tanks filled from the pumps and cardboard money changed hands. The proprietors now had several boys with them who did repairs. Each afternoon the cars were packed away either in or around the garage and set out again in the next activity period.

Progress of Interest

The interested group was taken to watch the activities in a real garage. There were discussions as to how garages get their supply of petrol and, after hearing about tankers and underground tanks, several children made a petrol tanker from a box and large tin.

Practice Work

A wall story about the making of the garage was used as reading material and garage picture-books were kept.

Length of Interest

The end of term concluded the interest which had lasted several weeks. After the holidays the large box was used as part of a puppet stage.

…s

…olds in a town school. Medium- …sks. Floor mats provided most of …n. This allowed more space for … use a corridor for play with large toys.

…nent included several wooden boxes on wheels …nforced with extra wooden slats. They were … pushing about dolls or loads of all sorts. One day… a couple of children jammed into the box, and anoth… g it along. " We're going up the street in a bus," they exp…ed. They held odd bits of paper in their hands for tickets.

Progress of Interest

The bus was so popular that the children arranged a row of small chairs in a queue where they waited with dolls and shopping bags for the bus to return. A second and third bus were eventually added, and their destinations varied. One went to the shops, another to the seaside, and another to the country. The ' seaside ' was the sand bin and when the children reached their destination, they played with the sand and sat their dolls down by the ' sea.' The country was a part of the room beside pictures of the country and the children sat on the floor to have picnics.

Teacher's Contribution

The teacher showed them labels which they could fix to their buses to show where they were going and she helped them to make cardboard tickets and to write 1d. or 2d. on them. She played games with them to show how many pennies were necessary for the different rides. The conductors often counted out their pennies while the class looked on. Counting out pennies became a favourite game.

Length of Interest

The interest never really finished but sometimes the buses were not used for several days or they were suddenly changed to ambulances when the main interest was in hospitals. The succeeding class took up the bus interest and played buses for long or short periods and the vehicles eventually became part of the permanent equipment.

E. R. Boyce.

A Railway Model

Age of Children

Seven-plus years. In a large town school.

How it originated

One morning in the early autumn Roger's father had a week-end holiday. As it was Roger's birthday, his father took him to London for a treat. The train was held up for a few minutes outside St. Pancras Station. During this time a thrilling event happened. Roger saw an engine reversed on a turn-table. Later in the day he was taken on the Underground Railway. Entering the Tube from Russell Square, he went down in a lift. At Oxford Street he had another new experience on coming up to the street on an escalator. The principal events of the day were stored in his memory, and came out in his free play with friends during ' choosing time ' the following week in school.

A group of about half a dozen boys, quietly and busily occupied, were not noticed by the teacher until one of them came to her and said, " Look, I have made a turn-table." " Do you mean a gramophone turn-table ? " she asked. " No ! A railway turn-table," was the answer. The teacher looked at the cork mat he was holding which had two Plasticine lines running across it. He led her to the table to see what they were doing.

Before her lay an elaborate network of rails made with Plasticine. It was so good that she suggested making it in more durable material.

Background

The next day three large cards were procured and laid side by side. Two boys set to work to paint the landscape. They painted a cornfield, with one corner brown where the corn had been cut, a cabbage-field, several fields of grass with rabbit holes in them, and a pond. Hedges of dark green divided the fields.

The train lines then had to be drawn parallel, and after experimenting unsuccessfully, the teacher suggested putting two pencils through holes made in a matchbox so that the distance between the lines would remain constant. With this, the boys drew lines all round the edge of the three cards making double tracks and junctions, with a place for the turn-table. Clay was used to make cows, sheep, horses, and rabbits, to put in the fields. A level-crossing was indicated by drawing a road to cross the railway with cardboard gates.

Model Engines

While this was in progress several other boys were employed in sawing up dowel rods and wooden laths into portions of two and two and a half inches respectively. Other boys then nailed the rods and laths together so that primitive engines came into being.

The next day the teacher bought some wooden button moulds which were nailed on for wheels. Drawing-pins made the buffers; staples and dress hooks formed the connections. A very small piece of Plasticine was glued on to each engine for a funnel and the whole enamelled.

Water Tank

By this time a railway book had been discovered in the cupboard by one of the children, with a page of diagrams of many things used on the railway. This was seized upon eagerly and Barrie was filled with a desire to make a water tank.

He found a powder paint tin which looked suitable. Then he followed the teacher about, asking how to make a hole in the bottom. She was too busy to attend to him at the time, so he found a large nail and hammered it in. By this time she was free to help him and together they made the hole larger with the aid of a pair of scissors.

He then hammered a wooden rod into the hole and nailed a flat piece of wood to the other end of the rod, so that it would stand.

The next thing was to enamel it. This done he required a rubber tube and went off to see whether one of the nursery teachers could spare him a bit. He returned triumphant, bearing a long piece of tubing and with permission to cut off as much as he required. He did this and the tank seemed complete until another look at the minute diagram revealed a ladder hooked on to the tank.

The teacher produced a roll of hat wire and Barrie proceeded to make the ladder by cutting two pieces of wire the same length and several smaller pieces also the same length which he bent on to the two longer ones to form rungs. The tops of the ladder were then bent over and hooked to the tank.

Other Articles

Signals were made by sawing wooden rods, nailing on a wooden stand, and making the signals with cardboard and wire.

A second and much superior turn-table was made after examining the book. This had a handle to turn the table and sides like a bridge.

Station

The station was made by two boys who nailed a box lid on a flat wooden platform. They cut doors in the cardboard lid (which was standing on its side), made wooden pillars, put on a roof, painted posters, made a bookstall and several other details, tickets and flags, etc.

Underground

A further inspiration was to make an underground station. A plank, with two lines made from wire, was placed under the table with its ends on the rungs of chairs. Suggestions came for a lift, escalator, steps, platform, seats, and posters. The children finished by decorating the station for Christmas.

The activity had lasted for four weeks.

N. Clarke.

Chapter III

IN THE NURSERY SCHOOL

THE NEEDS OF THE UNDER-FIVES

It is not suitable in a short chapter to deal at any length with the points to be kept in mind in translating the principles of early education into Nursery School practice. An attempt to do so has been made elsewhere.* All that will be attempted here is a brief reminder of one or two guiding principles for teachers of under-fives.

In dealing with children and in planning their day, it is necessary always to be fully conscious of the unity of the child—his wholeness. Otherwise the educative opportunities given to him and the teaching and training attempted must be incomplete and might probably be unhelpful. For instance, in training children in physical habits and in the daily performance of their toilet, in giving them meals and putting them to bed, it must never be forgotten that though the reason for these fixtures is to ensure cleanliness, food, and rest, the formation of each child's personality and his capacity to acquire good habits are affected by the way in which each thing is done. His intelligent co-operation and emotional satisfaction are therefore as important as his physical cleanliness, and harmful attitudes towards cleanliness and all bodily functions can be aroused where there is disregard of the child as a person, a living unity of body, mind, and spirit. He is never just a body to be washed or fed. In terms of daily practice, this involves many considerations. The bathroom, playrooms, and all equipment should be devised so as to stimulate and encourage self-reliance and independence. They should also enable the child to learn by doing, however much this tends to slow down the performance of routines. It is not getting things done that matters. Educative living, which the Nursery School should provide, should foster the habit of attacking intelligently, and as far as possible, independently, whatever has to be done. The whole day and everything the child does, from the moment he arrives in the morning until he goes home, must be so arranged as to make possible this thoughtful, purposeful action on the child's part.

There should be a total absence of drilling or directing

* *Life in the Nursery School.* Lillian de Lissa (Longmans).

children in the mass, of marshalling them into lines and of any routine that makes thinking behaviour unnecessary or impossible. In the bad old days, even in moving from room to room or out to the garden, children held on to one another, each clutching the skirt of the one ahead. Today they move freely as individuals and this individual self-direction is essential at all times. It is the mainspring of education, which is not something that an adult does to a child at specific moments and places. Education is, on the contrary, something a child acquires for himself, travelling under his own steam, planning and carrying through each activity as the necessity arises, selecting and using the material at hand for his requirements, adapting himself with intelligence to the needs of every situation and experiencing thereby the happy satisfaction of a completed act. If the habit of intelligent, full living is to be built up, the day's plans must provide ample time for children to undertake everything at their own pace. Visiting the toilet, selecting play material, and replacing it after use, setting tables or arranging flowers : each task must be undertaken thoughtfully and be free from pressure of time or of over-zealous teachers trying to impose adult standards, or of working slavishly to a time-table. There are daily fixtures that are unchanging, such as meals, sleep, toilet, and these have been referred to appropriately as forming a framework which gives the days stability and shape and within which freedom and elasticity in all other matters can exist. Such a framework of orderly arrangement is necessary to the child whose love of routine is strong, possibly because it gives him a feeling of protection and of safety. But the framework must never be allowed to become a cage through a teacher's misplaced zeal for having things done in an orderly way and by a preordained time. The adult's conception of order or speed of movement has little relation to children's needs, and in the cage which enthusiasm for order, tidiness, and punctuality can create, the spontaneity, the desire for self-reliant action, and the gaiety of the child can beat their wings in vain until the spirit is broken and the child becomes passive and lacking in initiative. Happy, healthy people are not produced in this way, nor good, useful citizens for a democratic state.

In giving children freedom and time to act for themselves, their need for guidance and for training must not be overlooked. The help that the adult can and must give each child in acquiring skilled movement, in adjusting himself socially, and generally in building up his pattern of behaviour is of first importance. Such guidance must be given to each child individually in ways suitable to his temperamental needs and with due regard to his age—the responsiveness of a two-year-old being so very different from that of the child of four. Individual teaching, important at all ages, is essential in nursery years when children differ so markedly from one another that group teaching is practically impossible. But it is necessary for other reasons, too, and particularly because of the desirability of helping each child to grow in his own way and to preserve his essential character. So the teacher's day should be spent watching all her children and coming forward to help each one personally when it becomes necessary. Her motive is to assist each one to gain skill and mastery over himself and to fit into his social world, but she also wishes to establish personal contact with him in the way that gives him the comforting feeling that he has an ally, a special friend who is guarding him, loving him, believing in him, and helping him to grow strong. The teacher's method of giving help should create this relationship between them. When the child lacks the feeling of security that such contact gives, when he feels alone and unprotected, this can seriously hamper growth by inhibiting action and producing a timid attitude of shrinking from life and its problems. It can also give rise to aggressive behaviour, cultivated by the child to give an illusion of strength and as a form of self-protection.

In planning the daily régime, care must be taken to provide a balanced day of activity and rest. In addition to the sleep period, there should be pauses throughout the day when children are quiet and relaxed. Such times should not occur too frequently and they should be designed to give more than bodily rest. The Montessori Silence Game, if properly taken to produce the complete relaxation that is part of it, can be a most refreshing pause and is usually thoroughly enjoyed by the children. There are other enjoyable things such as story-telling, nature talks and the showing of pictures or other objects of special interest, etc. At all these times the teacher is the prompter and director of everything that happens and the children give themselves to her leadership, which is itself a rest to children who are throughout so much of the day actively in charge of themselves. It is important for the teacher to keep all these times in true perspective as periods of relaxation and not to fall into the error of believing that because she is the leader these collective periods are *the real* learning times of the day. Children will undoubtedly learn much from them as they do from all their experiences, but, like most people, they learn most from activities in which they are the chief actors. If these collective periods are to be truly restful, they should be brief and vivid and be chosen to meet and satisfy children's real interests. If they are suitable the majority of children will always be eager to bring up their chairs and join in, though no one should be under an obligation to do so. Many children rest themselves in their own way and can be seen rolling or lying on the ground or sitting quietly, toy in arms, watching others, or wandering about doing nothing in particular. If collective periods are laboured or are so unwelcome that children do not willingly leave their play to join them, the teacher should seek the cause in her choice of subjects and her manner and methods of leading the periods. Unless she is childlike (this does not mean childish) and enjoys the things she chooses, there is little chance of the children doing so. These collective periods should not occur too frequently. Once in the morning and once in the afternoon is often enough.

The child's need to play alone and undisturbed for reasonably long periods every day is generally accepted as being of the greatest importance, for play is recognized to be the child's method of learning as it is also the outlet for his feeling. Play is usually varied. He finds emotional release in punishing dolls, banging hammers, splashing water, and making a great mess with sand and water. He also takes delight in delicately handling fragile objects—glass vases which can be filled with flowers, china cups and plates—and he finds as much fun in cleaning up a mess as in making it. The child needs various kinds of play material to meet changing needs and interests and freedom in the use of it. Dolls, teddies, and push carts are not enough. A child wishes to manipulate and take things to pieces. He needs to handle all manner of material and to experiment with many substances. Much of his play is a form of asking *how* and *what*, and his play material should help him to discover the answers to his questions. He needs, too, many tools: tubes, funnels, sieves, measure pots, for sand and water play; hammers, nails, glue, paste and all the paraphernalia necessary for playing at mummies and daddies, including mops and pails, brooms and polishers, garden tools, etc. The child who plays wholeheartedly prepares himself well for whatever lies ahead.

Finally, the Nursery School or Class must be a place for fun and laughter, good humour and good fellowship. In creating it the teacher, who should be a poised, happy person, plays a leading part in seeing that the children's approaches and dealings with one another are always kept on a friendly basis, that there are many occasions for laughter and that there is a genuine atmosphere of mutual goodwill. She can do a great deal to create this, without saying a word about it, merely by her own behaviour of unfailing gentleness and affection in her dealings with every child, and also by giving such corrections as may be necessary in ways that keep him ever aware both of other people and of her own affection for him. She should say, " Children like it better if you do . . ." " Do you think it would help more if you . . . ? " and so on, and she must give each suggestion in a way that convinces the child of her desire for his happiness and her belief in his good intent. True happiness, which must not be confused with mere pleasure, abides if it arises from deep sources. It is dependent on a sense that all is well, and the child who feels affection for those who care for him and is confident of their affection for him knows that all is well. Love spells protection to the child and gives rise to faith and belief. It is the soil in which the seeds of the spirit are nurtured and in which religion has its roots.

Lillian de Lissa.

Chapter IV

IN THE RURAL SCHOOL

I. A DAY OF ACTIVITY

FIFTY children, from four-and-a-half- to eight-years old, come to the small school in this country town.

There are two classes ; one for children from four-and-a-half to five-and-a-half and the other for those from six to eight years. Both classrooms are light and airy and are painted in pastel shades —green and cream. The 'little room' is rather small but we are fortunate in having a large main room which gives scope for the development of activity methods through which children can learn the art of living.

The School Setting

Since the atmosphere of a school, like that of a home, is of vital importance, we try to surround the children with things that are beautiful. Flowers there always are, and the Sistine Madonna occupies a central place on the wall.

The furniture is arranged informally. There is a good piano, a gramophone, a Nature Corner with snails, stick insects and mice, a doll's house made from orange boxes and furnished by the children, a dressing-up box, puppet theatre, shop, and a Reading Corner with a wide range of books suitable for different ages.

Perhaps a description of a day in our school may best illustrate how activity methods may be used in a rural school.

When the children come to school, they go either into the playground or the classroom, as they choose, and are soon playing horses, busy with bricks or dolls, arranging flowers or chatting in a ring round the fire. Often children will bring their mothers to see the aquarium or the white mice, and together they feed them with scraps which they have brought from home.

The bell rings and the children get ready for prayers. Here the little ones join us for a short assembly and then return to their own room to the tune of a nursery rhyme. The morning programme is very much the same each day, but the afternoons vary.

A Free Period

For the first period the children are quite free to choose what they would like to do. Some will paint, draw or read, while others will move tables and chairs to build a lorry, a double-decker bus or a house. The shop is generally used, sometimes for groceries, at other times as a post office or sweet shop.

Noise and movement there always will be as each child is pursuing his purposeful aim or discussing his findings with another.

This morning a group of girls and boys have built a caravan; one 'gypsy' has fallen down and broken his arm so the doctor must be fetched. "Will you be the nurse?" they ask me.

The large blackboard is not in use so two little girls are drawing a picture of a house and garden with some children at play. Two boys have dressed up and made a boat out of the upturned lid of the property-box and tell me, "We're pretending it's cold, so we're going across to where the polar bears live."

"Can we do a play?" ask the bigger girls and then proceed to announce, "This is who's in it." It is the Christmas story and they have borrowed the rocking-horse from the other room to take them to Bethlehem. Several children leave their bricks and drawing to come and watch. "Will you play some music to keep them company a bit?" asks Mary, and then, "We're ready to sing 'O come all ye faithful!'" "Who's going to be the inn-keeper?" is the next question to be decided, and the boys are invited to accept the parts of shepherds and kings. "Can we make our crowns this afternoon?" they ask.

Jennifer brings her book and asks, "Will you hear me read?" while another needs help to thread a needle to sew her apron.

Four small children have just come up from the lower class and a little girl of five-and-a-half is most anxious to look after them. She gives them each a 'busy book' in which they may draw or write as they choose, and invites one of them to share her pigeon-hole. Next, she begins to teach a boy the values of, 1, 2, and 3 with pictures, and comes to ask me to approve her efforts. "Can I have the star box?" she enquires as she corrects his sums.

There is some individual work, a few children are painting, two are drawing on the floor and another is continuing a story he began yesterday.

For this activity period there are only two rules for the children:

(i) they must put away their occupation when the bell rings;
(ii) they may not use other children's tables or chairs without asking them.

A few minutes before the end of the period they are told that it is nearly time to stop. Then I ring the bell (a tinkle is sufficient to attract their attention) and there is a ready silence while I tell them to put away their things and get ready for P.T.

P.T. Activities

The children change their shoes, take off their jerseys and choose from the games box a ball, hoop, or skipping rope and run into the playground. Already their initiative shows itself in the activities they devise during the lesson. Rollers (on which American cable was wound) are piled in steps for jumping and landing, and piles of two or three rollers are spanned with a plank for balancing. Across this plank is yet another which forms a see-saw or, if somebody sits on top, a chute down which the others slide on a mat. Old car or bicycle tyres from a nearby garage are sometimes used for hoops.

Number Activities

The children know that arithmetic comes next, so when they come back into the classroom they get out their sum books. Some who have done written arithmetic for several days prefer practical arithmetic today. There is a group round a fishing pond, chalked on the floor, complete with ducks. The rods were made from a stick, piece of string, and a wire hook. The fish are numbered and the catch is added up and one of the bigger children is invited to check the results.

A garage is always popular and a group of small boys carry this into the arithmetic activity by making a hill from a plank and a chair and drawing numbered chalk lines on the floor at varying distances from the plank to represent the track. The cars are then lined up and shot off from the ' hill ' and the number of miles written down to be added up.

The shop is in use with scales and a telephone made from two cocoa tins and a piece of string. A basket of goods is delivered to me on a scooter.

Other children are working from books while Jean and Monica ask if they can work out their sums on the big blackboard. They each fetch a little chair and stand up to the easel.

Lunch-time

It is nearly time for lunch. I ring the bell, tell the children to finish the sum they are doing, put away their books and get ready.

The children lay the cloths, each with a little pot of flowers, and every day there are two milkmaids who put on their aprons and take round the bottles of milk on a tray.

At playtime they go out (and all are encouraged to do so) but a few prefer to read or draw. While the children are out the room is given an airing.

In summer most of the children's day is spent out of doors. " Can we take our tables and chairs outside ? " is one of the first questions they ask on a warm day. They have lunch outside, too, and fetch books and apparatus as they are needed.

The playground is almost as big as : tennis court but unfortunately there is neither grass nor garden. It has an asphalt surface and is surrounded by a wall 5 ft. 6 ins. high. To prevent balls from bouncing into the adjoining garden we have fixed 5 ft. wire netting. There are logs, plants, and the rollers and car tyres with which the children can build and make toys. An engine, trolley, and a hobby horse have been made by the Grammar School woodwork class.

Writing Activities

After lunch comes the period for writing practice or for writing stories. The room is fairly quiet and most of the children are intent upon their work. Those who want to know how to spell a word ask another child or come to me. They have a piece of paper on which to try out such words and I correct these before the children write them in their dictionaries which they have made with 3-hole sewing as the need arose. " I must write a story about a parrot in a minute," says Bryan, who is still doing sums.

This is a reproduction of the story of a seven-year-old girl :

> Once there lived a little Knome he lived in a tiny hill. You know you sometimes get frightened well the Knome was getting frightened for at night ghosts crept out and stole the jewelry so the Knome made a trap and next night just as they came through the door and—S M A S H the ghosts were bang dead then the Knome had them for his dinner and stewed them.

Then follows a picture of two lone, thin ghosts with blank faces, each carrying a necklace from the room of the sleeping gnome.

The children make books connected with their centres of interest. For instance, a hospital interest produced a large book labelled " Our Hospital " with a picture by a child, and loose leaves were added from time to time, sometimes written with a paint-brush and sometimes with a thick crayon. The book was interleaved with pictures and then fastened. " Could we make a book of our own ? " they asked, and so they did. We combined to make up the sentences which I then wrote on the blackboard. The book went like this :

> We made a hospital from mats and blankets.
>
> We made some red medicine for Charles. He has caught chicken pox.

(Middlesex County Council and Tottenham Divisional Executive)

Water play.

Experimenting with various materials.

(W. Escott)

(*Ealing Education Committee*)

Left
Learning to read.

Below
Home play.

(*Middlesex County Council and Tottenham Divisional Executive*)

Graham fell off his bicycle into a ditch. We heard the telephone go and sent the ambulance right away, then we bandaged up his wounds.

This book was useful for both reading and acquiring the skill of writing, but the children's composition is quite free and has its beginning in story-writing.

As soon as they begin to enjoy writing the children will choose cards for themselves and copy them in their free time. Those who have done a piece of work which they know to be good are so pleased when it is appreciated. They are rewarded with a 'star' made from pieces of coloured gummed-paper.

The Scripture Story

At the end of the morning comes our Scripture story for I find that the children are more receptive at this time, and they will often discuss the story in relation to school life.

Dinner-time

Next comes the preparation for dinner. The children wash their hands and play outside while four of them lay the tables and put flowers on each one.

By this time the Supervisory Assistant and the server have arrived to help with the meal, and the containers are brought down on a trolley from the children's kitchen.

The children come in and sing grace and one child serves the staff table. They enjoy this and arrange to take it in turns to serve. Yesterday they put on cooks' hats for serving! Meanwhile from each of the other tables of six or eight a server is chosen. After dinner is over the children go out again to play.

The Afternoon Session

Afternoon school begins at 1.30 p.m. The first period is handwork. The boys make their crowns for the play and one of the shepherds wants to make a lamb as his present. For this modelling they use brick clay which is kept soaking in a bin. The angels need haloes, so two of them have asked for help in the fixing. The handwork lesson has now developed into a practical period.

The teacher of the smallest children has brought her pet rabbit to school. It is quite tame and hops about in the classroom. The children have brought crusts and cabbage leaves and invite him to eat from their hands.

A group of little boys ask to continue their building in the playground. They have been making a house from planks and sheets of zinc and now they want to live in it. "I'm a baby donkey," says one. "See, we're making different pens. I'm a bull," says another, and a few minutes afterwards, "I'm a little baby reindeer now," and the house becomes the reindeer's home. Soon there is a small house for the baby deer and one for Father Christmas. Nancy has now asked if she may write Father Christmas a letter.

Mary's little brother has a birthday tomorrow so she has taken paper to make a birthday card. Wanda joins her and they make one each.

David is reluctant to read at the request of Jennifer, but she has her way and he reads. After a little while, however, he escapes to make a church with bricks. He shows me the windows and I enquire about the people. "They aren't come yet," I am told. Donald and Billy, who have been sorting the logs to find suitable 'legs' for a seat, return with the plank, hammer, and nails to make it.

The bigger girls are making aprons from pieces of dyed hessian. Audrey is making a stuffed doll which she will dress, Susan has cut out a pair of slippers from red felt, while others are knitting, drawing, or painting. Charlotte, Jean, and Vera have made a house from the puppet theatre and are reading, 'while it is still light' since they have 'put the babies to bed.'

A Reading Activity Period

This is run on very informal lines. Not all the children read, but when I have heard one group they return to finish clearing up while I hear the next. Some of the little ones who are too small to read independently build their names with boxes of letters or draw in their 'busy books' until their turn comes.

Music

Playtime comes, and after break we have music. I play 'The Merry Peasant' and straightway they turn up the lids of their desks and prop up a book as they enter into the spirit of the music and 'play' too. To Beethoven's Minuet they ask, "Can we make up a dance?" and they dance either with a partner or by themselves. During Schubert's Cradle Song they invariably put their heads on their desks as if to sleep, and feel the lullaby. They enjoy interpreting music and ask, "Will you play the minuet of the little boy who was six?" and, "Can we have the one when he was grown up now?" We sing a few songs and then they bring up their chairs, seats, or mats into a ring for a story which concludes the afternoon.

After their good-bye hymn, music sends the girls to fetch their coats, and then the boys. They see that the playground is tidy and leave school to a march or a nursery rhyme. Michael and George ask if they can write to Peter tomorrow (he left on Friday when the family moved away), and Janet asks: "Do you think I could take my reading-book home and do a bit more?"

There are various good-byes and the building is quiet.

A Time for Reflection

I reflect on the day's activities and consider where they are likely to lead tomorrow:

(i) I note centres of interest which have arisen and are likely to develop; for example, the Christmas play;
(ii) I think out possible extensions of these so that class lessons may be adapted to the children's interests;
(iii) Is there any child who lacks an interest and why?

For example Jonathan, aged seven, seems to be at a standstill. He is the youngest of a family of grown-up brothers and sisters who, his mother tells me, often make fun of him. He is shy and needs bringing out. Can I make him feel we need his help? Will he be a king?

June, aged six, is an only child and inclined to be selfish and aggressive. Her mother is very co-operative and has been to discuss the matter with me. It appears that June is 'spoilt' at home by her father and she is inclined to be rude to her mother. A story bearing on this must be included tomorrow and she should have an opportunity of feeling the joy of sharing. Perhaps she can be a shepherdess.

Ben is seven and below average. He has not yet begun to read although he has a fair idea of numbers. He is very interested in nature study, particularly birds. He will take a bird book from the Reading Corner and find the egg which belongs to the bird of that name. Tomorrow I will suggest that he makes a simple bird book of his own to help his reading and writing.

A parent comes to tell me about her boy who will be returning tomorrow after an illness. We discuss the school party and decide to call a meeting of parents who would like to help.

There has been nothing spectacular about the day, but as is shown by the few illustrations above, the children are growing and developing and I have to plan to keep pace with their growing needs and demands.

Note :

Other afternoons might include percussion band when the children enjoy marching with their instruments. Sometimes they ask, " Can we go round the playground ? " and although I do not know why they ask, I see no reason to refuse them and they continue in perfect time, without actually being able to hear the music, and return to pick it up in the classroom as though they had never really been absent.

Poetry is another favourite lesson. The children enjoy the rhythm before understanding the context but they will often ask to dramatize a poem.

Puppets have an important place, too. These are often begun as a free activity and continued as a class activity with the production of a play. The puppet theatre was made to fit the children and the sill is 3 ft. 6 ins. high so that they can stand comfortably.

On a sunny afternoon would come a request for games in the recreation ground, five minutes distant, or, " Can we go for a nature walk ? " when we might go to the woods or pond-dip in a nearby pond.

Barbara V. R. Smith.

II. PROBLEMS OF THE NURSERY CLASS

The special needs of children at the pre-school or Nursery stage of development, and the methods of meeting these needs, are outlined elsewhere (see Chapter III), and as a rule there are Nursery-trained teachers to take care of such classes ; but it sometimes happens that in a small Rural School there may be a group of under-fives for whom no special provision of properly equipped Nursery, or trained teacher, is made. In many cases these children are included in the ' baby class ' with the five-year-olds, and so they often have to join in activities for which they are not ready, their own special needs are not considered, and they lose the benefit of this very important stage of their development, and are consequently retarded in their later school progress. Conditions in Rural Schools are so very different, and the number of children under five, the space, equipment, and teachers allowed for them vary so much, that it is impossible to lay down any rules of procedure which should be followed. Here, however, we can remind ourselves of the special needs of children at this stage, and suggest some of the ways in which a teacher in charge of the under-fives in a small Rural School, with all its handicaps and all its advantages, can try to meet these needs. They can only be suggestions, but every teacher with originality and the welfare of her children at heart should be able to select and adapt, so that each school may be working towards the same ends, although in widely different ways.

Fundamental Needs of Three- to Five-year-olds

Children between three and five, as has already been described, are growing away from dependence and the care given them as babies towards the sturdy self-reliance of little boys and girls. They need opportunities to use and develop their senses and big muscles, to get used to other children, to establish interests in the world around them, to use and understand speech; in short, to live fully through these years so that they are ready to pass on to the next stage with interest, confidence, and ability.

The fundamental needs of children at this stage can be briefly stated, as first, the need for a background of security, and secondly, having this, a need for opportunity to go forward to independence, new experience, and achievement. If we interpret these two needs in the widest sense we can evolve a plan for education which, however limited our means, will provide what our children need most to enable them to live and grow fully.

The Need for Security

First, the need for security; we should realize that this means more than that our children must be safe. We will assume that parents and teachers alike will try to ensure that the children are safe from common dangers of the country, from traffic and farm machinery, poison berries, an unfriendly bull, a deep mill-race, or whatever in the environment may imperil life and limb. In school we are, however, more concerned that the children shall *feel* safe and secure in the people who deal with them, in their environment, and in their own worth as persons. This requires, first and foremost, a teacher specially interested in them, who is understanding and sympathetic, reliable and friendly, someone who is always there when needed. She is not to be a second mother—too often an untrained teacher makes the mistake of 'over-mothering' the children, fussing and caring for them and helping in a way that keeps them babies. The teacher's function is rather to provide a safe background for the transition stage from home to school, for a child's feeling of security must be planted, not only in his reliance on other people, but in his dawning confidence in himself. For this he must come to know that he has a proper place in the school as he had at home, and there must be as much room and space as can be provided, where he belongs and which belongs to him. Even if the Nursery room is cramped or gloomy it can be helped by light paint and colour wash, suitable pictures at eye level, and equipment which, however simple and improvised, the children can reach themselves. There must be some sort of cloakroom (again, it may have to be improvised) where they can wash and dress at their own pace, unhurried by the needs of older children, and outdoor space where they can play apart from the more vigorous noise and movement of the big ones. Having their own place and status, their natural dignity must be respected, and they should not be known generally as the 'toddlers' or 'babies.' Where families are large, and the three- or four-year-old is already supplanted by other babies at home, it is all the more important that he should feel he has a place of real significance at school.

The Need for Experience

With this secure background, the children's chief need is for experience; the kind of experience which will enable them to exercise sense and muscles, to learn differences of colour and shape and size and texture, weight and density, to build and manipulate and create, to do things and to know about other people and how they do things, and besides knowing and doing, to learn to talk freely about what they know and do. And here the Rural School, whatever its deficiencies compared with the properly equipped and planned Nursery School, has priceless advantages, for all that Nature offers out of doors can be included as equipment for the Nursery Class. The country child need not be confined, as is his city brother, to a little sand in a tray, a little water in a zinc tank, and factory-made bricks and counters, but his teacher can look about the school and take note of whatever possibilities are offered. Where the setting is really rural, and places easily reached, the class should go regularly to a clearing in a nearby wood or spinney, to a corner of a meadow or a grassy hedge, to a sandy river bank, to play by a brook or spring or runnel, or to scramble and climb on a fallen tree. Regular visits at all times of the year help to develop the possibilities of any place; certain sheltered spots under trees and bushes become houses, stiles or wooden fences are climbing frames, a bank becomes a shop, a disused cattle trough a pond for boats. Shop-play with pebbles, leaves and flowers, cones and other country treasures, house-play with acorn dishes and hedgerow food, all provide stimulus for thought and imagination, as well as sensory experience far richer than is gained from artificial apparatus.

Besides this regular experience of outdoor play, the class can be taken on frequent expeditions to see whatever the environment can, from time to time, provide. Thus class and teacher may go to a nearby byre to visit a baby calf, to the pond to see the fluffy yellow ducklings, to watch trains at a level-crossing, a mill-wheel turning, a tractor ploughing, the blacksmith shoeing a horse. Each such experience provides something fresh to see and talk about; experience is widened and vocabulary enlarged within the setting of a real and familiar background. The children are helped to enjoyment of all that Nature has to offer, to know the seasons, to take part in the festivals of the year. Thus class and teacher again go out to gather primroses, or blackberries for mother, to get autumn leaves to brighten a winter classroom, to make a snowman or look at icicles, and always their experience is becoming richer and their perceptions keener.

Country children often suffer the disadvantages of slow speech and dull perception, because their experience and their contact with other people is limited. This need not be so if full advantage is taken of all the opportunities about them and if they are encouraged to talk freely to each other, to their teacher, and to all the friendly people they meet about them. These may be many and varied, with different turns of speech and ideas to stimulate the children; a cowman who lets them watch him milking, a hedger who gives them queer-shaped sticks, the vicar and visiting managers, an artist or an author who is staying in the village. All this means that the teacher herself must live in full the life of the village, know the people and enlist their interest in the children and their doings, and take her own part in the adult community.

Although we have stressed here the value of real experience in a rural environment, the school and Nursery room remain the base from which it all starts, and to which it all returns. Within the room will be found many of the same toys and apparatus to be found in any nursery, but richly supplemented by natural playthings, nuts, cones, berries and pebbles, feathers and flowers and leaves, sticks and odd pieces of wood from the wood-yard. These the children care for and arrange themselves, the teacher seeing to it that supplies are always fresh and that anything which is dusty or decayed is properly disposed of, so that the training in beauty and order which is Nature's own is continued indoors. Here, too, language training continues, and it is very important that the teacher cultivates a clear and pleasant voice, since hers is the one the children hear most of the time. They talk over with her their outdoor experiences, they hear her telling stories and learn from her songs and hymns, nursery rhymes, and singing games, and with these latter she is careful to keep to the local versions. The room should contain a Book Corner with plenty of picture-books, especially those with good pictures and photographs of farm and country, flowers, and animals, things the children see and know. Here they learn to handle books and care for them, they are encouraged to talk about the pictures, and they are laying the foundation for future interest in reading.

The best preparation for life is living, and our general aim is for each child to live fully through each stage of life as he comes to it. To ensure this for the Nursery child means, not only his happiness and well-being here and now, but the surest foundation for his future progress and development.

Elsa Walters.

and teacher again go out to gather quantities of the [illegible] for another, copper autumn leaves to brighten a winter classroom, to find a snowman or [illegible] and always their appreciation is to be made richer and their perception deeper.

Country children often suffer the disadvantage of being shy, stupid and dull [illegible] because their contacts with other people is limited. This is a [illegible] because [illegible] of the opportunities about them and if they are [illegible] encouraged to talk freely to each other [illegible] their family people they meet about them. There are just as many and varied [illegible] among the children, a [illegible] who [illegible] a house wife who [illegible] [illegible]. This means that the teacher herself must [illegible] village know their people [illegible] children and their [illegible] as a [illegible] community.

Although we have stressed here the value of the [illegible] in a rural environment, the [illegible] from the [illegible]. When the room will be [illegible] and questions to be found [illegible] natural [illegible] and leaves [illegible]. Here the [illegible], the teacher [illegible] who [illegible] [illegible]. It is very important that the teacher [illegible] stories and learn [illegible] and singing games, [illegible] local variants. The room should contain a [illegible] with plenty of picture-books, especially [illegible] poetry, and good [illegible] the children see and know. [illegible] they are [illegible] and [illegible].

The best preparation for life is living, and our [illegible] is for each child to live fully through each stage of life as he comes to it. To ensure this for the Nursery child [illegible] his happiness and well-being here and now, but [illegible] foundation for his future progress and development.

[illegible]

PART TWO

FROM FORMALITY TO ACTIVITY

Chapter V

ACTIVITY METHODS IN FORMAL SCHOOLS

I. ENRICHING THE CHILD'S BACKGROUND

FOR various reasons, it is not possible for many teachers to embark on a thorough-going activity curriculum. There are such physical limitations as lack of space and material. The problem of noise can be serious, especially where the Infant room adjoins the classrooms of older children. However, activity methods are very elastic. In fact, an important essential is that they should be adapted to suit each particular group of children in their particular school conditions. There is another essential, which must not be overlooked. The teacher must understand the underlying principles of the methods she is to introduce. If a whole school is to experiment, there must be general agreement as to aims and principles. These have been clearly stated and explained in Part One of this book. It is enough, therefore, to remind readers that respect for *inner* activity is all-important. Activity methods mean providing opportunities when the children can think, plan and choose for themselves; they are methods which stimulate mental alertness and they are methods which encourage friendly intercourse, co-operation and mutual helpfulness in the classroom. Teachers should be able to watch the children grow in confidence and become useful members of a community as a result of more informal methods and real experience. In this section we shall consider the modifications which can be made to suit classes working under difficulties and suggest how the principle of activity can be introduced into schools which still need to retain something of a formal setting.

Changes in the Handwork Lesson

For many years we have been accustomed to regard the handwork or 'occupations' period as a time of relaxation for teacher and pupils. This may be because there is no straining after results as there often is in the three-R subjects. It is a time when the children are sometimes allowed to be themselves within certain narrow limits; that is, they can model or draw what they like. For these reasons one good way of introducing activity is by reforming the handwork lesson. It has long been recognized that doing things with the hands is vitally important in the development of young children. Thinking does literally begin with doing things. The value of such practical activity is, however, considerably lessened when children have to do the things they are told to do and in the way they are shown. By removing the teacher's direction and allowing the children to do the things *they* like in the way *they* like, the experience of the handwork period can have a very valuable influence on the development of each child and his attitude to learning. In formal schools, the traditional handwork lesson can be changed to a 'creative handwork period' which will enliven the rest of the curriculum, give the teacher a much more interesting task and provide immense stimulus to the children.

Collecting Equipment

Pamphlets which provide reliable lists of suitable materials are marked (*) in the bibliography. These, however, are inserted as guides only, and no teacher should be daunted because some of the equipment is unobtainable. The practical plan is to assemble everything which the school can already offer, remembering that the children are not expected only to *make* things. The new interpretation of handwork includes all the things children like doing when they have the space, time, and necessary materials. They will sometimes play without any apparent purpose; they will paint pictures and perhaps spend long periods just looking at things. So, in addition to the usual school-cupboard equipment, they will need plenty of waste material: boxes, rags, sacking, cardboard of all sorts, bits of wood, old catalogues, as well as natural objects like stones, shells, cones, chestnuts, etc. They will want picture-books, a pocket lens, and little interesting things which can be magnified, a magnet and objects it will pick up and some that it will not, a kaleidoscope, a few small mirrors, sometimes an old nest and any curious things which stimulate investigation. If changes are to be made throughout the school, materials can perhaps be pooled and redistributed; the time-table may be rearranged so that such equipment as bricks, the large sand-tray, the screen house and a few large blackboards can be shared. If it is possible to buy anything new and there is no large building material in the school, I should certainly get bricks of assorted sizes (particularly big ones) and a good supply of damp sand in a large deep tray. Nursery classes are among the best-equipped rooms today and some of their educational toys might be shared while the youngest children are resting.

Arrangement of Equipment

The choice of materials partly makes up the 'instructive environment' which is referred to in the *Infant and Nursery School Report*, p. 141, and their arrangement is not so insignificant as might appear. The whole success of the creative handwork period depends on careful selection and display and on the sympathy of the teacher towards the free choice of the children. Permanent shelves or low-cupboard space save a great deal of time as the materials need only an occasional re-arrangement. Borrowed things can be set out just before the children need them.

Some materials are stimulating when put close together: large needles threaded with gay cotton and stuck into a width of hessian just above the rag-bag suggest making something with stuff; a few peg dolls in a box close by help a child without ideas to make up her mind about her next activity.

Length of Activity Period for Beginners

At first, the children will be slow to take advantage of their freedom; they may even say that " they do not know what to do." This indicates the failure of formal methods, not of activity methods, but we shall discuss the problem in a later paragraph. Until they are more used to initiating their own activities, forty minutes is roughly long enough, but the period should gradually be lengthened to at least an hour. The children do their own clearing up and they want time for putting away their half-finished jobs carefully. Seventy minutes, including clearing-up time, is most usual. In many schools, the period is repeated every day and twice a day for the five-year-olds. Teachers will probably find that twice or three times a week is enough at first. As the children's confidence increases, more weekly periods can be added until there is one each day. In congested classrooms, the painting lesson is kept separate from the rest of the creative work. This means that one handwork period of the old type is given up to painting and there are four activity periods. Of course, the free choice of work entirely rules out the ordinary handwork lesson.

Arrangement of Classroom

A large number of Infant rooms are now arranged with groups of desks instead of straight rows. In these days, no teacher should tolerate the screwed-to-the-floor desk. It is a simple matter to remedy, and once the furniture is movable, there is a possibility of more space, more movement, and more friendliness. The children sit facing each other in groups of six or eight. If there are steps in the room the desks are moved on to the flat, the teacher's seat, lesson equipment, Nature Table, etc. being arranged on the steps. If straight lines must, for any reason, be the rule throughout the morning session, a few older children will soon whisk the desks into groups before the afternoon when the free period often takes place. This is done in a large number of schools. (Stepping, by the way, is not difficult to remove. Many classrooms have been levelled in the last few years.)

The Creative Handwork Period

Some time before the first activity period, the experiment must be clearly explained to the children. In many schools, the children go straight to their freely-chosen occupation as they come into school at the beginning of the afternoon session. This does away with any overcrowding at the shelves. The children are warned about anything which they may not do, but if there is to be real benefit from the new approach, the 'don'ts' must be very few indeed. "Hammer on the floor, not on a desk," "Put down a sheet of newspaper before you use paste," "Ask before you take anything which someone else seems to be using," "Put your tools back after use," are legitimate rules. For the rest, the children should understand that they really are free to choose, to change when they want to, to talk in ordinary voices, to ask help from each other and from the teacher. The noise of doing things and the hum of conversation is absolutely necessary; where there is danger of disturbing another class, the time-table must be arranged so that the creative activity period coincides with an outdoor or hall period, a handicraft or housewifery lesson. When two classes are taught in one large room, the best plan is for both to have their activity period at the same time; Junior classes profit quite as much as Infants by such a period.

The Activities

At first, the children may not show any great originality; it takes some time for them to get used to the new conditions and to understand that they can do as they like. The better trained they are in doing what they are told, the slower they will be to express their interests and desires. Their sense of adventure is dulled, their power of taking the initiative is repressed and they may have very few ideas. We cannot expect original expression from barren mental backgrounds. Ideas are the result of living experiences at home, in the street and in school, and of imaginative experience in stories and stimulating conversation. If improvement seems slow, there may be a chance of loosening up the rest of the curriculum in the ways suggested in the notes on 'Expeditions' and 'Dramatization' in the second part of this chapter. In some way we must enrich the children's experience. Directing attention to any interest which does appear will stimulate fresh ventures (see under 'Vocabulary' on page 89). When the children persist in making and drawing the same thing continually, the materials may be at fault. Some more unusual equipment may be necessary; the material may want cleaning and brightening up.

On the other hand, there may be no such inhibitions. It is often noticed that children want to play with toys which are normally enjoyed by younger children. There is nothing disappointing in this; they are perhaps expressing desires which they have never been able to work out satisfactorily at the right stage. When they are ready, they will proceed to more mature work. Some children use only one sort of material for weeks on end and then follow up by using another kind of material for a long time. These are one-track-minded children and this is their way of expressing their inner needs. Some children hardly ever paint; they may prefer to build. These are usually the more practical-minded but they are being creative in their own way. Many children enjoy intervals of inactivity. This is disturbing to some teachers who are in the habit of associating idleness with subsequent mischief. The traditional pointers to naughtiness do not exist in a successful free creative period. There is no reason why any children should not stop to consider, to watch others, or to relax. In fact, one of the benefits of this sort of period is that it provides relaxation from the tension of continually attending and doing one's best and 'trying hard.' A great deal is accomplished when the striving ends and the relaxed mind comes into its own. A certain amount of aimless, restless activity is understandable; nevertheless, a child who constantly seems unable to settle down and become absorbed should receive some friendly attention. A few suggestions, showing something simple to make, working with the child for a few minutes, may prove helpful, but more often he needs different material or is ill or unhappy. Approval and friendly sympathy will probably solve the trouble as far as school is concerned.

The more successful the new work is, the more unorthodox will the classroom become in appearance. Uniformity is the key-note of the traditional classroom; now the emphasis is on variety, individuality and a tendency to co-operate in groups. Teachers who understand these methods are delighted when they notice that the children are beginning to work in small groups. This happens more often with the sixes and sevens than with the fives, and may be the sign that a centre of interest has emerged from individual activities. Instances of such interests and how they are used are to be found in Part One. The teacher makes a note of her observation and is able to use the awakening interest in other lessons. There may be several such interests going on in one classroom and yet some children will continue to pursue their individual activities or to play with a couple of friends in the doll corner. The essence of this period is to allow each child full independence of action providing the action does not seriously interfere with other children.

The Question of Skills

What, then, happens to the raffia work, the knitting, the weaving, and paper folding? It is a mistake to teach five-year-olds to make objects which involve careful, small movements; they have not yet developed the power of fine adjustment of the fingers. Theirs is a solid grasp of the hand. In their activity period, we see how contented they are with rough representations. A chair will do for a ship, a train, an aeroplane, or a bus; a couple of pieces of wood with a nail attached can be used for almost anything which is needed to complete a piece of dramatic play. But a change takes place during the sixth year and becomes more definite in the seventh year. By that time, many children want to make a neat job of their constructions. They ask for help, they paint only one side of an object and leave it to dry, they are careful not to smudge their work and often ask, "What can I use for so-and-so?" or, "How do I make this look like a real so-and-so?" In some classes teachers provide well-illustrated books so that the children can see for themselves just how things are put together. It is during these years that the teacher's superior skill is of value. There are many things that she should know how to do so that she can pass on her knowledge at the moment it is needed. The seven-year-old girl will spend much effort on furnishing a doll's house; it is then that she will welcome the teacher's instruction in weaving and knitting. It is an economy to teach a group rather than an individual: so anyone else who is interested should be invited to join the lesson. Raffia is a useful material to be hung up in bunches for plaiting, tying and stitching, but it is probably only used for its traditional purpose when some children want to make Christmas presents. Simple skills with woodwork tools should be part of every teacher's professional equipment; paper folding has its day when the children want to stock their toy shop. Teachers can discard none of their old knowledge but they will use it differently.

A New Skill

The successful teacher by activity methods learns a new skill; that of anticipating the needs of the children. She watches a group building houses from boxes and she helps when they cannot manage to cut their cardboard properly. Then she makes a note to remind herself that tomorrow the children will want stuff for curtains. When, therefore, they go to the rag-bag to find suitable material, they come across just what they need. Another day, there are several children making boats. Sometime later, the teacher asks them to show the rest. Altogether, the boats look like a small fleet. "Where are they going?" someone asks. When the children begin their activities on the following day, there will be enough blue cloth to lay down for a river, and boxes and wood to make the bridges. Several seven-year-old boys had chosen to make themselves carol books because they were going round the village carol-singing. "Which one are you writing

(*Ealing Education Committee*)

(*Ealing Education Committee*)

Above

A puppet theatre.

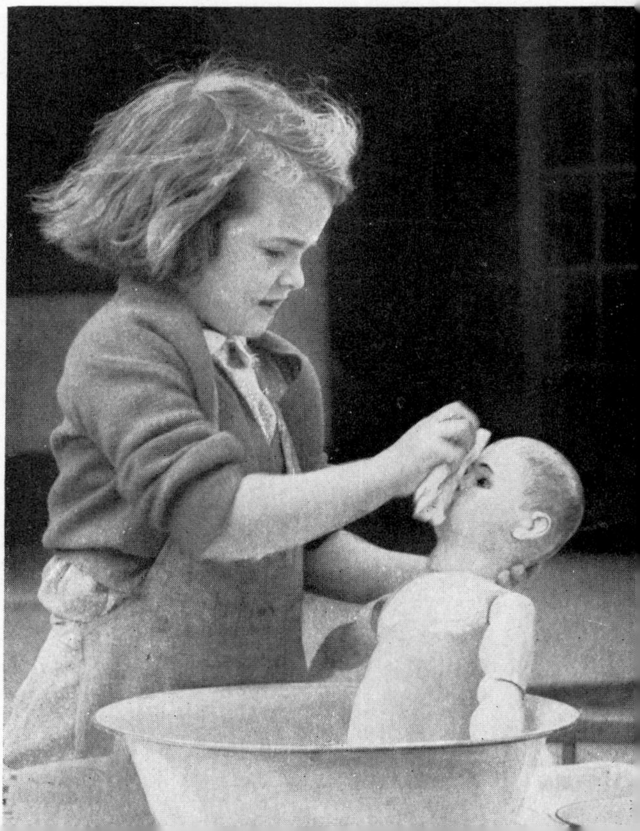

Right

Bathing Baby.

(Ealing Education Committee)

A Railway Journey: the booking office is on the left.

A " Ship " centre of interest.

(Miss Edith Coop

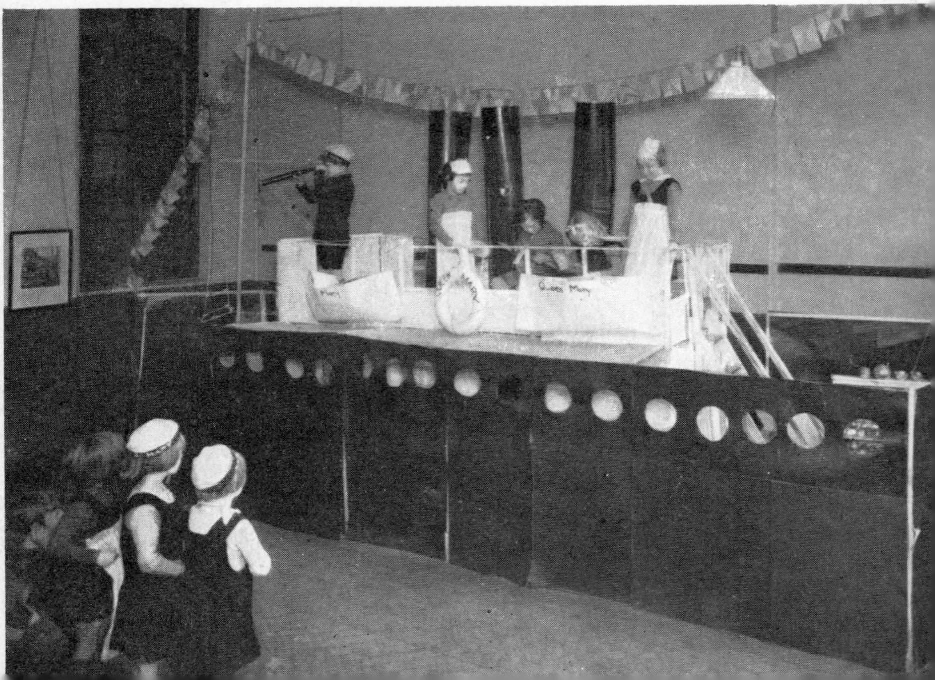

next?" asked their teacher. By the following day, there were copies of the carol which they required. The skilful teacher is constantly thinking ahead, and yet she is never disappointed if her efforts are ignored.

The Teacher's Work

The teacher can hardly be recognized in a busy classroom during the creative handwork period. She may be holding something for a child, sitting by a group to show them a new skill, she may take the part of customer in shop play or she may just be looking on. She is never hearing a few backward readers, for the slower the reader, the more precious is every minute of his activity time. Nor is she dictating how things are to be done. But she is observing her pupils and noticing how different they are from when they are attending to a blackboard lesson. It is a good plan to keep a notebook handy for reminders of new materials needed and new interests to be discussed. These notes are also useful as a record to replace the handwork syllabus.

During the creative handwork periods, the children will ask questions and carry on friendly conversations with the teacher. This is a very important part of her work; there is no better way of learning to talk than to talk, and no better way of imparting information than to do so at the exact moment of enquiry.

Finally, in spite of repetition, we must remind readers that the care and selection, as well as the arrangement, of equipment is one of the teacher's most important contributions to the success of activity methods.

Sharing Responsibility

Of course the children take their part in clearing up, cleaning, arranging, and collecting materials. Activity is a general term which includes a wide range of 'doing things.' In schools which are described in other chapters, the children take a large part in running their own classrooms. They help themselves whenever possible, not only in personal matters but in selecting occupations during most of the day. They help each other, talk together and move about freely both in and outside the classroom. This may be impractical in many schools, but the care of materials for this period is an opportunity for real experience which should not be ignored. A dustpan and brush, a few mops and rags, a pail and sponge will be necessary, but these are found in every school.

Summarizing the Value of the Creative Activity Period

What is the use of this free choice of activity compared with the handwork lesson?

(i) The children learn to think as they solve the practical problems presented by their self-chosen activities.

(ii) They practise independence.

(iii) They learn to share, to offer help, to appreciate another's efforts to co-operate. In a word, they are learning to live with others.

(iv) Through their choice of activity, they are given opportunities for relaxation, for expressing fantasies, for unravelling mental confusion and emotional troubles and for following their own particular interest. The rest from continual listening and trying allows the course of natural development to proceed quietly.

(v) They get practice in talking and the exchange of conversation.

(vi) They are accumulating real experience which is the basis of learning.

E. R. Boyce.

II. EXPLORING THE ENVIRONMENT

We have seen how the background of the children may be enriched with real experiences so that they have more ideas to bring to their creative efforts. Now we shall discuss how the formal school can provide those experiences.

Children are tremendously interested in their surroundings and in the happenings of the everyday world. As is pointed out in Chapter II, all activities arise spontaneously from one aspect or another of the environment. This desire to make the things they see, to ask questions, to pretend to be people they see about them, is all part of their great need to understand their environment. Every school, whatever its organization, seeks to do something to satisfy this need through story-telling, picture talks, and conversation. But it is first-hand contacts which are of paramount importance. In schools where a full activity programme operates, expeditions are arranged whenever the children show by their choice of occupation that they are especially interested in some aspect of their environment. They visit docks, railway stations, markets, and watch river traffic.

In the more formal school we canbegin with the opportunities which arise when the outside world comes into the school. Children who happen to be at play when fuel arrives, watch with deep interest as one after another sackful is tipped down into the cellars. The teachers of some Infant classes who notice the arrival of the coal truck, take the class out of doors to watch. Then they go below to see the coal as it tumbles into the cellar. Next day, they are allowed to watch the caretaker as he feeds the boiler and then they trace the course of the pipes which carry the hot water. They like to stand and stare for some time at the furnace and then they begin to ask questions.

The same good use can be made of any workmen who arrive in the school: the window cleaners, the piano tuner, electricians, telegraph boy, dustman, etc. Teachers in some modern schools welcome any interruption of this kind and put other lessons aside so that every possible advantage can be taken of the experience. After watching and asking questions, the children discuss with the teacher what they have seen and learn what happened before the men arrived and what will happen to them next. Children are very interested to hear about the disposal of rubbish and how the telegraph boy gets a message to deliver. If they are allowed a creative handwork lesson, the new ideas are often worked out constructively or dramatized.

From about their sixth year, natural phenomena are very interesting to children, and younger ones profit by any vivid experience connected with the weather, the sun, moon, stars, etc. Instead of trying to keep their attention away from the snow outside, or the wind which rattles at the window, we can deliberately use the distractions as part of their education. Regardless of the time-table, we can let them enjoy a light snowstorm one day, a good snow battle, and the creation of snowmen and houses on the following days; then as the fall melts they can take part in clearing up the playground. When their natural curiosity makes them collect lumps of ice and handfuls of snow, we can make the most of their inconvenient collections by suggesting that they put their treasures into pails. Very soon after, there are demands to know why the snow is now *dirty* water and the ice has melted. These are real investigations which stimulate thought and reasoning and add to the background of ideas on which we can build.

Wind is also very exciting for small children, especially in autumn when the leaves are torn from the trees. Every teacher knows how uncontrolled the children are on windy days; instead of trying to suppress their boisterous behaviour, we might allow them to experience the rough buffeting in the playground and to watch the whirlwind of leaves and to feel the strength of the gale as the dustbin lids bang over the asphalt.

"Come out and look at the clouds," "See how many shapes you can find," "The sun and moon are in the sky just now, we will go and look." The expeditions may take five minutes and the conversation which follows may take another ten minutes but it is a quarter of an hour of active learning and is a valuable part of the curriculum.

At times there are still more interesting experiences. Pigeons may build on a ledge of the school wall, unknown birds may come to the bird table, seedlings may suddenly show through in the window boxes; all such events are the occasion for an excursion out of doors and for a break in the routine of the day. Time-tables are not meant to control events; they are useful only as indications of the broad rhythm of the day and to encourage the balance of work and play. A speech training period, a blackboard lesson in arithmetic, or even a period of individual work can be sacrificed for an outdoor experience.

Expeditions

Short expeditions from the school into the neighbourhood can be arranged. Plans are made and explained to the children before they set off. For instance, the whole of a large Infant School in a built-up area was taken to see the spring bulbs in a strip of public garden about ten minutes' walk away. Arrangements were made for the children to go, a class at a time, in charge of a couple of teachers. They were told about the different kinds of flowers beforehand and where to look for them; it was also suggested that if they looked at the bushes they could find some which were in blossom. "I don't know what else you might see," said the teacher. "Just look out and tell us when you get back." In this way, the children went with minds prepared and so made the most of the experience. It is usually best to refrain from directing attention and explaining as the children watch; they observe more if uninterrupted. Sometimes they talk a great deal and ask questions; at other times they say little and see a great deal. It is also wise to leave the discussion of the outing until the following day. The children seem to want to ask more and to compare notes when they have had more time to assimilate the experience.

There are a number of expeditions which can be organized for the younger children within a few minutes' walk of most schools. For instance, they can go along the street to watch the postman empty the pillar box, to stand and watch the road-sweepers, to peer into man holes and down gratings, to stand and stare at a group of workmen laying a cable.

The older children can go farther afield to investigate more complicated activities. Permission is easily obtained for them to see what happens at the back of a general post office and behind a station booking office; to see a baker at work; to watch ships; to see a newspaper being printed or a tree being felled; to watch any machinery in action or being repaired. If an unusual operation is going on in the neighbourhood, it is an opportunity for a valuable expedition: when the snow-plough is at work; when specific building operations are in progress; when copper wire is being swung from pole to pole; when threshing is going on or a combine is at work.

One class of children enjoyed a whole series of planned visits to investigate the immediate neighbourhood of the school and their home. Each expedition was short and each group in the class had some special detail to discover: how the houses were numbered; which streets crossed others; where the traffic signs were situated and what they were; the positions of the shops, the fire hydrant, the letter boxes, etc.

These experiences, together with the use which is made of them, both directed by the teacher and undirected during the creative handwork period, form part of the active learning which we associate with modern schools and which can be introduced into formal schools without undue disturbance of the existing curriculum.

Investigation of the Classroom

Children do learn a good deal about their environment without leaving the classroom, but it is generally second-hand experience which young children often find confusing unless they have some ideas on which to build. No one would decry the efforts of teachers to inform their pupils through story-telling and pictures, but these alone are not sufficient. They depend too much on the activity of the adult instead of the activity, mental and physical, of the children. To correct this, teachers are trying to stimulate first-hand investigation by various classroom devices. Most common is the Nature Table, which is described in Chapter XV. Next, there is the Investigation Table referred to in Section I above. Any low surface is suitable so long as the children can see and touch easily. Some objects are supplied by the school and others are contributed by the children. They are often changed and shared with other classes. Magnets, lens, and a kaleidoscope have already been suggested. To these can be added scraps of clockwork engines, the insides of clocks and watches; measuring vessels and things to measure: dried beans, tape measure and spring ruler, a pair of scales and weights. The children's contributions often include nests, pretty stones, fossils, skeleton leaves, and oddments which have no interest for an adult but which, for various reasons, appeal to children. In the country, children regard empty cartridge cases as treasures and these are often brought for the investigation display.

The equipment of the table can be used during the creative activity period, but if there can be no such period then groups of children cluster round it before the sessions begin, and in bad weather when they cannot have the usual playtime. It must be strongly emphasized that this collection is to be handled and used for experiment; looking is of little value.

If a centre of interest develops which needs a Display Table, the equipment gives way for the time being to the current enthusiasm. A class of children who did not normally work on activity lines, undertook a centre of interest for two weeks each term. At one time they decided to investigate their own neighbourhood which was in the country. Their ages ranged from five to eleven and, while the older children were on the expeditions with maps or looking up names in the church, the little ones found out what they could about sheep which grazed in large numbers on the hills around. As the interest developed, the Investigation Table was used to display specimens of wool, local stone, pictures and photographs, specimens of the flora, etc. At the end of the two weeks the table formed part of an exhibition illustrating their work, and was on view to the other classes.

Another teacher, realizing the importance of the environment in education, abolished the usual routine while for several weeks the children undertook the study of 'roads.' In this case, the Investigation Table gave way to a scale model, made by the older children, of the roads and buildings in their immediate neighbourhood.

Other Real Experience

Without disturbing the formal nature of a class, the children can take a share in the care of their room and its equipment. These "exercises in practical life," as Dr. Montessori calls them, can include more than dusting, tidying, arrangement of flowers and the keeping of the weather chart and Nature Calendar, for the children can organize the collection of waste material for the creative handwork period and different children can be responsible for different sorts of materials: matchboxes, newspapers, cardboard, etc. They will write labels for the cartons into which their friends drop their contributions and put notices on the wall to tell the others when their supply needs replenishing. The distribution of the mid-morning milk can be undertaken by groups of children; after a little supervision they can be left to do the job independently. Volunteers can look after the individual apparatus and tend the Nature Table or keep the Display Tables in order. Percussion band instruments and physical training apparatus also need care. Every job of this sort is an opportunity for undirected action and first-hand experience.

Community Hours and the Work of the Head Teacher

The head teacher can do a great deal to stimulate activity methods in a school where the teachers prefer traditional methods. She can arrange frequent staff meetings and emphasize the aims which underlie progressive methods. She can inaugurate discussions on more progressive methods and arrange for her staff to see them in practice.

If the creative handwork period has been introduced, she can take the responsibility for one or two sorts of activity. For instance, one woodwork bench and several sets of tools may be all the school can raise. If the Woodwork Corner can be fitted up outside the classrooms, perhaps at the end of a cloakroom or corridor, the noise of the activity is banished from the rooms and the head teacher undertakes to supervise the children who work there. Sometimes, large constructional work is taken into the hall, where children from all classes work away together, and the head teacher gives friendly help.

It is her responsibility, also, to see that the utmost use is made of all space, outdoors and in the school. The hall and playground should be in constant use unless the weather is too bad for outside activity. If no physical training or music is going on in the hall, the space can be used for dramatic work or for play with large toys or for creative activity such as we have described. It is no unusual sight to see children using every yard of space in corridors, in porches, and so on. A time-table well displayed, showing teachers when they can take possession of these public places, is vastly more important than the lesson time-table.

It is also the head teacher's privilege to alter the appearance of the school outside the classrooms, if she wishes. Outward signs of activity can be misleading but, at least, they show that the children are being considered and that it is a children's place. Pictures, books, and flowers should be low enough for the children to see and touch ; any useless decoration can be replaced by the children's own paintings or pictures which will attract them. In one school the head teacher was responsible for several large aquaria which were kept on low tables in the hall so that the smallest children could see them.

If no other form of activity is possible, perhaps the head teacher can herself take charge of each class, for say an hour a week in the hall, when all the available toys and materials are assembled and where the children can choose and talk freely under her quiet supervision.

Schools of all types enjoy a 'community hour' weekly when every class can offer some form of entertainment or display for the benefit of the rest. There are plays, verse speaking, miming, percussion band, dancing, singing, as well as displays and explanations of things made. Each class notifies the head teacher a little beforehand about their contributions ; they choose their own announcer and, as far as possible, carry through their performance without any adult help.

Spoken English

We come now to discuss the relation between activity and the most important aspect of the young child's education. There is no doubt that in many cases the Infant School bears the heavy responsibility of speech re-education. Without any exaggeration, we can say that the majority of children who enter the schools at four or five years come with distorted, inarticulate speech habits. It rests with the school to transform this stilted half-audible language into clear, fluent, easy, confident speech. How is it to be done?

From the beginning, we have Nature on our side. During these early years children delight in talking, naming, asking questions, making up nonsense and playing with words and phrases. They are quick and eager to imitate both good and bad language; to catch mannerisms from each other and to adopt any sort of speech which attracts their attention. Talking and experimenting with the vocal organs is one of the inborn natural activities of early childhood. That is why "Don't talk" and its counterpart "Don't fidget" were once the constant admonitions of all adults in charge of young children in traditional schools.

We are learning now that it is hopeless and unprofitable to go against this stream of verbal activity. In other chapters there are accounts of schools which have entirely banished the rule of silence, knowing full well that to say, "Don't talk," is to mean, "Stop learning how to talk."

Teachers in traditional schools who wish to introduce a more modern curriculum must consider the question of verbal freedom. Activity and talking cannot be separated; young children especially have to talk as they do things. Moreover, if we realize our responsibility with regard to language development, we have to consider the fact that no amount of speech training replaces the simple method of just talking freely.

It is a good plan, in considering the day's programme, to see how often it is possible to allow the ordinary, friendly exchange of conversation which takes place when several children are playing together in a good home. We have already mentioned the possibility in connection with the creative handwork period. There seems to be no reason why a rule of silence should be enforced as children take off their outdoor clothes or dress to go home, as they wash their hands, pass along the corridors, or drink their mid-morning milk. There is no reason why they should not consult each other as they work their individual exercises or prepare their reading. In fact, the only time when silence is necessary is when they should be listening: during a story or talk, when instructions are given in music or physical training lessons, or when they should be attending to a blackboard lesson. Children who are used to talking whenever the more informal activities are in progress give immediate and voluntary attention without any repeated admonitions of "Don't talk" or "Sh-sh." Of course, they know from experience that they will hear something which interests them. Occasionally, it is necessary to give a reminder "Talk quietly" or to tell a child who is interrupting another child's concentration to "Get something to do."

When first lifting the ban on talking, children do tend to talk loudly, but this stage is soon over, especially if they are often asked to " talk in your ordinary voice."

The voice and attitude of the teacher has a deep influence on the speech of small children; they imitate her accents and the courtesy and friendliness implied in her tones. It is her friendliness also which breaks down speech inhibitions. Activity methods and a friendly attitude cannot be separated. There is no need to use a shrill, penetrating, unnatural voice to enforce discipline. It is replaced by a natural, friendly voice which suggests approval and understanding; and implies that the adult is on the side of children and ready to co-operate with them. This, in its turn, influences the atmosphere of the classroom and when children discover that they are members of a happy school group, wisely controlled by a cheerful adult, their speech quickly becomes clear and confident. The one-word answers, indistinctly given, are replaced by well-rounded sentences. As Gesell remarks, it is difficult to stop them talking.

Vocabulary

In schools where the curriculum must continue on traditional lines the handwork period described at the beginning of this chapter will give the teacher an opportunity of discovering the dominant interests of the children. The uses to which boxes and bricks are put, as well as the drawings and models, will show when groups of the class are concerned with trains, aeroplanes, animals, shops, etc. These topics can be substituted for the more orthodox ' conversation ' lesson or ' picture-talk.' In these discussions, the teacher stimulates the children, by questions and suggestions, to talk about their plans for carrying on their interest; she also encourages them to tell each other what they know about the subject. " Tell us what you are going to make next," says the teacher after a child has shown the others the ship he has made. " Another ship," he may reply. Then he is encouraged to speak continuously. " Tell us just how you are going to make it." This might be followed by a suggestion that somebody else should tell how they would make it. There should be interruptions; other children will want to give advice; somebody wants to argue and the teacher listens with approval. When her chance comes, she manages to talk about different sorts of ships, and she uses new words and mentions the various parts of ships by their right names. As the discussion proceeds, the children also speak of port-holes, rigging, gangways, cable, hatches, etc. and before the interest has progressed far a completely new set of words has been added to their vocabulary. They not only know them but can use them appropriately and follow a conversation which deals with them.

These discussions are usually given an informal character because the children are free to leave their desks and sit in a friendly group round the teacher. A few mats or small chairs and a spare teacher's chair can be useful. " Come on the speaker's chair and tell us all about it," encourages an inarticulate child to speak at greater length.

If the conditions of the school are such that even a free choice of handwork is impossible, the orthodox ' conversation ' lesson can be developed on freer lines by the substitution of a period when the children can exchange news from home and outside school. " Tell us what you did last night," or, " Where did you go on Sunday ? " asks the teacher and volunteers are encouraged to interest others (see *Infant and Nursery School Report*, p. 127). The framing of stimulating questions on the part of a skilful teacher can do a good deal to break down reserves, as can also her reminder : " Make John hear, he's right at the back." The question of audibility needs tact and patient encouragement. Too much attention and over-emphasis on ' trying hard ' makes some children still more voiceless. In schools where activity methods have been introduced gradually, children suddenly find the use of their ordinary voices. In the midst of a busy classroom during the creative handwork period, one child's voice will suddenly ring out loud and clear above the general hubbub. The rest stop to stare. " Was that you ? " asks a child. " Well done," commends the teacher. This child will probably be disturbing for a week or two as she continues to practise her lately-developed vocal powers on every possible occasion.

As schools adopt the more progressive methods, the old practice of ' hands up ' becomes a custom of the past. Children ask questions and make remarks in the classroom as naturally as they do at home. The informal news time would be a complete failure if the children had to wait their turn to speak with their hands in the air. They are just as capable of not interrupting or waiting their turn in discussion as adults and, if they are too eager at first, they soon learn by experience to consider others and to behave as members of a group.

Speech Training

Speech training lessons in formal schools sometimes defeat their ends by cramping the natural flow of language and inhibiting continuous, verbal expression. There is no need for this unhappy result if we think of speech training as a period of relaxation and activity on the children's part more than the teacher's. The fun which the children can enjoy as they play their games of animal noises in order to improve their articulation and enunciation is described in Chapter XI. Speech training rhymes are meant to be similarly used. All effort should come from the children; the teacher only suggests and controls a happy, carefree, almost boisterous lesson. The nonsense jingles which are meant to amuse the children and which appeal to their natural love of word-rubbish should be voluntarily repeated again and again for sheer delight in playing with language.

If noise and laughter are not welcome in the Infant class of a mixed school, the best plan is to take a few minutes' speech training daily, just before the children dress for going home. Then, they can repeat their jingles as much as they like as they go round their cloakroom. The exercises are of no use whatever unless they are practised, and practised again, because they are thoroughly enjoyed.

Dramatization

A royal road to clear speaking, and one which belongs essentially to activity methods, is by way of dramatization. Chapter XI tells how children in modern Infant Schools often set up their own small theatres and arrange their own plays. In notes on various centres of interest (Chapter II, III), there is a brief account of a class of seven-year-olds who were responsible for their own classroom stage and orchestra. In every school where an activity curriculum is in operation, the children at some time or another spontaneously organize one or another form of acting. Sometimes it is puppets, or the pictures, or street entertainers.

Dramatization after story-telling is usual in schools of all types. Because acting, or pretending, is one of the natural creative activities of children, it is a pity not to give it more time and attention, especially in formal schools where other interests have to be repressed. With skill on the teacher's part, the inner activity of the children can be stimulated until a play is really of their own making and producing.

Except in a class of mixed ages, the five-year-olds are too immature for organized acting; their dramatization is more of a 'let's pretend' game. In the Infant room of mixed ages, however, they can be quite important as the audience or they can mime the parts of animals, or join hands to make the walls of a castle or the boundary of a field. Six-year-olds are capable of making their own simple plays.

As an illustration, we will take a nursery rhyme: for example, *Little Miss Muffett*. Instead of filling up the last few minutes of the afternoon session with the dramatization of a complicated story which the children have just heard, we might leave the whole of the story period for play-making and acting. When the children have understood that they are making a whole play from *Little Miss Muffett*, the teacher begins by stimulating them to think of the scene in Miss Muffett's home. Where did she keep her tuffet? Where would she eat her curds and whey? What was she doing before? Perhaps her mother was busy in the kitchen and Miss Muffett was playing on the floor. Perhaps her mother noticed the time and said, "Miss Muffett, it's time you had your curds and whey." If she was a helpful child, she probably fetched her own bowl and spoon and her mother poured out her refreshment from her big jug. "Sit down and have it comfortably," suggested her mother. "Oh dear, I've nothing to sit on; your chair is too high." "Run and get your tuffet from the other room," suggested the mother. And that is why the tuffet was in the kitchen.

It is easy enough for a teacher to make up a sequence of ordinary events which are simple enough for six-year-olds to mime but it requires more skill to stimulate the children to make the play for themselves. The result depends on carefully-phrased questions. Teachers who work in this way use a notebook and take down all suggestions. Then with the help of the children, as much as possible is embodied in the play. No imaginary lesson can do justice to the actual planning of a class which is experienced in this sort of playmaking. The children make remarkable suggestions which are often quite practical.

Having a rough idea of the action, teacher and class discuss the dialogue. This is chiefly to give them plenty of suggestion rather than to compose definite words. The conversations may be settled but the children do not consider that they are unalterable. Original remarks are made during every performance, the children take up their cues very easily, and the play changes from day to day during the first few weeks. Then, suddenly, the words acquire an accepted form and if any character makes an innovation, the class insists that the 'proper' words shall be spoken.

Before the children act this scene, the whole class practise miming the action. If they have decided that mother is baking, they mix the dough and roll it out, then cut a shape and place it on an imaginary pie. They practise glancing at the clock, opening a drawer to get out a spoon, lifting up a heavy jug to pour liquid into a bowl. Individual children will practise looking for a suitable bowl, going out of the room and bringing back an imaginary tuffet. To keep the spontaneous character of the play, it is better for the teacher not to demonstrate the actions; children who are more creative than the rest can show the others. As far as possible, the teacher should remain in the background, stimulating but not detracting from the creative activity of the children.

When the scene is ready for its first rehearsal, as many children as possible are used. In this case, Miss Muffett might have a baby sister who sits and watches, or who plays near by. There may be a cat and a dog. This is where a few five-year-olds can take part ; they enjoy curling up like a cat or lying outstretched like a dog. Properties are unnecessary beyond what the room and the 'dressing-up box' can provide. This box of old finery is worth keeping in every school. It is an assortment of discarded clothes, hats, handbags, feathers, pieces of curtain, furs, buckles, and anything which can be used to transform a child into the character he is playing. Just a twist of material round the head will convince a rather shy child that he can make a success of his part ; a cardboard crown suggests a prince to the audience, even if the child who is acting is not very convincing.

Before the second performance of this scene, the class is invited to criticize. "I couldn't hear what she said." "The mother was good." "She didn't look as though she liked her curds and whey." "Who thinks they can do it better?" asks the teacher. "Have we got enough talking?" And so the play progresses.

The next lesson begins with Scene 1 before the discussion on Scene 2 and the rehearsal of the whole play. A good repertoire of dramatized rhymes is made and noted before a story-play is attempted. The following rhymes are very suitable because they deal with the familiar kitchen scene : *Little Jack Horner ; Old Mother Hubbard ; Polly, Put the Kettle on ; Little Polly Flinders. Lucy Locket* can also be set against a familiar background : the garden or playground or inside a house. The following are more difficult but make excellent plays of more than one scene : *The Queen of Hearts ; Tom, Tom the Piper's Son ; Six little Mice sat down to spin ; Little Bo-peep ; There was an Old Woman who lived in a Shoe ; Sing a Song of Sixpence ; Pussy Cat, Pussy Cat, where have you been?*

Dramatizing Stories

The stories which the children know very well are the best for conversion into plays. Small children can act only what they know from experience and their experience is very limited. The richer the school background, the more imaginative experience they will be able to assimilate and the more ambitious will be their plays. They are usually successful with plays about animals. As an example, we will discuss *The Musicians of Bremen.* The following notes indicate the way in which a large class of seven-year-olds worked out the play.

They already knew the story but it was retold in a form which made the dramatization easier. It was suggested to the children that they should make the story into a play. Direct speech was emphasized and the action made particularly clear.

SCENE 1. After a good deal of discussion they decided that the first scene should be the kitchen of the mill with the miller and his wife sitting round the fire discussing the killing of the old donkey. A few sticks and crumpled, red paper in the wastepaper basket did duty as the fire and the blackboard made a wall. On the other side of the wall, the donkey crouched up for some warmth as the heat penetrated into his 'stable.' This was how he came to overhear the plans for his death. The dialogue ran something like this:

Miller : The old donkey must go. He's getting too old for work and is not worth his keep. If we kill him, his skin will bring us in a bit.

Wife : Very well, let's kill him tomorrow morning.

The listening donkey shivers and his knees shake under him; his head droops and he makes off that very night. (There is some practice before the children learn how to slink away like a sad animal.)

The miller and his wife remain talking by the fire and then decide to go to bed. (The children practise miming the lighting of a candle, raking out the fire, and taking steps upstairs.)

Their place is taken by the huntsman and his wife. Their old dog crouches against the fire-back in the adjoining stable. He also overhears the plans for killing him the next morning as he is too old and useless to be kept. After the dog has crept away and the couple retired to bed, their place is again taken by two old ladies with their ancient cat in the stable. As they decide to drown him the following day, he too goes off and the old ladies go to bed.

SCENE II. This scene is supposed to take place out of doors and the only 'prop' necessary is something on which the cock can perch, a high chair or the window sill. The donkey enters (the children have to practise being 'old') and meets the dog. "Where are you going?" asks the donkey. The dog gives the sad story of the night before and tells how he is running away. "I'm going off, too," answers the donkey. "I'm going to join a town band." He suggests that the dog could join him if he could contribute something to the band. "I can bark. Listen!" replies the dog and he gives a good demonstration. So the donkey brays and the dog barks and they go on their way till they meet the cat. The conversation is repeated and the cat is asked to show what he can do. His "miaow" being considered satisfactory, the three continue round the room until the dog catches sight of the dejected-looking cock.

He explains why he looks so sad; his master is going to kill him for the pot. When he hears the plans of the three animals, he shows them he can still crow, and he too joins the band. The scene ends with a noisy demonstration of the animals' band.

SCENE III. The animals creep in; they are exhausted. The donkey persuades the cock to climb up and see what is ahead of them. After climbing on to the window sill (or teacher's desk) he looks everywhere, peering this way and that, and at last spies the lights of a cottage. He explains the direction to the cat who is told to creep round the house to find out if there is any food and shelter for the band. (A screen play-house or blackboard can represent the cottage.) He returns with cat-calls and tells of the great feast which the robbers are enjoying and the bags of gold which lie around. "I could just do with a loaf of fine white bread," says the donkey. "And I could just do with those chicken bones," says the dog. "I'd give anything for a dish of fish," remarks the cat. "Well," said the cock, "let's play our band to them. They may give us a bite of supper."

They creep up to the house; the dog perches on the donkey's back; the cock and the cat get up on chairs to peer into the window and they all make a terrific noise with their various calls.

The disturbed robbers (there can be six or seven hidden behind the screen) fly for their lives and hide all round the classroom.

SCENE IV. The animals settle into the house. The screen house or the blackboard is turned around so that the audience can see what is happening. First, the donkey draws the curtains. Then the animals feast and make suitable remarks. Finally, they decide where to sleep. When all is quiet (allow enough time to create a feeling of expectancy) the robbers tip-toe across the classroom and form a group near the house. In hoarse but audible whispers they discuss their plans. The Captain (wearing something which shows his office) commands one of the gang to investigate. He creeps in and tries to light a candle at the gleaming eyes of the cat who retaliates with disastrous results. The robber then falls over the dog who bites his leg, and collides with the donkey who begins to kick. The cock descends from the window sill and crows as loudly as he can. The robber returns to the dismayed gang outside and gives a dramatic account of what has happened. The gang creep away to their hiding places in the classroom and the animals settle again with audible snore.

This is the sort of robust dramatic activity which appeals to children who are reaching the gang stage and who have plenty of energy which needs to be turned to good account. *The Tale of a Turnip* also makes an excellent rollicking play. *The Three Billy Goats Gruff* is similar and has been successfully adapted and acted by six-year-olds. Other suitable stories are: *Rumpelstiltskin; The Sleeping Princess; Snow-White and the Seven Dwarfs; Snow-White and Rose-Red; Henny Penny; The Three Little Pigs; The Shoemaker and the Elves.*

With a little ingenuity, the number of characters can include a large proportion of the class. *The Musicians of Bremen* uses about half an ordinary class. A ring of children seated on the floor makes the room where the miller's daughter spins her straw, and her baby can have a nurse and the dwarf can have his companions; there can be more than one little pig in the apple orchard and each pig can meet several people on the road before he finds the man with suitable building material.

The audience is also active and it is their applause and criticism which does so much to improve the play. "Can't hear!" calls a child from the desks and at once an actor raises his voice and improves his enunciation.

E. R. Boyce.

III. ADAPTING THE 'BABY ROOM'

In schools where there is no specially organized Nursery class, it is still possible to build up a curriculum based on those principles which inspire the best type of Nursery Schools.

The under-fives need conditions where:

(i) they can practise a growing independence;
(ii) they can meet with experiences which lay the foundations for the more formal work of the other classes;
(iii) they can talk without restraint;
(iv) they can mix freely with each other and learn by experience how to be friendly and to share their toys;
(v) they can play with well-chosen equipment under the guidance of a wise and friendly adult.

Types of Activities for the Under-fives

Learning to be Independent

It is important to allow plenty of time for these activities and to consider them as part of the real work of the class. All the following demand considerable effort from young children who are naturally 'dawdlers.' The test of a teacher's work in this class is not how much she does for the children but how much she enables them to do for themselves.

(*a*) Dressing and undressing. Undressing is much easier. In bad weather when there are so many outdoor things to put on it helps if the children see each of them spread out in the order in which they are to go on. The second sleeve is very difficult and the teacher's help is legitimate.

(*b*) Taking off shoes before resting, and putting them on again. (Tying laces is too difficult.)

(*c*) Washing when dirty: hands, face, and knees.

(*d*) Putting on overalls for a dirty job, and aprons for water play.
(*e*) Cleaning up messes : water, paint, etc.
(*f*) Putting away playthings.
(*g*) Fetching toys and changing them for others.
(*h*) Arranging chairs and floor mats.
(*i*) Arranging milk meal and rest.
(*j*) Dusting, polishing, and scrubbing.
(*k*) Washing dolls' clothes.
(*l*) Sorting out crayons, cleaning brushes, and paint-mixing.

Equipment : Mops, brooms, pans, and dusters must be kept where the children can easily reach them and where they cannot get into disorder. Ordinary sizes are the best ; the handles can be cut down to about half. A loop for hanging and a separate hook for each is an excellent plan.

Play Activities

The first concern of the teacher of under-fives should be her attitude of friendly sympathy, and the next should be the arrangement and equipment of playthings and materials so that the children have free access to them and space to play as they wish.

In the following notes, various activities have been isolated to show their value to children in school. It is sometimes possible to observe just how a particular play activity increases a child's opportunity for making friends ; for freer or more articulate use of language or for greater control of his limbs and hands. But no one aspect of the child's development grows without his whole personality being affected. Two four-year-olds may stack up the bricks into a trolley and together they may push their load round the room. Here we have an act of advanced co-operation for that age, an exercise in physical control and adjustment, and first-hand experience of numbers, space, size, and distance. Probably, also, there will be an interchange of conversation. This overlapping goes on constantly and the benefits of free play activities can be recognized, not in isolated bits of knowledge and achievements, but in the all-round growing maturity of the children.

CREATIVE PLAY ACTIVITIES. Drawing, painting, and modelling materials are arranged so that the children can use them freely. Large pieces of clay or Plasticine are needed but if there are a good selection of other occupations, six to ten balls only are necessary for a class of forty children.

Pattern-making games, *e.g.* peg boards and mosaics, are displayed on a low shelf or table so that the children can see what there is to choose from. Medium and large coloured beads for bead-threading should be attractively displayed with a threader in glass jars.

Building materials are very important and among the most

used of all material. All shapes and sizes are needed, but large bricks are especially valuable. Odd pieces of boarding, laths, and plywood are excellent for roofs and bridges.

Damp sand, also for building and modelling, should be available. A good-sized trayful is the minimum, a lined box several inches deep is better and a pile out of doors is best of all.

DRAMATIC PLAY ACTIVITIES. A dressing-up box, with oddments of finery, handbags, shopping bag, bits of uniforms, aprons, and pieces of material and curtaining, is an important piece of equipment.

The home corner consists of a three-sided screen which the children can arrange as the walls of a room. A clothes-horse with an old curtain tacked round is sufficient, but a hole for a window is much appreciated. Boxes, which can be used as furniture, dolls, crockery, and a bed make up the furnishings, and the children will devise anything else they need.

If possible, there should be a few boxes on wheels to use as vehicles; also bus tickets. A simple shop can be made from a table or boxes and equipped with cardboard money, empty packets and tins, and something which can be weighed, *e.g.* conkers, shells, small stones, etc.

Activities which involve Intellectual Problems

(*a*) Dry sand and pouring utensils, measures.
(*b*) Jig-saws.

Activities which involve the beginnings of Reading

Picture-books, catalogues and very easy word-picture books are arranged together and, if space allows, a few small chairs are near at hand to form a Book Corner.

Outdoor Activities

Where there is a communicating door into the playground, and this is very desirable, the children are free to come and go as they wish during the free activities period. Otherwise, in fine weather, a daily period is devoted entirely to play in the open air. Large toys like scooters, tricycles, and wheelbarrows are excellent, as well as climbing apparatus, balls, ropes, push-and-pull toys, digging tools, if there is waste space, and sand and water.

Activities involving the care of natural things and enquiry into natural phenomena.

Growing plants in the room, unless there is a garden. The children watch and tend them, help to set them and trim off dead parts.

Sowing and tending quickly-growing seeds.

Collecting and arranging seasonal displays (with the teacher's help).

Keeping aquaria, set up by the teacher, but the inhabitants fed by the children under her direction. The children sometimes help to clean out the tanks.

The keeping of a very simple pictorial Nature chart.

Recording the weekly weather by pictures.

Verbal Activity

Talking is perhaps the most important activity of all. The children are allowed to talk in their ordinary voices most of the day. A signal is used if silence is required for the teacher to speak. A silence card or some similar sign hung up in a position agreed on by the children is better than a sharp noise like a bell, whistle, or hand-clapping. There will be silence during rest time and comparative quiet during story-telling and any other activities directed by the teacher. The children like to interrupt with their comments during verse and story times and the experienced teacher knows that these remarks are valuable and is able to embody them into her talk without disturbing the attention of the rest of the class.

Physical Activity

No restrictions are enforced during play periods except that the children must take care of school property and not interfere unduly with each other. They play with whom they like, wander where they will, sit or stand at their occupations and are generally as physically free as the space allows. Sometimes they are allowed to overflow with their large toys into corridors and the hall.

Directed Activity

This includes lessons in rhythmic movement, singing, rhymes (including number rhymes), informal speech training games, stories and picture-talks. They are entered on the programme as 'music' or 'English.'

Suggested Daily Routine (chiefly for four to five-year-olds)

(*Times are approximate*)

Morning

Until 10 a.m. Arrival, undressing, changing shoes, and washing and toilet, if necessary. Play activities and tidying room afterwards.

Until 10.30 a.m. Arranging room for milk meal; some children to wash hands; sing-song and finger plays, meal, rhymes, clearing away.

Until 11 a.m. Music, story, and speech training games.

Until 11.45 a.m. Play (out of doors preferably).

Preparation for home and afternoon school or preparation for dinner at school.

Afternoon

Rest, play (as much as possible out of doors), short period for rhymes or story or sing-song before leaving for home. Tidying and cleaning toys and room when necessary; washing, for children who need it.

If dinner is taken in school, all the children will need to wash and use the toilet.

When the Children are Five

Teachers who are used to this sort of school day for the under-fives sometimes doubt the wisdom of carrying the play activity period into the next class. " Isn't something more formal and more like work better for them ? " they ask.

Formality is introduced gradually and each year the time-table shows that the school supplies the need of growing children for more routine. The five-year-olds have their physical training period and they join in the school assembly. There may be a short period of directed activity when they are introduced to their first reading experience. The sixes and sevens like to feel they are progressing with the three R's, so we set aside their practice times. But at each age the children still need a long, daily period when they are free to choose their activities, to work or play with companions of their own choosing, to create what they like, and to do anything or nothing.

' Work ' and ' play ' are interchangeable terms where young children are concerned. They often call play their ' work ' and the activity time is spoken of as ' My own time.'

Changing Character of the Activity Period

In schools where each class has its ' free ' period, teachers find that the character of the ' work-play ' changes with the age of the children. The *under-fives* have few group interests. They may play side by side or with one companion. Some children may spend time just watching others. There are wide differences also in the length of time they spend in one occupation. They may use one kind of material for a few minutes only and pass to something else which holds their interest for thirty minutes. The skilful teacher leaves them undisturbed, knowing that their capacity for more and more sustained attention develops as they continue to become absorbed in their play.

The *five-year-olds* often return for several days to the same interest, an indication of how much more capable they can be at sustained effort and attention. They are also better at playing with others but it is not often that more than two five-year-olds share in one purpose at the same time. Three together often end in trouble, and the teacher has to protect one from the other two. In a class of mixed ages, the fives respond well to the older children and agreeably accept a small part in a group activity. But they do not stay for long; they walk away directly they are bored. It would be unwise to force them to co-operate in large groups at this age.

The *six-year-olds* approach their material with a more mature attitude. They still like a good deal of dramatic play but they also like to experiment, to handle lots of different materials, and to try out new ways with familiar things. On the whole they are more creative; they make more things and are more particular about the look of their constructions. They concentrate for long periods on their paintings and will add daily to something they are modelling. Among a class of six-year-olds there are usually several groups the members of which are full of ideas and plans. In many cases these plans are too ambitious but this is no reason for interference. The children begin with great enthusiasm and then get confused. Their eagerness disappears and they want to give up their purpose. This is the point at which the teacher helps by giving them encouragement and simple directions. Perhaps a few suggestions and some information are needed to clarify the plans. There may be other setbacks before their purpose is complete and the teacher helps them on until their plans are brought to a satisfactory conclusion.

A simple reference library of illustrations is very useful at this age. Boys want to see just what a particular aeroplane looks like before they make one and girls like to get ideas for dressing-up clothes which they tack up from discarded materials and sacking.

Six-year-olds appreciate a chance to talk about their interests and to show what they have made. They can organize visits from another class to see their finished model set out and they are delighted to give their own explanations. They should always be given the opportunity for performing a play they have planned and rehearsed.

While they are much better at group activities, the groups are still unorganized. Perhaps the leaders, who are often a couple of real friends, begin a centre of interest and four or five others appear to co-operate. But many of these may go off to another interest at any moment and the rest of the group do not even enquire when they are returning. Fresh children appear from time to time. Only the originators may continue till the plans are complete. There will certainly be some children who play alone for most of the time. In a group of mixed ages, six-year-olds are liable to bully younger children and the teacher has to protect them.

Seven-year-olds like to be getting on with things to do and to feel that something is expected of them. The day becomes more organized and includes very short periods of group blackboard drills in tables, handwriting, word-study, etc. They like a well-planned day and respond excellently when given a set time in which to do their three-R practice work. A blackboard notice tells them each day what they are to do and they work through their 'assignment' with enjoyment. In spite of the more formal day, the free activity period is still very important.

Constructive activities are chosen more often than in the younger classes. Unlike the sixes, the sevens are not concerned with the finished article but are intensely interested in the actual making. Woodwork tools are the favourites. They try to get their models to look like the real thing; they handle them carefully, and if paint is used, it is put on skilfully. Brushes are chosen with care and are washed before different colours are used. Dirty water is constantly changed. They are proud of their masterpieces but are ready to take them to pieces to make something else. As a rule, there is less make-believe activity in this class.

The children are now better at planning and can follow a discussion dealing with ways and means. They want the teacher to give them hints and to make suggestions which they may or may not accept. As many as five will co-operate seriously together in carrying out their own purpose and the teacher can do a good deal to help by encouraging and praising the whole group. When their combined efforts are complete, they experience a happy feeling of shared achievement.

While a whole class is unlikely to join spontaneously in one interest, it does no harm if the teacher suggests a class centre of interest, provided that it is made clear that everyone is free to join in or leave when he wishes. In most classes it is found that several group interests go on simultaneously and that a good proportion of the children join with one companion or frequently play alone.

This is an age of invention as well as of experiment. The boys are constantly 'rigging' things up and utilizing odds and ends: boxes and cartons and pieces of electrical equipment. Paper and cardboard modelling are popular. The teacher's work, therefore, includes more hints on *how* things are done. She should be able to manipulate woodwork tools and be ready to show how to weave stuff, model in cardboard and clay and paper, and so on. In fact, the traditional equipment of the teacher of Infant School handwork is very useful in this class.

The reference library begun in the class of six-year-olds becomes increasingly important. Some children can follow printed information and instructions. Seven-year-olds want hard facts and their choice of activities shows how far they are concerned with reality. By books and pictures, expeditions and explanations, and through stories, we do our best to satisfy their enquiries.

E. R. Boyce.

Chapter VI

HOW THE CHANGE-OVER WAS MADE

It will be apparent from previous chapters that careful preparation and planning are necessary before a change-over from formal to activity methods can be made. Each school must plan individually according to its needs, but the following descriptions of how the change-over was made in (1) a large Town School and (2) a two-class Rural School are included in practical illustration.

I. IN A LARGE TOWN SCHOOL

The first glimpse of my new school showed a modern building lending itself to children's activities, many of which could be carried on out of doors on the verandahs and on the lawn. A strip of grass on the farther side of a large concrete playground immediately suggested an ideal site for the children's own gardens.

I longed to start these little ones on education according to the three A's: age, ability, and aptitude. Above all, I wanted to write a large A for education through activity. However, I realized that it would be wise to introduce changes gradually. First, it was essential to talk over ideas with the staff; the circulation of books, articles and even paragraphs dealing with pioneer education efforts was most helpful in starting staff discussions. Gradually a fairly general desire to adopt activity methods was shown. So we decided to start with one class and we chose the youngest children, aged four years and nine months to five years.

First Changes

Room and Furniture

The teacher of these young children willingly returned all formal three-R apparatus to the stock room. The furniture was then considered. It was felt that colour must be introduced. So the drab brown chairs were painted in bright colours. Surplus blackboards, placed across two small tables, were used to make large tables. These were painted attractively on one side only. They were turned over when surfaces were needed for drawing with chalk.

Cupboard doors were very wide and took up much space when open. So several of them were removed and replaced by gay curtains. The uninteresting tiles on one wall were covered with paper attractive to children. Some of the brown paint on the woodwork of the room was repainted in a fresh green. No more could be done to the room itself at this time owing to general restrictions and shortages.

Play Equipment

Next, we considered what equipment the children would need for their play and experimenting.

SAND AND WATER. Surplus blackboards were converted by the school carpenter into a deep trolley. This was filled with dry sand and various implements, such as spoons, sieves, and containers of different sizes. Two zinc-lined trays were found in the stock room and the carpenter put these on legs. Into one went the wet sand and suitable implements. The second one was used to hold water, jugs, funnels, rubber tubing, and bottles of various sizes.

CLAY. A zinc-lined clay box was bought and red and white clay, ready for modelling, was placed in it. Close by was a boxful of pastry-cutters of all shapes and sizes and butter-pats of different designs.

BRICKS. Building-bricks and odd chunks of wood were collected and placed in a large box on wheels. Large compressed cardboard containers, thrown out from the school canteen, were painted for use as building-bricks too.

PLAY-HOUSE. Across one corner of the room was placed a screen house. Gradually we were able to equip this with suitable furniture: dolls and beds, crockery and several domestic utensils. A little later the children wanted two rooms, a bedroom and a living-room, and so we fixed up a dividing curtain inside the house.

PAINTING. Two home-made, double-sided, painting-easels were placed in the room. Some sheets of kitchen paper were clipped on to them. A few jam jars were filled with powder paint though at first a range of only five colours was available: red, yellow, blue, green, and brown. A large painting-brush was provided for each jar.

Mathematical Equipment

To simplify class organization and to ensure that the children had opportunities for gaining mathematical concepts through activities, we decided to separate all games and activities which had a mathematical bias. These were kept in special cupboards. In selecting these we kept in mind the following concepts and skills which we considered desirable for the children to attain: space, size, shape, capacity, volume, weight, measurement, understanding of fractions, and counting.

It may be helpful to give details of equipment under these headings. *Spatial* conception could be gained through play with big toys, hoops, scooters, prams, wheelbarrows, etc. For comparison of *size* we collected various bottles of different sizes with their stoppers, graded rings, various locks, and keys to fit them, and a set of cotton-reels prepared by sticking two together, three together, four together and so on. We also provided tins of beads to be threaded, some containing beads of two sizes, some of three, and some of four sizes. We also found some manufactured apparatus useful. To give experience of *shape* we provided building-bricks; some of these were purchased in sets and others were just odd pieces of wood we were able to collect. We also included easy jig-saw puzzles and tile mosaics. Tins were filled with beads, some containing round and square beads and some round, square, and oval ones. We made some shape insets with two pieces of plywood and also included some manufactured apparatus.

Play with sand and water gave experience in *capacity* and *volume*. To stimulate activity we provided different-sized beakers and spoons and different-sized bottles, funnels, and jugs.

Heavy and light objects and free play with scales in the shop gave experience in *weight*. At this stage we did not introduce actual weights, reserving these for the five-and-a-half to six-year-olds.

Constructive play with building-bricks and waste materials gave rise to practical situations introducing the need for simple *measurement*. Practice games were provided too. We collected a box of ribbons of different lengths to be matched with lengths painted on a board or on the wall. Another box contained paper to be measured and cut to lengths as painted on a board.

During free play with clay many occasions for incidental learning about *fractions* arose: sharing one piece between two or three children, etc. Insets with the wood cut into halves and quarters of a square, an oblong and a circle were also placed on the shelves.

Every possible occasion was used for *counting*: skipping, ball bouncing, bead threading, etc. We also provided tins of beads to be threaded in twos and threes or fours, etc., the directions for threading being given by a picture on a small piece of wood fastened to the end of the threader. Later, Number symbols were used as well.

As an introduction to *Number* symbols we provided games of observation: picture dominoes, picture matching, matching bus tickets, playing cards, etc. Later, we placed Number jig-saws and Number insets in the cupboards. In the Book Corner, too, we placed Number picture-books.

The first stages of scoring were introduced in this room, too.

The children played with skittles and drew pictures of those they knocked down. When they understood Number symbols, they wrote down the number of the skittles they knocked down.

Reading Environment

The room would not have been complete without a Book Corner. We arranged two tables in one corner and displayed picture-books there. Many books were home-made and contained pictures with one or two explanatory words. Later, it was possible to make a screen for this corner, too, which gave it an air of greater importance to the children.

Various notices were printed and hung in appropriate places, such as: ‘ Please shut this door,’ ‘ You may wash here,’ and ‘ Hang up your towel.’ One large card was prepared with the words: ‘ Silence, please,’ and used when needed.

Several sheets of kitchen paper were fastened together under an attractive cover. This became the class ‘ News Book.’ Later on, other books were made about the children's various activities: ‘ Our Wendy House Book,’ ‘ Our Pool Book ’ (arising from water play), ‘ Our Book of Paintings,’ and so on.

Introducing Activities to the Children

All these additions to the room were introduced gradually, and definite lessons were given on the activities when introduced. For instance, when bathing the baby doll was suggested, the teacher gave a demonstration not only of how to do the washing but also of assembling and putting away all the things needed. The class helped to decide where tools and objects for each activity should be kept. They soon saw the wisdom of keeping “ a place for everything and everything in its place.”

Daily Programme

The adoption of a daily programme was essential. This gave a sense of security to the children and was so planned that the children had periods of vigorous activity alternating with restful periods. The teacher understood, however, that if the children's interest demanded a departure from this programme, there was no need to adhere to it rigidly.

Observation and Records

From the beginning, the teacher observed the children carefully while they were playing, experimenting, and constructing. Through observation of gestures, movements, speech, attitudes to toys and to playmates, duration of attention, paintings and drawings, the teacher came to understand her children and their respective stages of development physically, socially, and intellectually. A system of individual records was adopted, including notes on general intelligence, special interests, social development, health, home conditions and, later on, attainments. At the end of each month the teacher wrote a general account of the class activities.

Later Developments

The experiment in this first room stimulated staff discussions and the parents' interest and criticism were aroused. So we called a parents' meeting and explained, as far as possible, the underlying principles of the play-activity approach to formal work. Many became most co-operative. One parent volunteered to spend an afternoon every week in school to help us with the painting and has kept this up for two years. Others were helpful in providing wood and materials and others again gave donations to the school fund. Gradually colour schemes were worked out in other classrooms and the hall was also re-decorated in attractive colours.

Art

We were anxious that all the children should have the opportunity of expressing themselves through art. The staff saw that this was not mere ' expression ' but was really the children's way to educate themselves. What they experienced they expressed and so understood more clearly. The staff read and discussed books on this subject and Cizek's method was mainly followed in school. Large brushes were in very short supply and we often had to use newspaper to paint on instead of kitchen paper. But we were fortunate in having a spare classroom which was set aside for art work. Each class had its allotted time for using this room and at other times it was used by individual children when they felt the need to use this means of expression. Soon the children's own pictures added to the colourfulness and interest of the school.

Woodwork

On the verandah near my room we made a Woodwork Corner. Here we placed home-made work-benches and a tool rack. At first, we gave the children hammers, saws, pincers, and nails. Later we added gimlets, screws, and screwdrivers, and rulers for the seven-year-olds. A tea-chest was filled with odd pieces of wood supplied mostly by the parents. When a ceiling had to be repaired in one classroom, the workmen gave us the old laths. Each class had definite times for sending small groups to this corner, where they worked under my supervision. At first I prepared a book for them which I labelled ' Things to make ' illustrating it with pictures and sketches. Very soon the children discarded this as they found that they had ideas they wished to carry out themselves. Another book entitled 'Things we have made' was more popular and the children regularly recorded their achievements.

As general activities increased in the school, some teachers found it necessary to supply their own Woodwork Corners in the classrooms.

One class of seven-year-olds have undertaken to build and equip a large, screen house to be placed in one corner of the hall and to be used exclusively for reading. They have called it 'The Library House.' Some old black-out frames have been used to make this and the children are keeping a book recording all the details of its construction. Planning it, selecting frames all the same size, and two half-frames for a door, fixing the hinges, distempering and painting it provide many problems for them. Next term they will tackle making the furniture for it and making and selecting some of the books to be placed there.

Mastering the Tool Subjects

Mathematics

After nine months we decided to introduce further changes in the children's mathematical training. The youngest children, the five-year-olds, had already been provided with opportunities for gaining many mathematical concepts, as described above. We realized that the sixes and sevens needed more to do than daily practice with sum cards.

The mathematical concepts, described in the work of the five-year-olds, were again kept in mind and we also added the following: money, time, and scoring. Clearer conceptions were expected from the sixes and even greater accuracy from the sevens. With the box of different-sized beakers, sand, and a spoon we provided written instructions, *e.g.*, "Find out how many spoonfuls in A. Write it in your book." Definite instruction was given about liquid measures and for a while one of the shops became a dairy. This enabled the children to apply what they had learned at once and in a real situation. Similarly, instruction was given about weights and a shop was equipped with weights, scales, and goods to be weighed. In order to shop more efficiently the children were shown how to make simple bills and how to use money.

Further experience in measuring was obtained through the use of a measuring board with the question: "How tall are you?" The children recorded their own heights and those of visitors, too. At the height of the children's interest, one teacher took the opportunity of converting a shop into a draper's shop and gave definite instructions in inches, feet, and yards.

Many scoring games were made. These included skittles,

ring board, quoits, spinning tops, ball games, fishing, and many original games similar to ludo.

Whenever practicable, the seven-year-olds were given written instructions and were encouraged to record their findings.

Drawing, Writing, and Reading

Realizing that the children's natural desire to draw could be used as an approach to writing and reading, we introduced the following scheme throughout the school.

FIVE TO FIVE-AND-A-HALF YEARS (*approximately*). The children were given books of plain paper and were encouraged to draw pictures and to talk about them to the teacher. It was enlightening to listen to the almost continuous flow of speech while the children were drawing.

FIVE-AND-A-HALF TO SIX YEARS (*approximately*). The drawings were continued as before, but now the teacher wrote words in the book which the child wished to say about his drawing. Later the children were encouraged to copy the teacher's writing.

SIX TO SIX-AND-A-HALF YEARS (*approximately*). Drawings were continued, but half the page was now left for writing about the pictures. The teacher wrote on slips of paper whatever the children wanted to say and they were encouraged to write the words they knew by themselves.

SIX-AND-A-HALF TO SEVEN-AND-A-HALF YEARS (*approximately*). The drawings now became smaller and more space was left for writing. The children were encouraged to weave stories around their pictures. Individual word books were now started in which the pages were lettered alphabetically. When a child wanted to know how to write a word the teacher wrote it on the page in his book corresponding to its initial letter. When that word was needed again the child could refer to his book. Thus the children built up their own little dictionaries.

This scheme led to the writing of many fluent and original stories.

A 'school post box' was also organized. Letters passed between classes, individual children, and teachers. A child, as postman, was responsible for collecting and delivering these letters daily. Invitations to attend plays, puppet shows, art exhibitions, etc., were received in this way.

The 'class news books' and records of activities increased and the seven-year-olds wrote their own. These made valuable reading material of vital interest to the children.

Two Years after the 'Change-over'

Today, two years after the new method was introduced, a quick glance round reveals the following scene:

The five-year-olds are actively experimenting with sand, water, or clay; some building with bricks on the lawn, others playing with large toys; one group playing in the Wendy House and yet others sitting quietly with picture-books or jig-saw puzzles.

The sixes are completing the stage, the scenery and the properties for the play they are producing, which will soon be performed in front of the parents.

The older sixes are happily engaged in the art room completing their experiences by expressing them through the medium of paint.

The sevens are making glove puppets and a stage. Some of them are writing little plays for the puppets.

The older sevens are scattered; some are reading, some working in the Woodwork Corner, and some tending their garden.

Yet another class is singing and dancing in the hall.

Many changes have taken place, yet we realize that we have only started to make school a place where our children can live, love, and learn. As we discover more about the children, their needs, and their ways of learning, so must our life in school inevitably change, too.

Dorothy Davis.

II. IN A TWO-CLASS RURAL SCHOOL

My first impressions of the children were that they were pleasant and well-behaved. They responded willingly to suggestions but were evidently not accustomed to thinking for themselves. They had a certain skill in the three R's, but had little ability to express themselves freely. They put up their hands to attract my attention, but it was clear that they did not feel free to approach me in any other way. I knew that we could make very little headway until our relationship was established on a natural basis.

I wanted the children to use their initiative, develop their individuality and discover their own creative powers, but I realized that the process must be gradual.

In the classroom I began with a choice within certain lessons. Writing cards were made from coloured cardboard with a picture and a poem or a nursery rhyme, and the children were invited to choose any card for writing practice. I encouraged the children to move, if necessary, during a lesson, and to give in their own books rather than wait for them to be collected. For art, there was a choice of paper of different sizes, of crayons or paint and, later, of their own illustrations. In arithmetic, a textbook from which the children worked individually was given in with their written work. Games were included in the scheme and the children soon fitted up a shop.

Now came the need for these children to be responsible for their own books. Hitherto they had been neatly kept in piles which were collected after each lesson and not given out until they were needed the next day, but I felt that the value of learning to care for their own things was of greater importance, so I sacrificed this well-kept appearance in favour of the much-handled, rather dog-eared books which are often produced. Pigeon-holes were then fixed and each child labelled his own with coloured, gummed paper.

I gave the children a free period one afternoon to see how they would use it. Most of them moved about, a few painted and some of the girls continued their needlework. Other children needed suggestions but they got busy in different ways.

That this experience was enjoyed and would be profitable was quite evident, so after some months I arranged a short period of undirected activity each morning after the Scripture lesson. Here the children made trains and drew railway lines on the floor, dressed up and had tea parties, drew pictures or continued their writing.

Later on, I found that they would get out a piece of work before school began and were often disappointed at having to put it away for a class lesson. At this point I decided to give them a free period at the beginning of each day and to move the Scripture lesson to the end of the morning. The children were happy in this arrangement and gave more attention to the Scripture lesson, having been free to express themselves first.

In the little room, too, the four-and-a-half- to five-and-a-half-year-olds were longing to *do* things. For most of the children, playtime had provided the only release for their pent-up energies. The playground was quite bare, with a good surface, but with no interesting crannies or apparatus. So a brick sand-pit was provided and there the children would build, sometimes alone, sometimes in co-operation with others, and they used it more often than in their recognized playtimes. A group of boys asked me to go and see their city of Troy. It was complete with walls and a moat and a wooden horse standing outside the drainage hole. (This was a story they had heard several weeks before.)

We also collected planks and rollers from the coils of American cable for steps, bridges, and see-saws, and motor tyres for hoops. Now the physical training lesson centres round this apparatus from which the children devise their own activities.

Music played an important part in the change-over. It told the children when to get ready for dinner, and when to stand for their good-bye hymn or to fetch their hats and coats at the end of the afternoon. We collected a percussion band; through this the children developed a sense of rhythm and knew the joy of playing together. I took singing in the usual way except that the chairs were arranged informally to avoid the atmosphere of a lesson.

The time-table now became elastic because I found that by using the children's interests as they emerged, the activity formed part of their natural growth.

" Can we do a play ? "—and this they will organize entirely by themselves. Tables are pushed together and covered with mats to form a stage. Rows of chairs are arranged for the audience, paper tickets bought and sold, and a ticket collector who tears them in half meets the queue as it proceeds to the performance.

Puppets have been another interest. All the children enjoy making them, and they arrange the show independent of grown-up supervision.

There is a purposeful air as the children go about their activities. A group of them made a house from tables and rugs and a little girl came to me with a pram made from a box, saying, " Miss S——, the baby's come by you to sleep. Will you call us if she wakes up and cries ? We've got to go and shake the rugs, then wash John's hair."

Some who have been drawing or painting will ask if they can pin up their pictures or take them home. There is a space on the wall for their own drawings.

We fitted up a Reading Corner from an orange box which we painted, and the county library provides a box of illustrated story-books. The children make good use of these and I find the books a great incentive to their reading. Said Joan: " Can I have a piece of paper to write the name down ? Then if they don't bring them back I can go round the ' houses.' "

The originality and freshness in their stories and letter-writing are a direct outcome of this atmosphere of freedom. Stories tell either of their own activities or of those living purely in their imagination (see Chapter IV). They write letters of invitation for their parties and open days, letters to their mothers (instead of a message), and letters of thanks for toys, etc.

We are still short of equipment in many ways, but the Grammar School woodwork class has helped with toys. The following is a letter which followed their arrival.

DEAR MR. F——,

Thank you very much for making the engine and the rocking horse and the truck They are all very nice I think I have not had a ride yet but I will soon have one I hope The baby's have got them. Well that is all I can say now so goodby.

Love from
ROSEMARY.

It has been interesting to watch how the children's art has grown more lively and interesting as their imagination has developed. Some children weave stories round their pictures while others express hopes or fears or joys. This commentary came from Michael, aged six:

> "A little boy jumped out of his pram and ran away. He got lost all night but a lorry driver found him and took him back. He nearly ran into a tree and said, 'Who's been writing his name on this tree? Put him in prison!' but the policeman said, 'No, he's been a good boy. He helped me to pick my apples.'"

Quickly the children developed poise and self-confidence and their powers of concentration in class lessons increased. I used to arrange work for the children but invariably there was a deviation from the plan. The children might ask, "Can we go on with our sewing? We will do sums this afternoon," or, "Can I draw a picture?" so I found that a notebook with a record of the children's inclinations, activities, and sayings was valuable for reference when planning school work.

Having built a house or a camp, the children will often ask: "Can we do our writing in our house?" Accordingly they are not frustrated and can give their whole attention to the work. Often they sit on the floor and make a table from a chair, or sit in a 'boat' and do their reading. Much of their work radiates from a centre of interest which usually arises from their undirected activities.

Handwork and art activities are pursued each day. Many activities now take place under the name of handwork; washing the dolls' clothes, pegging them out and ironing them, or organizing a play or a wedding party. There are times when the children will dress up and spend the whole day in fantasy during practice periods and class lessons. "I'm a princess," says one. "I'm a policeman," says another, while others will be kings or soldiers.

Nature study is all-important to the children, and since they are so fortunate as to live in the country, there is an opportunity of using this environment to stimulate their interest in living things. We set up a Nature Corner and an aquarium, and fixed a bird table in the playground. We have permission to visit a nearby pond and here the children catch fish, snails, tadpoles and sometimes a dragonfly larva. They will bring scraps of meat with which to feed these creatures, and bits of cheese, etc. for the mice.

Sometimes we go to a large wood not far from the school where the children will observe a squirrel's drey or a bird's nest. They learn to handle plants and flowers with care and this sympathetic attitude towards Nature is deepening their sense of wonder and reverence. We can only set their feet on the paths of discovery; we cannot hope to go all the way with them.

When the children had gained poise and independence, I began to feel that they could take a more active part in their morning worship and I asked them if they would like to make up a prayer. They suggested that a different boy or girl should do this each week. We think them out together and their prayers are generally little acts of thanksgiving, like Jennifer's this morning:

> "Thank you, Father God, for the little lambs,
> and the snowdrops and the blue sky——
> *Miss S——, that's not enough!*"
> (So I whispered)—" and the birds."

The children are quite sincere and there is a real feeling of reverence in their worship.

It is said that a child's attitude to life is formed by the time he is seven; he needs time therefore to make friends with this strange universe, and only as the teaching of subjects leads towards this goal should it be permitted before this age.

Barbara V. R. Smith.

* * *

The teacher who uses activity methods needs to have clearly and constantly in mind the fundamental nature of her work—the direction of the growing child towards integration of the whole personality. The first essential for healthy all-round growth is an atmosphere of well-being and security (which the teacher should provide). Help in co-ordinating the children's experiences and in supplementing knowledge are also important functions of the teacher.

The following sections are designed to aid teachers in these aspects of their work.

PART THREE

THE RELIGIOUS TRAINING OF YOUNG CHILDREN

Chapter VII

THE AIM OF RELIGIOUS TRAINING

And they brought young children to him that he should touch them.

THE whole aim of religious training is to do just this ; to bring the children to a state where they will naturally reach out towards God, as those children long ago must have drawn nearer to Jesus when they saw him. For religion is an experience, an understanding, a perceiving. It depends not upon precept and lesson, but upon the atmosphere in which the child lives. Therefore it cannot be gauged by the number of times Scripture appears on the time-table, nor is it chiefly carried out in morning assembly though these periods should be focal points ; but it gains reality and depth from the way in which the whole day is lived, and its truths may be apprehended in any lesson or any experience which is truly orientated : *I am come that they might have life, and that they might have it more abundantly.*

Yet how much reason have we given to the child to think that religion is a matter of living fully ? Have we not rather made it appear an affair of standing very still and quiet while others sing hymns he does not know, or say prayers he does not understand, to a God who is far away ?

A young child must feel love, courage, honesty, patience, forgiveness, and faithfulness before he can learn about them as qualities ; but we have to remember that, while words are difficult to him, impressions of actions strike on his soul far more accurately and clearly than they do on our less sensitive ones.

The First Essential of Religious Training

The first essential of religious training is that parents and, after them, teachers shall live a life which is in itself an effort to follow the teaching they would give their children. Fortunately, children seem to have a strong intuitive sense of what the adults round them are aiming at, and when we fail, as we often must, they are quick to perceive that we ' did not mean it.' Nevertheless, a grave responsibility lies upon each of us and it is obvious that what we do with our private lives is going to matter very much indeed in this kind of training of the children.

We have to see also that the words and analogies we use do really bear for the children the meaning we have given them.

Whereas to many of us the Fatherhood of God is a very precious attribute, to some young children ' father ' may not be the loving provider of good. He may be a strange, or even a frightening or angry man to be avoided. One little girl was puzzled by allusions in school to ' the Lord God.' She confided to her mother that she knew who God was, and she had seen the Lord Mayor, but she could not find out who this ' Lord God ' was.

The Growth of Wonder and Awe

In our schools we must provide also for the growth of wonder and awe. Flowers in the classroom and in the garden, the wonders of growth on the Nature Table and out of doors, the beauty of a sky seen at playtime, pictures, poetry, the joy of a mathematical truth understood for the first time, all these experiences, and many more, may lead to a fuller appreciation of the God who has said, " So are my ways higher than your ways and my thoughts than your thoughts," and who yet is with us to rejoice at the least of our joys, or to feel for the least of our sorrows.

Without love and reverence no amount of Bible teaching can be fruitful ; but with it, any good lesson may lead teacher and children on together in the pilgrimage towards the Giver of love and wisdom.

Morning assembly will grow differently according to the needs and opportunities of different schools. Here the needs of the Nursery and Infant School children must be carefully distinguished from those of the Juniors who enjoy being part of a large body. Set prayers in the Nursery are rarely in place, except as they arise spontaneously (as they often will in a free and happy atmosphere) out of news, or at grace-time before mid-morning lunch. Simple verses of praise to God may be learnt so that teacher and children can sing their thanks to God when desire arises. Occasional joining with the older ones at their assembly, especially when a Harvest Festival or some other special service has been arranged, may be a great joy and a stimulus to thoughts about God and worship.

Morning Assembly

Children of six and seven begin to enjoy and understand a regular morning assembly if it is arranged for them with care. Hymns will be short so that the children may know by heart a good variety, the prayer must be simple but have dignity. Sometimes it is a good thing to use an easy form of litany. A response like, " Hear our prayer," or, " Thank you, Lord," often gives children a feeling of greater responsibility. A short period of silence "for praying our own prayers in our hearts" is often a good thing.

One form of service which has been found useful is this:

(i) Hymn.
(ii) Reading (a few verses from the Bible, a poem, a short story or parable) or music, or singing by a group of children.
(iii) A few moments of silence.
(iv) A prayer read by the teacher, or a litany or a prayer said by all together.
(v) A second hymn or a sung prayer.

For children of this age it is often the hymn which is the vehicle of worship they understand best, and it is worth spending much time and trouble in searching for words and music which are both suitable and beautiful. Any hymn book may yield a few, and often some verses may be taken from a hymn where the whole is too difficult.

Above all, in planning the morning assembly the teacher must have within her the sense of reverence. The appearance of the room, the type of music played before and after, and her own sense that this is the service of God, all help to provide an atmosphere of worship. Especially is this a time when beautiful flowers or a fine picture may be of value. A child's mind will often wander from the words of the service, but if he carries away from assembly a beauty seen rather than heard, he has still gained something.

Some teachers have brought in the older children to help with the planning and carrying out of the assembly. This needs careful preparation, but once it has been tried, the joy of the children in their own service is so great that it is likely to become a weekly function. They listen with greater attention to the services planned by others when they have tried planning for themselves.

A really live daily service means that the Scripture period gains in life too, because it is a time when the children have opportunity to learn the words and tunes of new hymns to sing, to suggest subjects for prayers or readings at future assemblies. It gives the teacher a time to talk over and, if necessary, fill out the day's reading, or perhaps to prepare the way for the morrow's service. Children's best worship is often active and this is a good time to plan the tidying of the room for the assembly for the next day or week.

Bible Stories

Some Scripture lessons must, however, be kept for stories, for there can be a very real joy in the sharing of Bible stories between teacher and class.

Very few Bible stories have any place in the Nursery, except the Christmas story which comes to hush the excitement of that time, as we think whose birthday it is we are about to celebrate. The story of the baby in the stable is one of the very few which is universal and ageless in its interest. For the rest, it is useful to remember that a mother can tell many stories to the children on her knee which a teacher cannot safely repeat to a roomful of twenty children, because the mother can watch and guide the reactions of her own child, and can smooth away perplexities which no teacher of a class can possibly make sure of detecting. In the Nursery Class, stories of boys and girls, whose lives are more or less like their own, do far more to show children what we mean by loving and forgiving, and being self-controlled, than can Bible stories about people whose way of life was so different from their own. The wise teacher will, however, often speak of God and Jesus to the children. She will answer their questions as truthfully and seriously as she can. She will often talk to them as occasion arises about what Jesus said of birds and flowers and children. They will begin to feel that this God of whom they often hear is real and good though they cannot see or hear him.

At six, children begin to love stories from the Bible. In choosing these a teacher must ask herself searchingly what idea of God the chosen story is going to convey to a mind little experienced in the ways of the world. It is by these stories that she will give examples of the kind of thought and behaviour God wants from us, and she will have to leave aside for later on all those Bible stories which need an understanding of primitive society and beliefs for their full appreciation. In preparing her lesson she will consider carefully what she must tell or show the children in order to help them to understand the story as a child in Palestine two thousand years ago might have understood it. Pictures may be bought from various sources listed in the Bibliography. If pictures are on the classroom walls for several days before the lesson, the children have time to assimilate the idea of costume or countryside, and in the lesson a mere allusion is enough to help them to get the setting of the story right according to the picture.

The stories Jesus told are much loved by children of six or even younger. *The Lost Lamb* and *The Lost Coin* (from *The Little Bible Books*, S.C.M. Press) give an inexperienced teacher an idea of how to tell some of the parables so that children love and understand them, and at the same time build up a background of knowledge of how life was lived in Jesus' time on earth. The baking of bread, the building and sweeping of houses, the patching of wineskins and bottling of wine, are all concrete affairs interesting to young and practical beings, and in this way a storehouse of information is gathered which will later illuminate the reading of the Bible. When a parable has been told in such a way that the children can picture it happening, even in a far country long ago, the teacher will often be wise to take her Bible saying, "Now I will read you that story from the Bible, the way Jesus told it."

Stories should be told many times—indeed they are asked for again and again—and after a while the children may join in softly as the teacher reads from the Bible until at last they may know a whole parable well enough for a group of them to say it at assembly.

Some of the stories from the life of Jesus are suitable to be told in school to children: for example, the healing of Jairus' daughter, the lad who gave Jesus the loaves and fishes, the mother who brought her children to Jesus, and the story of Zaccheus, the man who was too short to see in a crowd, a disability with which any child can sympathize.

Stories of cruelty and pain should be left till a child is older. At this age they will either trouble him too much or else he will not understand enough for them to arouse any feeling at all. The tales Mary told to Jesus when he was little are also much loved. Here again a careful choice must be made of these which show the God of Jesus and not the dimly perceived Judge of the early Hebrews. The story of Ishmael, the tease, with its example of mother love finding an answering love in God; of Jacob, the lonely boy with his vision of the ladder to heaven; the story of Joseph who had faith and forgave; of Moses, the baby in the bulrushes; of Samuel, the boy who heard God's voice; of David who overcame the giant: all these are wonderful tales to tell and to hear and each has also a message for quite young children, a message of God's loving care for his children, and his call to be steadfast and kind.

The true expression of work for religious training is a life lived with finer understanding. In this matter, more than in any other, the teacher is sowing seeds about whose growth she is not likely to know anything at all for many years. Quick results are all too often spurious ones. She must sow in faith and wait.

Barbara Priestman.

Chapter VIII

RELIGIOUS FESTIVALS

I. CHRISTMAS, EASTER, AND SUMMER

Christmas

IN the *National Basic Outline of Religious Instruction* we are told that in teaching Infants, " use should be made of the festivals during the year, *e.g.* Christmas, Easter, Whitsuntide, and Harvest."

Christmas, of course, comes first in popularity with the child. There is a glamour about Christmas, a richness, a satisfaction that no other festival can offer to the child in the same way. The Christmas season is indeed a great opportunity for the religious training of children.

Dickens, in his *Christmas Carol*, sums up Christmas in these words : " I have always thought of Christmas-time—apart from the veneration due to its sacred name and origin, if anything belonging to it can be apart from that—as a good time ; a kind, forgiving, charitable, pleasant time."

Christmas to the child means happiness and giving, or rather getting. We can use these attributes simply and naturally in introducing the child to the Christmas story, or in recapturing its delight.

Our message to the children is quite clear : " Unto us a child is born " (*Isaiah*, ix, 6). And the meaning behind it is God's love, as we think of it in the words of the familiar hymn :

> Love came down at Christmas,
> Love, all lovely, love divine.

Let us see how we can interpret this to the children in preparing them for Christmas. We might plan it under three headings : the setting, the stories, and the child's own expression.

The Setting

It is usual to decorate the schoolroom for Christmas. We shall want some of this decoration to remind the children of the birth of Christ. Pictures might help, so far as they give the right suggestion and are not merely ' illustrating the subject.' Little cribs or big ones, built in sand-trays or old sugar-boxes, are much appreciated by small children. A background made of stone or brick or brown paper is very effective, and the children can peep inside as the shepherds did on the first Christmas night.

The manger is best made of wood or cardboard, so that the figure of the baby can be put into it and covered with some real bits of cloth. It is very nice to have real straw and a tiny light, disguised as a lantern.

The figures for the crib can be either bought or cut out of a cardboard set. A gifted teacher can easily make some out of Plasticine or clay.

Music played for the children's Christmas games and singing can also be used to great advantage. Some old carols, too difficult for the little ones to sing, make most suitable 'background' music. "Away in a Manger" is a deservedly popular hymn, as both tune and words are just right for the younger children. There are, however, many other delightful hymns that the children will enjoy singing during the Christmas season.

Stories

When we think of the Christmas stories, three stand vividly out in our minds: "The Nativity," "The Shepherds," and, later on, "The Wise Men."

They are ideal stories to tell to small children. They contain movement, expectancy, and a certain amount of repetition. They are simple in detail, direct in narrative, and interesting in background. They have purpose and finality.

Naturally many children will have heard them before, but often it is only the bare outline or one particular incident that the child remembers. His delight in the details is for the teacher to recapture.

The stories are satisfying and they should not be hurried. Quite often it will be useful to tell them from a different angle. For instance, in telling the story of the nativity and the traditional animals in the cave, the story might go something like this, possibly told around the model of the crib, and adding the figures as the story progresses:

Teacher, standing by the crib, in view of all the class, and putting in the figures, as she introduces them:

"Here is a small house; we call it a crib; it is a kind of shed in a rock. Once upon a time, an ox and a donkey lived there together. Here they are; the ox is big and brown and the donkey is small and grey. They ate straw out of this little box here, the manger, and they slept on the floor, side by side.

"One night, the big door was shut tight, for it was very cold outside. But it was nice and warm inside, where the ox and donkey slept. It was dark and very quiet, but suddenly the ox and the donkey lifted up their heads and listened. They could hear footsteps—someone was coming. They could hear them —step, step, step, step—coming nearer and nearer. Two people were coming; here they are. We know who they are, don't we? They are Mary and Joseph.

"They had come a long way and they were very tired; they walked so slowly. There was no room for them in the houses, so they came to this little place, where the ox and the donkey lived. When they came to the door, they opened it softly and looked in. What did they see? Why, the ox and the donkey lying on the floor. So they went inside, too. Joseph hung up his lantern and Mary looked around. When she saw the box with the straw inside she was very pleased. She thought it would be nice and warm made into a little bed. For Mary had a lovely secret, but we know it, don't we? Who was going to sleep in this little bed? Yes—the Baby Jesus."

And so, slowly, the story might develop. The ox and the donkey watched the preparations and later they came close to see the baby. The children also want to come closer, and their interest and curiosity, together with their pleasure, help them to take a real part in the Christmas story.

The other stories will as readily spring to life and offer the children an opportunity for willing, spontaneous worship. They will gladly join with the shepherds and, later, with the wise men in joyous praise.

The Child's Own Expression

This will naturally be aroused by the message of the Christmas stories, which clearly invite the children 'to come,' 'to see,' 'to worship,' 'to say "thank you"' and 'to give.'

We should plan our Christmas activities for the children in such a way that they find plenty of opportunity for expressing all the activities just mentioned.

It will help to introduce movement into Christmas worship: a march around to see the crib, model, or pictures; acting at being shepherds or wise men or other people desirous of seeing the lovely new baby.

Children might pretend to be shepherds, "all sitting on the ground," while the teacher (or an older child) appears as an angel to tell them of the glad happenings.

Such action around the stories can be varied in all sorts of ways.

There is no difficulty in making Christmas worship real to the children. 'Thank you's' are there, on the tip of their tongues, before we invite them. It is natural to sing "Praise Him" when there are lights and silver stars around and, perhaps, even a little Christmas tree all bright with chains and balls. But Christmas should not be all 'getting.' It must be 'giving' too. "God so loved the world, that he gave . . ." True love always implies giving, and it is quite natural for a child who knows the security of love to give readily and enjoy giving.

The children may be helped to make Christmas cards to take

home to mother, or have a simple toy service for children in hospital or in a home. It may be possible to make small presents for someone at home, an old granny or baby sister.

Christmas is very close to us. The children look forward to it with joyful expectancy. There is excitement in waiting and there is mystery, too. Children's hearts are very ready for the real message of Christmas ; it seems to fit into the general happiness. Of course the truth is that happiness fits into the meaning of Christmas. The two are blended together. The tidings that we have for the children are in fact " tidings of great joy."

Let us share in this joy ourselves, as we help the children in our care to come close to the crib and look at the Baby Jesus.

Easter

Joy is the keynote of Easter and, as recorded in the New Testament, the story is a triumph of life over death, joy over sorrow. Small children as a rule do not grasp the reality of death. When they do, they often rebel against it. In this way the story of the Resurrection will be gladly and fully acceptable to them, but the mystery of the message behind the story will be beyond the children's understanding.

Joy will remain and find a quick response in the children. For small children are eager to enjoy life and will gladly accept the suggestion of a happy festival.

Nature helps greatly to emphasize such happiness, for spring is a time of awakening and all round there will be the first flowers, green fields, fresh grass, and leaves. To small children these signs are ever new and full of wonder, for last year's spring is too far away to be remembered.

But the true, pure joy of the Easter story has come, as it mostly comes, through pain. This pain is a stumbling block to many who teach small children. Naturally, it would be wrong to dwell upon it, but should it be mentioned at all? Can young children grasp it? Is it wise to bring it to their notice? A teacher will, of course, answer these questions in her own way and reach her own conclusion. Yet it is interesting to notice how children from their early days have to experience the realities of life; the floor is hard, the fire is hot, the wind is strong, and all these bring unexpected disappointments to the child, as he falls, or burns his finger or loses a treasured paper doll. In this way, as the child grows older, valuable lessons of life are learnt—moral lessons. The child very soon discovers that pain has a place in the world. Floods of tears and heartbreak are often part of the ritual when saying good-bye to mother, if she goes away. But the lesson of pain goes deeper than that and gradually becomes purposeful and full of meaning.

A little girl, just six years old, discovered this for herself. She was embroidering a tray-cloth for her grandmother's birthday. Accidentally she pricked her finger and, seeing some blood, began to cry. But quite suddenly, she checked her tears and said : " It does not matter, 'cos I love granny so much."

In this way a new experience can guide a child into the way of truth and such explorations into reality are necessary to make children unafraid and self-reliant.

Even if it is decided to leave all idea of pain out of the Easter story, the children might bring it in themselves, if they have heard about it elsewhere. But in any case the talk around Easter will be about life and strength and joy.

A beautiful Easter picture will help the presentation of the story, or better still, a model of an Easter garden. The tomb (brown and grey) is at the back, and may be made of stiff paper. In the foreground a lovely garden may be arranged in damp moss or sand. Dwarf plants, short flowering branches, grasses and small flowers massed together in tiny paste-jars make a delightful garden, much enjoyed by children.

The Approach

It seems best to approach the subject from the point of view of one of the friends of Jesus. This brings it closer to the children, for it includes them in the story. They, too, are his friends. If it is decided to see the Easter scene with the eyes of Mary Magdalene, the story might develop something like this, while teacher points to picture or model : " What a lovely garden, full of trees and flowers." (Children will love to point out and describe details.) " Early in the morning, Mary came to this garden to look for Jesus. She was very sad and unhappy for she loved Jesus and she had seen him die on the Cross and now she thought that she would never see him again. So she stood and cried. We all cry sometimes when we are hurt or sad. When we cry, tears fall down our cheeks, and what do we do ? We wipe them away. This is what Mary did. And suddenly—she found she was not alone. Jesus stood close to her." (A little pause.) " But of course Mary could not see who it was, for she was crying. She thought it was the gardener and she asked him if he knew where Jesus was. But it was Jesus himself standing there, and he spoke to her : ' Mary.' Then she turned round and how happy she was ! . . ." So the story enters into joy.

A more active and deliberate approach can be achieved if the narrative follows the two disciples, Peter and John. If desired, the death of Jesus can be referred to more definitely, for it will often be found that many children have heard about the Crucifixion.

Without dwelling on the subject, the teacher might start the story in this way, acting it out with the model, or pointing to the picture: " This is a beautiful garden and this is a quiet cave where Mother Mary saw the body of Jesus put to rest after he died on the Cross. But when some women who loved Jesus came to look for him they were very surprised. The tomb was empty. Jesus was not there. He was risen from the dead. He was alive! They were so happy that they ran all the way back to tell the others. . . . When Peter and John heard it, they came running into the garden as quickly as they could. . . ."

So the happy news spread, and the children identify themselves with those who share in this joyful victory—share in it they must, if the lesson is to be real.

A great deal will naturally depend on the amount of knowledge the children already have of the New Testament story, but even if this knowledge is inadequate a great deal can be taught in the school. For the message of sorrow turned into joy is an important one.

A flower procession is a simple expression and is much enjoyed by the babies, walking around, singing an Easter song or a joyful hymn, each waving a spring flower.

The older children can help to make an Easter garden, and tend and water the flowers. A verse of an Easter hymn, or a short Easter prayer can be learnt. " Spreading the happy news " can be made into simple drama.

Easter provides a valuable lesson in the appreciation of spiritual joys. In crowded towns and busy days our small children derive their pleasures all too often from material things: the pictures, a shopping expedition, new clothes, toys, and sweets. There seems no room left for simple gladness that springs from the heart and is easily shared by young children.

The Easter story in the spring setting can give the children that sense of wonder and happiness. Like the corn-filled valleys in the 65th Psalm, they will be so full of delight that, watching them, we shall be able to use the psalmist's very words: " They shout for joy, they also sing."

Summer Festivals

A group of Nursery School children were busy in their playroom on a bright summer morning. Sunshine was streaming in through the wide-open windows, birds were singing outside, the air was fragrant, and the sky a deep, unclouded blue. The young teacher stood silent, enraptured by the loveliness around her. The children, catching her mood, became silent too, and for a brief moment nothing was heard but the song of the birds. Then, quite suddenly, a small, fair-haired little girl near the teacher started singing; " All things bright and beautiful."

The teacher and the other children all joined in and their joy found expression in fitting words.

Joy and laughter are natural to small children, and as they are strongly suggestible, a happy mood is very contagious. A joyous beginning augurs well for the rest of the day.

So when summer comes with the parks and fields all green and gay, to the child's wondering eye this transformed nature is a joyful experience.

Teachers of young children notice constantly how beauty of nature delights them. Usually small things appeal to children most—a bright flower, a light-winged butterfly, a goldfish in a pond, a little cherry-tree in full bloom. Children can often be found standing silent, entranced, in front of one of these, as if a magic circle were drawn around them. Beauty is a stimulus to worship; there is often but one step from wonder to prayer. How natural it is for small children during the time of thanksgiving to offer their 'Thank you's' for bits of loveliness that they have seen and remembered.

The connection between beauty and God comes spontaneously to the child's mind. A boy of six, while walking in a public park which was ablaze with flowers, said suddenly: "This must be God's very own garden!" Yet this particular child lived in a home where God was almost unknown, and his own religious knowledge was scanty.

It seems that the young child's vividness of imagination helps him to reach out to things unseen, and to arrive at conclusions which are sometimes incomprehensible to the adult mind.

Yet, observing that "all things bright and beautiful" draw the child nearer to God, it is wise for the teacher to use this stimulus as a natural step to worship.

Summer days are crowded with lovely experiences to delight a child's heart, but these are often missed and lost during the hum and bustle of everyday routine. Silence is perhaps the best way to approach all beauteous things, so that the children's attention can be wholly absorbed by them. Then, later, through spontaneous play, that self-chosen occupation of all normal children, these memorable experiences can be relived and stored away.

So we come to consider the possibility of some special lessons, where summer beauty will lead to joy and praise and find expression in thanksgiving and worship.

A lesson centred around God, the giver of all good things, can be planned somewhat on these lines: a big picture of a summer garden or meadow can provide the teacher with her subject-matter, turning the lesson into a picture talk. There should be flowers on the table, sufficient for each child to have one. This lesson should be timed to take place when the children's delight in summer flowers and sunshine is at its highest. " God is good and kind. . . . He makes the sun to shine and the flowers to grow. He wants us to be kind, too, and happy, enjoying all his good gifts. . . . We shall love him and praise him and sing to him. . . ."

The natural culmination to this kind of occasion is a gay procession all around the classroom, waving flowers for banners and singing a familiar hymn of praise.

Another type of lesson is a quiet, simple nature talk about little things that grow in the earth. Such a lesson is best taken on a sunny day. If the sun actually shines into the room, the children's attention could be drawn to the sun's rays and their lovely play of light. This time a small garden can be arranged in a sand-tray or, better still, soil can be used in which the plants will continue to grow, and a nature story told to the children about the growing plants. After the story, the children can be flowers themselves and, to soft music, open their buds in the sunshine. Prayer comes easily after such lessons. Having talked about " creatures great and small," having enjoyed teacher's story about " things wise and wonderful," the very next step is to think of the good God who made them all.

The mind of the young child is unhampered by doubts and criticisms. His faith is simple and natural and full of joy. Eagerly he looks out on to the world decked in summer beauty, as he sings:

> How great is God Almighty
> Who hath made all things well.

E. Yanovsky.

II. HARVEST AND OTHER OCCASIONS

Some knowledge of their heavenly Father, and a real consciousness of his enfolding love can be imparted to young children if religious training is woven into the daily round. For this, teachers find it helpful to have a ' Central Thought ' which is associated with the time of the year and with the general interests or projects of the school. It can be adapted to the needs of every class, and forms a strong link binding all the children together. In illustration a brief outline for the months of September (Harvest Festival), October, and November is given here.

September

In September, the children come back fresh from the holidays and full of the joy of harvest—golden sheaves carried to stack and barn, ripe fruits gathered and stored, the homely harvest of garden and field made safe for the winter. Will not our first thought be thankfulness, and will not that naturally be our ' Central Thought ' for the month ?

There will be our Harvest Thanksgiving, when we bring into school our best as an offering to the Giver of all good things. We shall speak to him and say ' Thank you ' in our prayer and worship, and we shall consider *how* we are able to offer our gifts to the heavenly Father—" Inasmuch as ye have done it." The lovely glowing fruit of the harvest, piled up in such profusion around us when we gather in school for morning worship, will be given back to our heavenly Father as a token of our love and thankfulness. How ? They will be given in the way Jesus said they might be given. They may be sent to our own sick children, or to the children's hospital, or we may possibly use them for the benefit of the blind or the crippled. The children themselves will have suggestions to make.

In some cases it may be possible to link the school with the wider circle of religious life in church or chapel. Then at close of school on Friday afternoon, groups of happy children may carry into God's house the gifts they have brought during the week, and themselves lay them in a special corner, ready for the ' grown-up ' Harvest Festival on the Sunday. This helps to form one more link between school and home, and deepens the consciousness of the one great Christian family.

It is a happy thought to invite parents to come and join in the morning worship on the final day of our Harvest Thanksgiving for many of them have helped to make it real and beautiful.

During this month there will be stories of the cornfields : Joseph and his brethren, and the corn in Egypt, our Lord walking " through the cornfields waving gold," and talking about them, the feeding of the Five Thousand, Elijah in the wilderness, and with the older children, the story of Ruth and Naomi.

As we learn and sing our harvest hymns, even the Nursery children will be able to join in saying " Thank you for the world so sweet," and so be drawn into the happy circle of those who are seeing in the harvest and " all good gifts around us " the token of God's love and care.

October

This will lead us on to ask how we can show our thankfulness, " not only with our lips, but in our lives." We shall think of other gifts God has given us : our health and strength, eyes to see the beautiful world, and ears to hear its music, feet to run about and play, hands with skilful fingers to make all sorts of things. How shall we use them ? Kindly, helpfully, lovingly. " Be ye kind one to another "—so here is our ' Central Thought ' for October : Kindliness, ' living together ' in love and friendship.

We think of our Lord's constant thoughtfulness and care for

others: his loving hands laid in blessing on little children, or in healing on the sick, the lame and the blind, his feet walking weary miles that he might minister to the people, his eyes always seeing those who needed his help, and his ears always hearing their prayer.

The children will enjoy the story of the Good Samaritan, and other stories of love and kindness, and we shall sing, "God whose name is Love," and of the "Mothers of Salem" who brought their children to Jesus, and we shall learn the gracious words he said to them.

November

November is the dark month. We lay our brown bulbs in the earth, leave them in the dark, and realize that we must wait patiently for many weeks.

Let us now go far away from fog and darkness to a hot sunny land—the land where Jesus lived. There, out on the hills of Galilee, we may meet the shepherds—the Eastern shepherds—those familiar and well-loved figures whom Jesus knew so well, and to whom he so often likened himself. We can remember again the lovely story of Jesus and the children. We may tell the children that it was said of Jesus that: "He shall feed his flock like a shepherd, and he shall gather the lambs with his arm."

Nearly all the Old Testament characters of whom the children hear in their Bible stories were shepherds: Abraham, Isaac, Jacob, Joseph and his brethren, Moses, and above all David, the shepherd who became a king.

Let us learn all we can about the Eastern shepherd: his dress, his weapons, his brave unselfish life, and his tender care for his sheep. Then we may carry a vivid picture in our minds of all that is implied in that dearest of all names our Lord gave himself, 'The Good Shepherd,' and we shall know *why* those shepherds were out on the hills of Bethlehem at midnight.

Lucy Diamond.

PART FOUR

THE PHYSICAL NEEDS OF YOUNG CHILDREN

Chapter IX

THE HEALTH OF THE YOUNG CHILD

EVERY growing organism is subjected to two main influences, those of heredity and environment. We cannot alter a child's heredity, but we can modify his environment very considerably. In the past, heredity was thought to be the more potent force of the two, but recent researches, especially those in relation to the effect of varying the nutrition of pregnant animals upon the subsequent structural and functional development of their offspring, have opened up wide fields of speculation with regard to the relative importance of genetic and environmental factors in the causation of certain congenital deformities, which we have hitherto regarded as due exclusively to inherited genes. We know that we can accelerate physical growth by judicious feeding. Recent American work shows that there are grounds for believing that mental development can be delayed by malnutrition and encouraged by more favourable environmental factors. These new observations can only make us the more determined to give every child the environmental benefits we would each wish to give to our own children.

It is essential, in speaking of the child's physical development, to remember that growth of mind and body is one single and indivisible process, and that it is impossible to consider one without the other. The development of muscular skills, for instance, with which the educational psychologist is rightly concerned, depends upon the physical state of the muscles themselves, the physical maturation of the nerves which conduct the impulses to and from the muscles, and the physical development of the cortex of the brain which controls and co-ordinates all muscular activity and relaxation. The healthy child is not only the happiest one, but also the one who is best able to benefit from his education. It is necessary, therefore, to provide for the growing child, without overstimulating him, the fullest opportunities for physical and mental activity, with suitable periods of relaxation; and also to give him the best environmental conditions, since these will encourage him to develop at his own optimum rate.

Fundamental Needs

In order to ensure mere physical survival five things are essential: shelter, food, fresh air and sunshine, exercise and rest, and good health habits. If the child is deprived of any one of these, no matter how well endowed he may otherwise be, he will cease to exist. But mere existence is not our aim for the children. We wish to develop their potentialities to the full, not only for the child's own sake but for the good of the nation.

Shelter

This word is used to imply much more than mere protection from extremes of climate. It includes all that love and wise guidance we give to the young and helpless. It includes, too, *warmth* and the equipment of our schoolrooms, kitchen and sanitary provision, and suitable clothing. We have, as yet, little power to decide the sort of building we consider best for our children. When social conditions permit it, and public opinion has been sufficiently educated to understand the children's needs, we may reach that stage of good sense in which we erect only temporary school buildings on the lines of the prefabricated day-nurseries, so that every eight or ten years, as our ideas change, we can pull them down and rebuild without any serious financial loss. Every schoolroom should have immediate access to the garden or outdoor playing-space ; it should be warm, sunny, cheerful and well ventilated, within reasonable distance of the assembly hall, indoor recreation rooms, dining-hall, kitchen, cloakroom, and sanitary offices. These last should be connected with the main building by covered verandahs or passages. There should be adequate washing accommodation with hot water and individual towels ; there should be facilities for drying wet clothing ; each school should have its own kitchen.

The children's *clothing* should be light and loose enough to allow full muscular activity and full circulation of air between the various layers and the surface of the skin. Above all, it should be warm and washable. It should be adapted to the seasons, so that the children are well wrapped up against the wind and rain in winter, but wear the minimum compatible with comfort in summer. The head and eyes should be protected in strong sunshine, and the legs and arms should be covered out of doors in winter. Growing feet need special consideration. They must never be cramped into shoes too small, nor forced to shuffle about in footgear too large. Most important of all, children must never be allowed to wear shoes which have been trodden down unevenly. If possible they should never wear shoes which have belonged to someone else, but since this ideal is impossible nowadays, at least every pair should be made straight and weatherproof before being passed on to a younger child. Shoes should have a straight inner border, plenty of toe room, a firm but flexible sole, a stout heel, and should fit snugly round the ankle. Any abnormality of walking or wearing down should be watched for, and if the child tends to turn over on one side, he should be immediately referred to the nearest clinic for expert advice. Stockings should fit properly without being too tight, or the feet will be cold. A warm vest should be worn next to the skin in winter, and the boys need underpants beneath their trousers just as much as the girls need warm knickers beneath their frocks. All clothing worn by day should be removed at night, and bedwear should be warm and comfortable. In school, children should learn to wipe their feet when they come in from the garden, to change wet shoes and stockings, to hang their outdoor clothes on their own pegs, to do up their own hooks and laces, and even, as they grow old enough to use a needle, to sew on their own buttons. An overall or dungarees for school wear will add to the child's pride of individual possession, and will also increase his enjoyment in sand and water play, since he will not have to bother about possible damage to his clothes.

Food

Nothing in child care is more impressive than the rapid improvement in health and spirits of the undernourished child who, for the first time, is provided with an intelligently planned dietary. In the course of a few weeks a thin, pale, listless, backward, pliant little creature is changed into a noisy, active, rosy, bright-eyed, obstreperous young person full of vigour and independence. There is no need here to enlarge upon the constituents of a balanced diet, or upon the average number of calories considered desirable at each age period, but it is important to think in terms of fresh food, of milk, eggs and butter, meat, vegetables, bread and cheese, fruit; to remember that the growing child needs a larger supply of the *proteins* of eggs and meat in proportion to his total intake than the adult, since he must build new tissues as well as repair the old; that he needs an ample supply of milk to provide the vitamin D and calcium and phosphorus which will prevent rickets and make strong bones and teeth; that he needs the iron and vitamin C of fruit and vegetables to make red blood and healthy teeth, gums and blood-vessels. In other words, it is essential that the young child should be given his full allowances of school dinners, school milk, cod-liver oil, and orange juice, and it is the teacher's responsibility to see that each child in her care receives his proper share. It is also essential that an adequate supply of drinking-water is available at all times.

The feeding of school children, however, involves more than the actual intake of food. It includes training in good habits of eating, of willingness to try unusual foods, of civilized behaviour and table-manners, of consideration for other people by assisting in the service of meals, of washing hands before food, laying tables and clearing away, and of washing up. When they are older, simple lessons in cooking—as, for instance, the preparation of camp meals—will provide much interest and amusement. It is desirable that each school should have its own kitchen. Mass-cooked meals delivered in containers, no matter how scientifically designed, can never be as good as those freshly prepared and cooked in smaller quantities on the school premises, under the supervision of an experienced headmistress. Moreover, the cook should be the familiar friend of the children and her kitchen part of their educational environment. She will learn much from seeing how they eat the food she has prepared for them, and they will learn from observation the essentials of good housekeeping.

Fresh Air and Sunshine

The need for fresh air has always been realized, since it was known that oxygen derived from the atmosphere was necessary to the tissues, but only recently have the fuller implications of outdoor life and sunlight been understood. Recent research has shown that the ultra-violet rays of the spectrum are amongst the most powerful germicidal agents that we possess; and also that the body needs the tonic effect of cool, constantly moving air on its surface just as much as the lungs need oxygen, and that the possibilities of airborne infection are reduced to a minimum in the open air. Hence the enormous importance of keeping our children out of doors in the daylight and air at all times unless the inclemency of the weather makes it completely impossible. At present there is far too much indoor teaching, largely because school buildings are not designed on common-sense principles, but often from sheer habit and lack of imagination. The successful treatment of heart cases and of tubercular and crippled children in open-air hospital schools has shown how well even the most fragile children tolerate this life, and thrive upon it. How much more desirable, then, to accustom our healthy children to an outdoor existence in order to prevent the diseases we now treat in this way. When one comes to analyse the time-table there are very few lessons which really necessitate indoor existence, and if we insisted that our schools should be constructed on open-air principles there are not many weeks of the year in which the children would have to be shut away from the sun and air during the best hours of the day. In the meantime we must exercise our ingenuity to see that they are out of doors as much as possible.

Exercise and Rest

Unless the body muscles are fully exercised and then periodically rested in order to remove the accumulated products of fatigue, they will not develop. We have all seen the effects of enforced inactivity of muscles in the arm which has been broken and obliged to remain immobile in a splint. The need for exercise in children implies also the need for *space*, and for some sort of simple apparatus to climb up and slide down, to push and to pull. Outdoor playing space is the most important, as we have seen, but provision for wet weather romping indoors should also be made in a shed or covered verandah, or in the school hall. It is also necessary that children should be provided with large apparatus, such as jungle gyms, ladders, ropes, planks, slides, barrels, hoops, boxes, bricks, wheelbarrows, trucks, tricycles, and scooters. The child knows instinctively how best to develop his own muscles, and no amount of ' drill ' and formal exercises will be as beneficial as his own unrestricted play. For this reason the bare ' prison-yard ' playgrounds so commonly seen in Infant Schools are little short of tragic. Under-eights do not usually attempt muscular feats beyond their capacity. It is the ten-year-olds who 'dare ' each other to perform dangerous tricks, although perhaps they would not be so ready to climb glass-topped walls or lamp posts, or play ' last across the road ' among the lorries and buses, if we provided them with more interesting apparatus in their playgrounds.

It is interesting to note that as soon as the child has taught himself any muscular skill, which he does by first imitating what he has seen slightly older children do, he will immediately proceed to make his task harder. This imitation of older children, by the way, is a point which should be remembered in the planning of Nursery-Infant groups ; these should never be restricted to single-age units. In this way the child progresses to the more difficult skills at his own rate. Thus, he will first learn to pull a wooden toy by a string, or to push it along the floor with his hands, while he crawls or staggers after it. Later, he chooses larger and heavier toys on wheels which he pushes or pulls with increased steadiness and control. Then he piles bricks or sand in his truck to make it heavier still, and, finally, he gives rides to his companions, pushing or pulling with astonishing vigour and precision of balance. Provision for play with sand, water, clay and soil is equally desirable. All the time he is learning about light and heavy, size and shape, hard and soft, rough and smooth, high and low, that wheels go round and cubes stand firm, that square pegs cannot be forced into round holes. At the same time he is promoting the efficient working of every organ in his body, his brain, heart, lungs, skin, digestion, bones, joints, muscles and nerves.

After all this intensive activity it is obvious that he will need periods of rest and relaxation. For older children quieter play with picture-books, paints, jig-saw puzzles, blocks, Plasticine and needlework will provide rest for the larger muscles and activity for the smaller ones ; but younger children will also need a period of rest on a stretcher bed. The nap is best taken after dinner and preferably in the open air, but if the children must sleep indoors the beds should be as widely spaced as possible—three feet between is a reasonable distance—and they should be alternately 'topped and tailed' so that no child can cough germs directly into his neighbour's face. The children should have their own blankets which should be large enough to pass under them and cover them completely on top. The educational value of the rest period can be as important as that of the school meal, since the child learns in this way the necessity for regular hours of rest, the comfort of a bed to himself and how to relax easily and completely.

Other Theories on Afternoon Rest: Recently, certain child psychologists have shown a tendency to question the value of the traditional afternoon nap, and for older children quieter play with picture-books, paints, jig-saw puzzles, blocks, Plasticine and needlework, will provide sufficient rest for the larger muscles while exercising the finer ones; but, in the writer's considered opinion, children of Nursery School age need a period of complete muscular relaxation on a stretcher bed. The nap should not be unduly prolonged; an hour is usually sufficient. It is best taken after dinner.

A child who first resists taking the afternoon nap, either from a feeling of insecurity or because he has not been accustomed to relaxing after his midday meal, may be dealt with in the same way as the child with a feeding difficulty. Starting with a quiet period of sitting down with table toys, he should later be encouraged to have ten to fifteen minutes rest on his stretcher while his companions take their nap, and then gradually this period may be increased to the usual hour.

Good Health Habits

These are essential in order to prevent loss of life or physical efficiency by infection or accident. The increasing rarity of severe epidemics of cholera, typhus, and typhoid fever, even before we possessed D.D.T. and the new drugs, is due entirely to the better hygiene of the masses and the improved sanitation of our cities. Scabies and the head louse still cause us considerable trouble in the Primary School, but with the new insecticides they could be banished altogether if all of us, doctors, nurses, and teachers made one grand concerted effort to treat the cases promptly and to educate the parents and the children.

The first principle of good health is cleanliness of the skin, hair, nails, teeth, nose, mouth, lungs, and alimentary system. This complete bodily cleanliness implies cleanliness of the child's environment and his clothing. It is neither necessary nor desirable to make him over-conscious of cleanliness. A certain amount of dirt will inevitably be collected in the course of the day's activities. The principal point to remember is that this dirt must not be allowed to enter the child's body with his food and drink, or through an abrasion in his skin.

In school these precautions may be simplified into training in habits of hand-washing after visiting the toilet and before food, and of tidying before dinner and tooth brushing before rest. These toilet activities can be made as exciting as any other. Each child will need to possess his own towel, marked with his own symbol and kept on his own peg, with his tooth-brush and mug close by. Learning to use them correctly will involve the acquisition of several new skills and the training in good habits should last him a lifetime.

Preventing Infection

The importance of frequent medical inspection needs no emphasis, but is outside the scope of the present chapter. It is essential, however, that the teacher should know something of the recent research in the spread of infection and its prevention in order to appreciate the need for strict supervision of all the Nursery staff, especially the kitchen workers and the Nursery helpers, since it is upon these field workers that the health of the children ultimately depends. Without the necessary high intelligence and background of knowledge it is often difficult for them to understand the principles underlying the routine imposed upon them. It is the teacher's duty to explain them as simply as possible, and then to insist that the smallest detail is faithfully carried out. One careless kitchen worker may cause an epidemic of typhoid or dysentery involving the loss of precious life. One child with a sore throat permitted to cough at his neighbour may spread a virulent type of scarlet fever or diphtheria resulting in permanent damage to the heart or nervous system of his victims.

Infection is spread in three ways, by *inhalation* (airborne, breathed into the throat or lungs), by *ingestion* (through the mouth by the agency of infected china, cutlery, food, or drink), and by *inoculation* (or direct contact, as in skin diseases by the entry of germs through the abraded skin).

Inhalation

Coughs, colds, and other respiratory diseases such as pneumonia and, most grave of all, tuberculosis, and nearly all the common fevers are spread by airborne infection. The germs of these diseases inhabit the nose and throat, often without causing any serious inconvenience to the carrier, who has, in the course of time, developed an immunity to certain strains of bacteria. Whenever we cough, sneeze, shout, or even breathe hard, we eject into the atmosphere a spray of heavily infected ' droplets.' Some of these are large enough to be visible and so heavy that they immediately fall to the ground, where they mingle with the dust, and are sent back into the air in clouds when the floor is swept. Others fall on to clothing, apparatus, toys, books, etc. Some droplets are so fine that they remain suspended in the air, where the moisture rapidly evaporates, leaving perhaps a microscopic fragment of dried mucus with germs clinging to it, or the germ itself floating about in the atmosphere. These are known as ' droplet nuclei.' It will be seen that, dangerous as the dust and droplet nuclei may be, the most massive dose of germs will be derived from direct contact with a sneeze or cough, from using an infected handkerchief, or putting into the mouth some infected toy or utensil. The hands which have covered the mouth or manipulated the handkerchief will also be heavily infected. The younger the child the greater the risk of infection, since he has not yet had time to develop that immunity which eventually results from the body's natural defensive reactions to continual minute doses of bacterial poison. Hence it is vitally important that every possible precaution should be taken against his receiving a large dose of any infective agent. In practice, this apparently formidable task may be simplified by keeping the Nursery-Infant units small and widening the age-range of each group, so that those of the most vulnerable age are not crowded together ; by keeping the children out of doors, and spacing them as widely as possible during meals and sleep , and by ensuring adequate ventilation whenever the children are indoors. In the open air, droplets are so swiftly diluted and dispersed that the risk is reduced to a minimum. The correct use of the handkerchief should be taught. Each child should have his own handkerchief which should be boiled in due course. If destructible ones are used they should be immediately burned or disposed of. Cod-liver oil spoons and crockery should be boiled, toys scrubbed frequently and put outside to dry, blankets laundered periodically and dried out of doors, and hands regularly washed. Children and staff suffering from colds should be rigidly excluded. The upper respiratory catarrhs have proved our biggest medical problem in Nursery work, and until we can control them the provision of further Nursery Schools and Classes, however desirable from other points of view, must remain open to serious criticism.

Ingestion

This is sometimes graphically described as bowel-to-mouth infection, since it always implies the taking into the mouth of germs derived from the excreta. It includes the dysenteries, enteric fevers, threadworms and probably infantile paralysis. It was bowel-to-mouth infection we most dreaded when it was decided to open large numbers of war-time Nurseries, but fortunately the anticipated large-scale epidemics did not materialize because these infections can be more easily controlled than airborne infection by good kitchen and Nursery hygiene. The principal point to remember in school is that these germs can only be introduced directly by infected hands, food, drink, or eating utensils, and therefore strict cleanliness of all these things will effectively prevent any trouble. In the Nursery and Infant School this involves handwashing before food and after toilet, and scrupulous cleanliness of dishes and food itself. These high standards particularly apply to kitchen staff. The Medical Research Council recently advised that a notice should be fixed to the back of every lavatory door saying, ' Next, wash your hands.' In the Nursery this might be stated even more forcibly : ' A child's life may depend on it. Wash your hands.' The staff should be provided with soap and individual towels and adequate wash-bowl accommodation. They must not wash in the kitchen sink. The Nursery helpers must also understand the necessity of washing their own hands after attending to the children in the toilet-rooms. If possible the cutlery and crockery used in the dining-rooms should be boiled. The new Ministry of Education rinsing sinks have been specially designed with this purpose in view.

Inoculation

Infection by direct contact, once so serious in the Infant School, is now becoming rare as a result of more adequate inspection, exclusion and treatment. Impetigo, scabies, and the head louse can be controlled by the new drugs, benzl benzoate lethane, D.D.T., and gamexane. Perfect cleanliness of the hands, caps and clothing; short hair, short nails, and individual pegs and toilet appointments in school are the best preventives against contact infection. In some areas these diseases have almost died out but the problem family is still with us, and in these cases the teachers and health visitors will need to be particularly watchful, for the sake of the unfortunate children themselves, and of their companions whom they may infect.

Safety First

Training in traffic sense and the prevention of accidents can form the basis of many exciting activities in school. Those of us who have had the delightful experience of seeing a safety-first demonstration in a Nursery-Infant School can bear witness to its usefulness as training in muscular control, dramatic expression, alertness of eye and ear, fluency of speech, practice in writing down reports, and a score of other educational activities.

The future of any nation lies in the mental and physical vigour of its children. It is at once our grave responsibility and our happy privilege to protect and guide the youth of this people. If we, who have knowledge, training, and intelligence, fail in our duty, the whole destiny of the race is imperilled. The fight for better conditions in our schools—for meals and milk, for warm, bright, airy buildings, for improved equipment and civilized sanitary accommodation, for increased facilities for outdoor life and less rigid time-tables, and most of all for more expert training of our student teachers by experienced Child Welfare officers—may be weary and difficult, but for those of us who live long enough to see our visions take shape in the future, the reward will be correspondingly great.

Mary D. Sheridan.

Nursery children make their own arrangements.

(*Photographs: Dr. A. L. Smallwood and Miss C. E. Cooke*)

Net and parallel ropes combined. (Infants.)

Nursery children use ladders they can erect themselves.

Six-year-olds have much the same tastes.

Chapter X

PHYSICAL EDUCATION

DURING the war and post-war years physical education has been developing in line with, and as part of, the general educational methods of today. Children are not taught a series of exercises, but are given the opportunity to experience movement, either freely, as in Nursery Schools, or with guidance, called 'training,' in Infant and Junior Schools.

Physical education is, as the name implies, concerned with the full development of the child, physically, emotionally, socially, and mentally. Young children have a great need for physical activity, not only as an aid to physical development and poise, but also as an outlet for their energy and initiative.

In Nursery Schools

In many Nursery Schools the children are free to plan their own time-table, and to make use of all materials and apparatus that can be provided, whenever they wish.

In such schools many children choose not only the first part of the day, as well as the period following their rest in the afternoon, for the more energetic forms of muscular activity, but also moments between concentrated use of carpentry or painting materials, involving the finer controlled movements.

For instance, Peter, occupied in making a wooden motor car, frequently feels the need for vigorous and satisfying muscular activity and so runs outside to swing, climb, or jump before settling down to continue his constructive efforts.

Given the opportunity to climb, this is often one of the most popular occupations, especially if the apparatus is such that it allows the children to hang by their legs. Nets and parallel ropes are most useful for this purpose, but short ladders supported by two boxes are not only more easily procured, but enable children hanging by their legs to swing backwards and forwards in this unexpectedly popular position.

The ability to relax, so marked in very young children, is a vital safeguard from accidents. When jumping off boxes or steps, they frequently sit down and roll over quite easily, without any damage being done.

It is interesting to watch them considering from what height they can safely land, and being quite free to find this out for themselves, their self-confidence is maintained and they relax with ease on landing.

Ladders, planks, climbing-frames, duckboards, and boxes can all be provided at little or no cost by the enterprising teacher, especially if the interest and help of the parents are encouraged. Some fathers may be carpenters, or window-cleaners, and when short ladders are required, are valuable friends.

There should be ample material, both indoors and out, for the children to be able to experiment in all types of movement, from climbing large nets to painting and carpentering.

The social training involved must be seen to be fully understood. Nursery children working under suitable conditions show their innate sense of co-operation and understanding of each other's capabilities, and if allowed to experience their own potentialities, will come to no harm provided the apparatus they use is strongly constructed.

The result of allowing timid children to do what they wish on the apparatus, when they wish, and in their own time, will show in their greater freedom of movement and power of relaxation. They may spend a long satisfying period standing on the bottom rung of a net. Children backward in speech have found, by mastering physical difficulties, that they could also master difficulties of speech. Children suffering from bad home backgrounds have sometimes found mixing with other children no easy matter, and have been self-assertive and even violent. These children have been greatly helped by having the opportunity for violent exercise in adventurous and harmless form. Sometimes they will spend the greater part of the day, or many days, climbing and swinging, before they gradually settle down to quieter occupations.

Teachers of older children can learn a great deal by watching Nursery children in action. It is so easy to have preconceived ideas on movement suitable for certain age groups, but these ideas are well and truly shattered by visiting well-equipped Nursery Schools.

In Infant Schools

There is no reason to suppose that children reaching the age of five have suddenly no further need of physical activity, and yet it often happens that movement is stopped rather than encouraged when they reach that age.

Unfortunately, the large numbers in the classes of today, as well as the shortage of space, do not make it easy for young children to lead an uncramped school life.

Nursery methods often have to be abandoned, with the result that the time allotted to physical education is reduced to set periods of twenty to thirty minutes once or twice daily instead of constant opportunities being given to experience fully the joy of creative movement.

It has been suggested in the *Syllabus of Physical Training for Schools* (1933) that two daily lessons of fifteen to twenty minutes should be given to little children, one in the morning and the other in the afternoon.

Free movement cannot be taken when children are dressed in heavy footwear and much clothing, so that to get the full value of an active lesson it is essential for the children to be suitably dressed, *i.e.* with not more than knickers and vest or a jersey in cold weather, and rubber shoes or light sandals out of doors, or bare feet if conditions are suitable indoors.

This changing takes a few minutes, and many schools give a period of not less than twenty-five to thirty minutes at least three times a week in the mornings, as well as several periods of twenty to thirty minutes per week in the afternoons.

Knickers made up from black-out material, put on over the child's own pair, might be worn in cold weather, giving comfort to the anxious parent and freedom of movement to the child.

The value of big apparatus for climbing and hanging purposes has proved so great in developing the child, not only physically, but also socially and creatively, that it should be included in the lessons whenever possible.

Nursery School children have no difficulty in relaxing, because they are confident in their own skill and have no fear, but older children sometimes lose this ability to relax, which should be fostered and even taught. It is a vital factor in securing good health. Children so obviously enjoy the adventure and skill involved in all types of climbing apparatus, that experiments have been taking place in all parts of the country to provide suitable material for their use.

Aims and Organization of the P.T. Period

Training in mobility, relaxation, and general development are the chief aims of the teacher concerned in the physical education of Infants. The results are far-reaching if, in addition to her knowledge, she is able to allow her children to experience movement in its widest sense.

When using climbing apparatus to its best advantage in a short period, it is advisable to have not more than seven children in any one group. This ensures that there are never too many children for any one piece of apparatus, and that the whole group has enough room to be actively employed at the same time.

At least half the lesson might be allotted to group work, allowing for two changes to other apparatus in one day. Thus the children would get three types of activity in one lesson.

Group work needs to be so planned that some form of heave, some skill with small apparatus such as balls or hoops, and some activity such as jumping or somersaulting are included for each child.

The teacher should be free to watch all activities, and it is advisable that on any apparatus high above the ground the children should be left entirely free to choose their own activity.

Any coaching of skipping, somersaults, etc., should come earlier in the lesson with the class as a whole.

The lesson should begin in the classroom where the children are encouraged to leave all unnecessary clothing, so that, as they enter the playground or hall, taking with them all the apparatus they are likely to need, there will be no time lost in setting to work practising skills with balls, skittles, bean bags, bats, hoops, etc., or possibly turning cartwheels or trying another activity of their own choice.

The value of having adequate small apparatus in daily use cannot be stressed too much. It is during this free part of the lesson that the teacher is able to find out what type of activity appeals most to her children, what movements they are weakest in, and how the children respond to difficulties. In this part of the lesson, too, encouragement can be given to the timid child who has possibly suffered from too much help at home.

The next part of the lesson is given to training in footwork when, possibly without shoes, running, jumping, general mobility, and relaxation are practised, the work being based on the more informal movements in the lessons of the *1933 Syllabus*, with constant use of small apparatus and the necessary training involved.

The second part of the lesson can be devoted to the group work suggested before, and can end with a quiet movement for the class as a whole.

Care of the apparatus is a most important factor. Children should be encouraged to bring it out and, when possible, to set it up by themselves. It should be put carefully away or left where it is easily available for the next class.

Even such things as ladder-stands can easily be painted by the older Infants, and so made more durable. A pride in the care of their apparatus goes a long way to prolong its life. This care of the apparatus should not be left to a few children but should be the concern of the whole class.

Some teachers are worried by the possibility that Nursery School children, able to perform feats on the apparatus, will have nothing left to learn in the Infant or Junior School, and will therefore lose interest.

These are perhaps early days to deny the possibility emphatically, but at present there is little sign of children losing interest in anything that is worth while.

A small child enjoys playing cricket, but this does not mean that at fifty years of age he will necessarily be tired of it, or have outgrown it. If a child should show signs of tiring of any activity, the teacher will be wise to give him a higher standard to aim at, or possibly, in some cases, be ready to make other suggestions.

Movements can be more skilfully performed, or tried in couples, different ways of combining apparatus may be attempted. The surprising evolutions of children on ropes are endless.

As a result of purposeful lessons, the child's resource and initiative are developed, he gains in self-confidence, and therefore in ease of movement, which in its turn affects poise and posture. Socially, he becomes interested in other members of his group and their achievements; his consideration for other members using the same piece of apparatus is developed, not learnt, because this consideration was noticeable in the Nursery stage. It is a usual occurrence to see children steadying a piece of apparatus for other daring members of the group, although by so doing they may miss their own turn.

Asthma and other nervous diseases have been greatly relieved by the confidence gained when children have found that they could walk along a pole, or achieve some simple feat on the apparatus, which to them had seemed impossible.

Another type of lesson, often taken in the afternoon, consists of either games and games training, or dance movements. Games lessons consist of simple games of chase, or ball games, preceded by some form of games training, such as throwing, catching, dodging, aiming. Here again it should be stressed that, to give useful training, practice is necessary, and for this it is essential that there should be enough small apparatus for each child to get the maximum amount of turns. Climbing and balancing apparatus might also be included in a games period, as well as some form of athletic training, such as running and jumping.

Dancing lessons must of necessity vary according to the qualifications of the teacher. Whatever type is chosen, all the children must be able to take part. Children love moving to music and simple tunes played in good rhythm should be within the scope of most teachers, but if this is not the case, movement training in a creative form might be given with or without percussion. One of the chief aims should be to encourage the children to experiment in the widest possible variety of movements.

Stimulating Interest

When preparing a lesson for Infants, the teacher must bear in mind the needs of her class, physically, psychologically and emotionally. It may be that in taking over a new class, she finds the children lifeless and lacking in interest. There are many factors that may have been the cause of this, but the first essential, whatever the cause, is to arouse interest.

The use of small apparatus at the beginning of the lesson almost invariably provides this interest for all except the very timid child, even though the ability to use it skilfully may be almost entirely lacking. It is sometimes thought that the children are not ' ready ' for apparatus, and in consequence it is not used, and the children continue to show a lack of initiative and response. Children's ideas may formulate slowly and in the early stages little skill may be shown, but if given the opportunity, they will at least be able to experience movement, with all that this involves.

The very timid child may perhaps take several days before he lets himself go, but every time he even picks up a ball he may be acquiring self-confidence and a sense of achievement, which in the case of another child may be seen more clearly when he runs through a moving hoop for the first time. An occasional demonstration by a child who has thought of a new activity, or achieved a known one, does much to stimulate interest. Training, as suggested before, can come later in the lesson.

Ability to Relax

Some children may have lost the ability to relax, which shows itself in awkward, jerky movements. Free play with apparatus will improve this also, and all the big body movements such as crawling, rocking, and practice in relaxation itself, will soon produce a marked improvement in general physical development and poise.

A noisy class is probably suffering from too much inactivity and lack of real interest in the matter in hand. The use of small apparatus at the beginning of the lesson would again be of great value, not only from the point of view of interest but also as an outlet to the emotions, and as a form of self-control. In this case the teacher would be wise to limit the apparatus to one type, for instance, balls, so that she could give the children some definite aim, the achievement of which demanded concentration, and in this way gain the attention of the class.

Introducing Group Work

If the class has never worked in groups, and if this is found to be essential where climbing apparatus is used, group games might be taken, the children running back to their own ' homes ' in any game of chase. Small apparatus, well spaced, can be used, the children working in their own groups, or rather using balls, ropes, etc. belonging to any particular ' home,' and running behind their ' home ' line at a given signal, after first putting the apparatus tidy for the next group. Then when directed, they can begin work straight away with another piece of apparatus.

This momentary stillness in their 'homes' not only gives the teacher a chance to see that no apparatus is left about, but is also a valuable way of ensuring that the children can respond quickly to an outside stimulus, and, if not too prolonged, gives a certain poise to the class.

The question of dress and footwear is a difficult one, especially in winter, when many halls that might be available are used not only for singing lessons but also for assembly and dinners. Splinters and dirt are naturally a great hindrance to bare-foot work, and while it might be possible to remove shoes and socks for foot exercises, running in bare feet on a floor of this common type is not as a general rule to be recommended.

If suitable shoes are not provided by the school, and it is surely better for children to provide their own, a meeting with the parents, at which a demonstration of children's work is given, goes a long way to gain their support in providing the children with suitable knickers and shoes. No child should be allowed to climb apparatus with unsuitable shoes.

Suggested Apparatus

For Nursery School

6 or more strong boxes (varying sizes)

6–8 motor tyres

1 slide

1 climbing-frame (portable)

1 jungle gym and/or climbing-net

1 or more sets parallel rope-ladders (4 ft. high)

1 or 2 swings and/or vertical ladders

6–8 short ladders

1 wire rope (for suspending tyres) 4- 5 ft. high

Strong adult barrows

For Infant School

2 ladders (not more than 11 ft. long)
Strong boxes and/or steady benches or tables
Strong desk (old type) on which to hook a plank
1 plank
2 large door mats (for somersaults)
Individual fibre mats (for lying movements especially outside)
Parallel ropes or rope ladders (14 ft. long)
1 pole (pine, 11 ft. long)
2 pole stands ($3\frac{1}{2}$ ft. high)
4 sets jumping-stands (approx. 1–$1\frac{1}{2}$ ft. high, with canes)
1 balancing bar
8 syrup tins, with string (for stilts and aiming purposes)
Quoits, bean bags, balls, ropes, bats, hoops, hoop sticks, etc. (1 per child)

C. E. Cooke.

PART FIVE

SUBJECTS AND SKILLS IN RELATION TO ACTIVITIES

Chapter XI

LANGUAGE DEVELOPMENT

THE development of language in all its aspects is one of the most important contributions the Nursery and Infant School can offer in its programme. It should include: conversation, stories, dramatization, poetry, and speech training.

Conversation

Conversation is a widely misused term. Children cannot converse to order in a twenty-minute section of a daily time-table; the result, by this method, is stilted, artificial, and a 'subject.' Freedom must be given to enable children to talk, argue, quarrel and agree for a very large part of the day. Only in this way can they develop a skill to enable them to talk intelligently in later life, for skills must be practised continually to be effective. This approach is of the greatest importance in the Nursery and Infant School, because young children often say things before they are aware of their significance; thoughts follow verbal utterance in the solving of problems in the same way that many children must *hear* what they read before it means anything. If children are encouraged and stimulated in their talking, many opportunities will arise for the extension of vocabulary and for improvement in clarity of expression.

Let us glance at a daily programme. Most healthy children come into school with positive friendly feelings towards their fellows and teachers; some are excited about an expedition they have had during the week-end, or something that has happened in the street, or a birthday that is impending. Adventures can be recounted and greetings can be exchanged, and a very important link is formed between school and home. Undoubtedly the same thing happens at the other end; children rush home full of something interesting that has happened in school. In free-play periods where children are at liberty to choose materials of many varied kinds, and where centres of interest develop, a good deal of intelligent speech arises. It is interesting and enlightening for the teacher to stand by and jot down snatches of conversation between children engrossed in a communal activity.

To take a specific example from a group of seven-year-old children: a little girl had brought along to school a nurse's outfit which had been a birthday gift. The other girls were envious and, during the play period, all the odd pieces of white ' stuff ' were converted into nurses' head-dresses and aprons. Tables and boxes were converted into beds and a ' hospital ' idea was born. Each day something was added, and at the end of a fortnight the room contained doctors, sisters, almoner, dispensary, medicine bottles, stethoscopes, patients with injured legs, arms, etc., as well as ambulances, stretchers and all those things associated with hospitals. This proved a real interest as many of the children had experienced a period in a real hospital. The dramatic play that followed was rich in imaginative situations and verbal expression. The teacher was consulted on various points of technique and her advice was sought when, for instance, the children wanted to know how to make the stretcher strong enough to carry a ' body.'

Great value in verbal training comes from the discussions which precede and follow the working out of these interests; if the wheel keeps coming off, for example, what is the best method of making it secure? Is it better to use a nail or a screw? In addition to emotional satisfaction, much intellectual curiosity is awakened in the solving of these problems. The children who at first are less able to discuss ideas will gain a good deal by listening to others, and it is astonishing how, in time, these children throw off their reserve and forget themselves in their own enthusiasm for the job in hand. If a fairly large portion of the time-table is allowed for this type of work at the point where play and work merge into one, language development follows with amazing rapidity. The teaching of reading must surely wait until children can talk well to each other and to adults in a natural and easy manner.

There is a more directed form of speech activity which comes under the heading of ' News.' This has some value in that children talk individually to a large group and acquire the habit of speaking clearly and distinctly; otherwise they soon know that they cannot be heard. Short items of news can be written down by the teacher and kept either in the form of a News Sheet or a News Book. These can be illustrated in various ways, and so a record is kept based on the children's own vocabulary.

In the more formal practice periods where the children are learning the skills of reading, writing and number, speech again has a valuable part to play. It is unnatural and stultifying for children to work silently; as has been mentioned before, thoughts and ideas orten come after verbal expression or simultaneously with it. Provided that there is purpose and interest in the task, speech will arise out of it. The getting and putting away of apparatus, the consultation of reference books and dictionaries, the give-and-take necessary in helping one's neighbour, entail social awareness, and develop a co-operative spirit in the classroom. Long periods of silence should have no place in Infant Schools.

Stories

As stories have such a wide appeal for children they need to be given an important place in the time-table. This is an occasion when children learn to listen with concentration and absorption. The ability to listen is often dissipated by the constant use of the radio and the hustle of modern life, but in story-telling we can usually command a listening, receptive audience. The children enter imaginatively into new situations, and delight in re-living the old ones. In the development of language, stories can serve several useful purposes; for they are the means by which the vocabulary can be extended beyond the children's everyday speech. The more cultural and aesthetic language employed in stories and poetry needs to be introduced alongside the more prosaic, so that children can delight, as early as possible, in the beauty of English. Stories involving repetition are of great value, the children being able to join in at will. Examples are: *The Three Little Pigs*, *The Gingerbread Boy*, *Little Black Sambo*, and many others to be found in the Elizabeth Clark books; when memorized, these lead naturally to dramatization. Stories with a Nature interest and background can often be read for handwork activities. Six-year-old children who had heard and delighted in episodes from *The Wind in the Willows* wanted to make Toad's house in the wood, and eventually a large model was constructed, consisting of earth, twigs, stream, badger, mole, etc. This proved a lively interest and was constantly being re-arranged by whoever was in charge.

Many stories lend themselves to dramatization which is an activity of infinite value in the Infant School.

Dramatization

In every classroom there should be a dressing-up box containing odd pieces of material of all shapes and sizes which can be adapted to many uses: pieces of curtain suitable for weddings, silks and satins for kings' cloaks and queens' gowns, and so on. In the play period children can use these properties for their free groupings in make-believe situations. If the children are very enthusiastic about acting they will sometimes ask for a proper stage to use. This can be made by placing tables together in sufficient number to give a fairly good area, fixing side and top slats for front curtains and putting up a backcloth. I saw a group of six- to seven-year-old children working this scheme out for themselves. They painted a most exciting backcloth in gay designs and set it up in the classroom. The stage interest lasted a whole term, and groups took turns to make up and put on plays. This was carried out entirely by the children.

Another group of children decided to work out a play so that they could present it to other classes. They chose to dramatize *The Pied Piper* and, with the teacher's help, all the scenes were worked out, and each member of the class had a part either acting or stage-managing. During activity play periods the properties and stage were made, as well as a ticket office, tickets, money, and programmes. When the play was ready for presentation, invitations were sent out to another class and tickets were sold. The seating was arranged in numbers and the audience took their places and bought programmes. There was a small percussion band to act as an orchestra before the curtain rose. The whole performance was a delight to watch and this was reflected in the faces of the audience. It was so enthusiastically received that the other classes demanded repeat performances which were accordingly given ; it reached the ears of the parents and they were also invited.

In the early stages it is quite useful to mime stories using the language of the body in gesture. Children can get themselves into character more easily this way, since thinking of what to say sometimes holds up action. Let them act characters : kings, queens, princesses, soldiers, policemen, old men, fat men, drummer boys, etc., the whole class taking part. Then simple situations can be mimed : in the autumn, a road-sweeper sweeping up leaves in piles, putting them into a wheelbarrow and emptying them on to a heap ; in the winter, children making snowballs, having a snow-fight and making a snow-man. Simple stories like St. George and the Dragon can also be used, where all the children take all the characters in turn as the story proceeds. In this way a sequence is built up, and when the characters really talk the movement flows more easily. If a story is told well, with a good feeling for character and situation, the children experience little or no difficulty in finding words to express themselves. By this means, children at the top of the Infant School can organize and carry out excellent dramatic work.

Poetry

Poetry is a means by which children can be brought into contact with the more imaginative and aesthetic aspect of language ; we need to lay foundations for a real and lasting appreciation of this highest form of verbal expression. How can we set about it ? Children must experience and enjoy poetry. The toddler jogging upon his mother's knee delights in the sensation of *Ride a Cock Horse* ; the rhythm and fascination of the sounds, although meaningless intellectually, give pleasure in response. Nursery rhymes with a rhythmical quality are the foundations upon which we can build. As in the play periods children are actively doing, and by movement are perfecting movements, so in rhythmic periods children can enter into the joys of poetry through their bodies. Let them use the natural responses of running, walking, skipping, jumping, rocking, and galloping to express the feeling in poetry. To give a few examples of this, the following poems lend themselves to these rhythms :

Skipping :	*To market, to market* . .	Mother Goose Rhymes
	Hey, diddle, diddle . .	” ” ”
	A cat came fiddling out of a barn	” ” ”
	In the far corner, close by the swings	H. Wolfe
	What is the matter with Mary Jane ?	A. A. Milne
Walking :	*James, James, Morrison, Morrison*	” ”
	When Ann and I go out a walk	H. Wolfe
	Rub-a-dub-dub . . .	Mother Goose Rhymes
	The Grand Old Duke of York	Nursery Rhyme
Running :	*In Fleet Street* . .	E. Farjeon
	Up the Airy Mountain .	W. Allingham
	Wee Willie Winkie . .	Mother Goose Rhymes
	Duck's Ditty . . .	K. Grahame
Jumping :	*John had great big waterproof boots on*	A. A. Milne
	Here am I, little jumping Joan	Mother Goose Rhymes
	Jack be nimble . . .	” ” ”
	Humpty Dumpty . .	” ” ”
Rocking :	*Hush-a-bye, baby* . .	” ” ”
	Hush-a-bye, birdie, croon, croon	” ” ”
	O Timothy Tim . . .	A. A. Milne
	Silver	W. de la Mare
Galloping :	*I had a little pony* . .	Mother Goose Rhymes
	How they brought the good news	R. Browning
	Huski, Hi (from *Widdy Widdy Wurky*)	Rose Fyleman

The teacher must speak these verses clearly and with a good feeling for their rhythmic quality. The children will respond as they would to musical rhythms, and at the same time will be learning to speak the poems with true appreciation.

Poems with refrains can develop from the simple rhythms ; in these, two contrasting rhythms can be used. Take a rhyme such as :

John Cook he had a little grey mare,
Hee, haw, hum.

The first line might suggest a skipping rhythm and the refrain three jumps. It makes good fun if the teacher speaks the line while the children skip, and then they respond with the refrain, jumping as they speak it. Similar treatment can be used in the following, of which the first two lines are quoted:

A farmer went trotting upon his grey mare
Bumpety, bumpety, bump. — Nursery Rhyme

Here are crocuses, white, gold, grey.
O dear me, says Marjorie May. — W. de la Mare

Grandmother had a little grey billygoat,
Dinkums, Dunkums, little grey billygoat. — Rose Fyleman

There was an owl lived in an oak,
Wisky, warky, weedle. — Nursery Rhyme

Three black crows sat on a tree,
Billy Magree Magraw. — " "

The children are quick to suggest different movements and rhythms to fit into the refrains, and the nonsense words often used give, incidentally, good practice in speech sounds. It is through rhythm and musical sounds that poetry first appeals and it is not necessary to have an intellectual understanding of every word in poetical speech; emotional satisfaction comes first.

Later, poems can be used for group or individual speaking, when a good time-sense is developed, and there is a feeling for the spoken and silent beat. These poems are useful for this purpose:

The House that Jack built	Nursery Rhyme
Cock Robin	" "
See the Robbers passing by . . .	"
Friday Street	E. Farjeon
Blackfriars	"
King's Cross	"
The North Wind	"
The Yellowhammer	"

Through movement in poetry, children gain a joyful appreciation and learn to speak with confidence and clarity. It is essential to choose the best, and to avoid the sentimental and cheap verse which is sometimes included in children's anthologies.

Speech Training

Speech Training is often placed on the time-table as a set subject. Sometimes the formality of the routine is such that children are not allowed to practise speech during the day; it would seem pointless to train speech under these circumstances, the effort expended being of little value. It is by listening to children talking and noting where mistakes are made that help can be given where necessary.

(*Photographs by Miss C. E. Cooke*)

Infants appreciate this position, in which they can stretch the spine.

The relaxation needed to walk along the pole has a curative effect on asthma.

Nursery children love climbing.

Poise.

Relaxation.

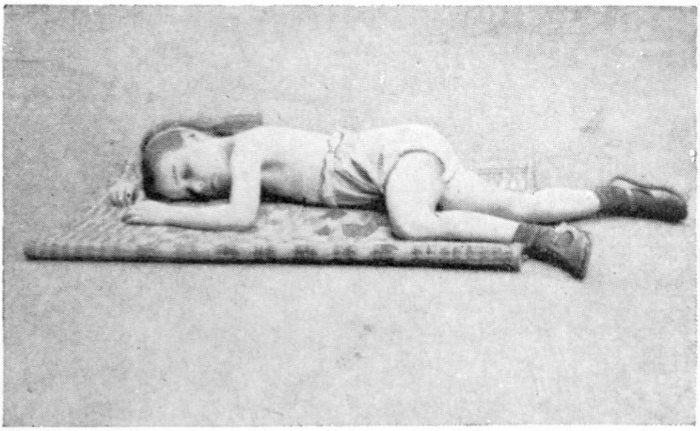

The see-saw used as a storming board.

The Rocking Horse: Mats are essential for mobility training. (6–7 year olds.)

The chief faults that arise, slovenly diction, and the substitution of one sound for another, are the result of hearing poor speech in the home and street, and of the encouragement sometimes given to baby talk. Opportunities must be provided in school for helping the children to overcome these difficulties and achieve clear, distinct articulation. The teacher must herself possess a pleasing, vital voice with good variety in tone so that the children will benefit by listening. This can be used to advantage in story-telling time when reception is at a high level.

Finger Plays and Jingles are a means by which fun is extracted from the repetition of good nonsense verse. An example is :

The more it snows
(Tiddely pom),
The more it goes
(Tiddely pom),
The more it goes
(Tiddely pom)
On snowing.
And nobody knows
(Tiddely pom),
How cold my toes
(Tiddely pom),
How cold my toes
(Tiddely pom),
Are growing.

A. A. MILNE.

'Tiddely Pom' gives a good vowel and nasal resonance. Other examples can be taken from verses by Edward Lear, Lewis Carroll, and Rodney Bennett. The children are playing with sounds, and while it is good fun, at the same time they are gaining control over their vocal organs, especially lips and tongue. A short ten-minute practice every day is better than a longer period at less frequent intervals. Where speech is naturally good very little practice will be needed. Children must not be made to feel self-conscious about their faults, or harm may be done to their spontaneity of expression.

Games of the following type, which give much pleasure and amusement, can be used :

An imaginary visit to the zoo : reproducing animal noises.

Calling out street cries : coal, papers, milk, any old clothes, etc.

Reproducing mechanical noises : trains, aeroplanes, cars, drills, etc.

In exploring the possibilities of these approaches, it can be seen that children will talk naturally and easily in school, exercising their vocabulary ; by listening to a good voice they will be aware of its pleasing effect ; by being brought into contact with the beauties of poetic language, a foundation will be laid of true appreciation.

P. M. Rolfe.

Chapter XII

STORIES AND VERSE

STORIES are the answers we give to the spoken and unspoken enquiries of children into the nature of the world around them. Their unspoken questions are closely connected with their spontaneous activities. Their games of make-believe, their simple constructions with bricks, their play with the furniture, their cuddlies, oddments of rubbish, and pots and pans, all indicate how their minds are working. If we watch their activities closely over a period, we come to the conclusion that they are not only concerned with the things they see and the sounds they hear, but with the manifold relations which exist between themselves and their environment, and between the adults they know best. Stories, if wisely chosen, do offer facts and information, but their most important function is to clarify the way everything is connected with everything else.

Although stories are of vital importance they are not real experience, but they are closely related to all first-hand knowledge. As they listen, children use the little they know of real life to help them to understand something slightly different in the story. And every fresh explanation presented by a story told in a way they can appreciate, sheds light on some detail of the real life around them.

But stories provide *imaginary* experience which can be of immense value in education. The extent of its usefulness, however, depends entirely on the choice of stories told and, in a less degree, on the skill of the story-teller. At its best, story-telling is a means of enlightenment and relaxation, as well as a release from emotional tension. An unsuitable choice of stories leads to mental confusion and emotional disturbance.

Finally, stories awaken the minds of children, already vastly interested in words, to the delights of literature and to the beauty of their mother-tongue. This appreciation, however, depends on the form and language in which the stories are told. At each level of development, there is a story form which appeals more strongly than any other. There are also characteristics of sound and pattern which make a poem more attractive at one stage than another. In dealing with the younger children we shall consider verse as one form of stories—stories which are organized into particular patterns.

It is impossible to discuss stories without reference to the children who listen to them. We must know our children before we are able to select the language and form of stories and before we are able to interest them in their content. The mental needs of the child should dictate the sort of story we choose and each story should reflect something of the nature of the child who listens. In considering the two-year-old, we have to ask ourselves : " What sort of language can he follow ? What use can he make of a story ? Do the ideas in the story awaken any response ? Can he interpret what he hears ? " It is the answers to these questions which suggest the sort of stories the children need to hear and how they should be told.

Two-Year-Olds

At this age, words do not exist apart from action. Play and chatter go on simultaneously ; each seems to rely on the other. The experience of the moment seems to inspire the words which would never be uttered without the activity.

" 'Dis funny mat, (*bang, bang, on the table*)
'dis funny 'poon, (*bang, bang*)
'dis funny fork," (*bang, bang*)

—went the chant as a two-year-old picked up each object on her dinner-table and used it as a banging weapon. Their whole waking life is spent in ceaseless activity accompanied by some sort of sing-song vocalization. They think in terms of what they need at the moment and of every immediate interest. These interests, which are often fleeting but which constantly recur, are only expressed by action and sound. When trains claim the children's attention, they become trains ; they ' chug ' as they travel ; they ' hiss ' and ' shunt ' and ' bang ' as they stop at stations. They suddenly change to cows, aeroplanes, bulldozers or tractors, and then fresh refrains are invented.

If we listen carefully, we notice that all their vocalization is in the present tense. Josephine was playing with her rag doll and the sing-song soliloquy which accompanied her activity went like this :

" Josey put baby to bed. Baby good. Josey loves baby. Baby drink. Good baby. Baby go byes."

They may recall something which happened yesterday but they still speak of it in the present. Josephine was fascinated by a cart-horse which grazed near the cottage gate. One wet day, she stood on the window-sill for a long time watching Pleasance. The next day her talk was all of the horse. " Josey see Pleasance. Josey's horsie. Pleasance eat grass. Josey see at window.

Pleasance wet. Josey see." There is no past or future for the two-year-olds ; they have no idea of time.

Nor do they understand the use of ' I ' because they cannot separate themselves from what is not themselves. Nothing beyond them is understood unless it affects them. They speak of themselves by name and respond more quickly if adults do the same, instead of using ' you.' All pronouns are most confusing to them. It is, " Martin get down," not, " I get down." Mothers unconsciously adopt the language which is natural to this age, when they say, " Martin's bedtime. Martin turn on tap for bath," and so on.

They love the repetition of words and delight in simple sound patterns. Their own rhythmical banging never fails to fascinate them and they will repeat a phrase with a distinct pattern over and over again. " Sheep ! sheep ! " exclaimed a two-year-old in the bus.

" Some little ones, some big ones.
Some little ones, some big ones.
Some little ones, some big ones."

The refrain went on and on and came to rest with the satisfactory remark, " They go baa-baa-baa."

Stories

Where can we find stories to suit such limited experience, which overcome the difficulty of tense, which do not use pronouns, which can be told just at the moment of interest and yet which give pleasure by the rhythm and repetitive sound patterns ? Here and there we come across isolated stories which serve as types but there are no story collections which are really suitable for two-year-olds. Nor should we wish for them. The best stories are those which are made up especially for a particular child or group. Parents often do this without realizing the significance of their efforts. To encourage a child to attend to his dressing and to take his share of the activity, a mother will string together the words which describe the action, adding the refrain which captivates his attention :

" Andrew pops in his head. That's right !
Andrew puts in this arm. That's right !
Andrew puts in this arm. That's right !
Andrew's vest is right on.
Now Andrew's socks.
This foot. That's right," and so on.

Children tell themselves these kind of stories. Martin was sitting precariously on his mother's knee as she was putting on his socks and shoes. All the time, he kept up a running commentary, partly conversation, partly soliloquy :

"Martin's shoe falling down,
Look, shoe falling down.
Mother, put it on.
Martin's sock falling down,
Sock falling down,
Mother pull it on.
Martin falling down.
Martin falling down.
Mother get Martin up.
Up! up! up! up! up!
Martin up!"

This is the sort of story for the two-year-old group in the Nursery Class, a recital of a series of familiar events told in a way which interests the children. No plot is necessary but the events must happen to themselves or to children just like them. Stories about the nursery toys and school pets; about the familiar people who come in from the world outside, like the milkman, and the nurse; stories from the day's routine, like resting, feeding, playing, dressing, washing, going home, and coming to school; all such subjects make short simple stories when told with repetition and rhythm. Every member of a group can be named:

"Bella gets the ladder and puts it up.
John climbs up the ladder.
Mary climbs up the ladder.
John takes his Teddy up the ladder, too."

Of course, it is impossible to make children of this age listen to a story if they are uninterested, and teachers have to be prepared for part of the group to wander off to some play of their own. By far the most successful plan is to tell the story as the action is taking place, just as mothers do in the home, and just as the children do themselves. When Mary gets into trouble with her fingers which will not go into the proper holes in the glove, her teacher begins a story about the awkward fingers as she gently persuades Mary to co-operate with her. The rest of the group cluster round to see and hear; they throw out an occasional remark and look curiously at their own gloves and experiment a little. There is no set time or place for story-telling at this age; any time may be the occasion for a rhyme or tale.

Learning from Stories

By keeping our stories within the boundaries of the children's limited experience, we deepen their feelings of safety and confidence. Hearing about the familiar world and themselves, or children like themselves, strengthens a sense of belonging which leads to a clearer understanding of relationships generally. Such simple statements as, "Mother brings Betty to the nursery, then she goes home to mind Baby Jean," holds a world of reassuring ideas for all the children who have recently joined the school. They also provide imaginary experience. Although the details of a story may be drawn from first-hand experience, they can be arranged in many sorts of situations. The first adventure story to be appreciated is the re-living of a past happy experience. For instance, the fun of a playtime in the snow is told again in story form some time during the next day.

This recall of past activity has another function. Because the happenings are so well understood, children realize the full significance and power of words to interest and enchant them. At the same time, and through the habit they acquire of attending to the story-teller, they sense the meaning of difficult expressions. For instance, the two-year-old does not use or understand such adverbs as 'under,' 'by,' 'upon,' and at first they hold no meaning for him. While telling a story, the teacher may pick up a cuddly to push it under a child's chair as she explains: "Golly crept along under Ann's chair." Such incidents occur very often and gradually understanding develops. Other confusions disappear slowly, partly through story-telling and partly through the exchange of conversation between adults, and adults and children. Ideas of time come very slowly indeed, but plurals are realized fairly early.

The pleasurable experience which comes from hearing attractive sound patterns and strong repetitive rhythm with recurring refrains is the beginning of literary appreciation. It rests with the teacher to weave the pattern of her stories as she creates their content.

Rhymes

It is easier to select rhymes than stories for this age. Finger plays, face, toe, and feet games are most suitable because they associate action and rhythmic pattern with the parts of the child's body which interest him most. *This little pig went to market*, *Pitty patty colt*, *Harry whistle*, *Brow Brinkey*, and *Eye winker*, are among the best-known. Nursery rhymes which are suitable because they deal with familiar ideas and because their strong, swinging rhythm is associated with clapping are, *Pat-a cake*, and *Clap hands till Daddy comes home*. A more advanced type is:

"Two little dickey birds
Sitting on a wall."

The success of this sort of rhyme depends entirely upon the action and the sing-song sound. The disappearance of first one forefinger and then the other, followed by their return, is an exciting real experience and commands immediate attention. *Imsey Wimsey Spider* and *Peek-a-boo* belong to the same group.

Whichever rhymes we choose, we must use them with the appropriate action in the same way that children experiment with words as they play.

Three-Year-Olds

This division into ages is for the purpose of discussion only. The reader will understand that there is no sharp change in the development of children because they attain their next birthday. The growth of each child's mental powers depends on inner forces and external experience and there are wide individual differences. This is particularly noticeable in the development of language. Boys are often slower than girls in the use and understanding of speech. Home environment counts a good deal ; some parents talk to each other and to their children much more than others. Intelligent children in these homes accumulate a greater store of ideas and can express themselves and follow the more involved parts of speech. Only-children suffer from a lack of companionship of older and more articulate companions. Others enjoy a greater breadth of experience than usual ; they are taken for expeditions and go away for holidays and are allowed to join in the activities of the parents. In spite of these differences, it is possible to generalize with confidence. Modern scientific, psychological research has provided us with a series of norms which inform us what the great majority are like and what they can do at various ages. The summary of children's characteristics is not therefore a matter of opinion. The writer has checked her own experience with these norms in the effort to provide as accurate a picture as possible.

The experience of three-year-olds has widened considerably. For one thing, they are more confident of their skill to get about, and so they explore farther and with greater independence. Their passion for investigation brings them into contact with many kinds of objects and materials, and their energetic physical experiments produce all sorts of situations which present concrete problems, usually solved by the trial and error method.

They observe many more details than two-year-olds, as we see if we watch their make-believe and dramatic play. They know a great deal more about adult activities and take more notice of other children, although they do not play much with one another. They are particularly interested in everything around them which moves, makes noises, or does something dramatic. In turn, they express this interest in vigorous noise and action. In the Nursery Class, they put chairs together to make a car, and then find some object to use as a steering-wheel or imitate the action with commendable accuracy. As an imaginary door is shut, they shout ' bang ' ; when the brakes are applied, they imitate a ' scrunch.' There may be no hooter but they hoot very effectively. They play at being animals or workmen or members of a family, all with deep seriousness. When they are dogs, they find themselves a kennel, call their food 'bones,' answer by barking and walk on all fours. As workmen they fiddle and tinker or they dig or haul along trucks full of material. They move house, take up roads and mend gates. If they are 'fathers' they go out to work and return home demanding attention and refreshment; mothers occupy themselves with shopping, tea-parties and baby-minding. Letters are scribbled and poked under the door of the play-house. In all such play, they show how much more they realize of the relationship between people and things and the general way of living.

Like two-year-olds, they talk as they play and do things, and it is still more soliloquy than conversation. But in order to complete an activity to their satisfaction, they will often throw out remarks and demands to members of the group who are busy round them. "Get up! get up! It's time to get up," or, "Shut the shop. Lock the door. Time to pack up." In listening to their running commentaries, which are addressed to no one in particular, we notice that their vocabulary has extended considerably. They can use adjectives and adverbs, and are sorting out the confusion of 'you' when it means 'me.' The realization of 'not I' is gradually dawning. After a story, someone will say, "John went to school with his red boots on. Not me. No, *John*."

This does not mean, however, that they have ceased to confuse words and ideas. They are constantly puzzled by the idioms in the language of grown-ups and have not sufficient control of words to ask for explanations or to follow if these were given. How often teachers feel helpless to explain when a three-year-old asks, 'Why?' which usually means 'How?' So much explanation involves other sets of ideas which we know will only confuse him more. Children of this age are probably more puzzled by what they hear than at any other age. Their interest in language compels them to pay attention as adults talk, yet they lack the understanding and the skill and persistence in questioning of the four-year-olds.

Stories

Stories for three-year-olds must therefore still begin from their own adventures in a world which they know and they must continue to be told in terms of action. But far more detail can be introduced; the children welcome some slightly descriptive adjectives when we first tell a story and then insist upon the same words at every re-telling. "Betty put on her best blue coat with the red buttons," is the sort of detail which attracts them. Characteristic noises always delight them. "Clip-clop, clip-clop, went the old horse down the road." "Pit-pat, pit-pat came

John's feet along the garden path." "Cluck, cluck, cluck said the hen."

It is useless to attempt the entirely unfamiliar in stories for this age although they need not deal exclusively with the child and his immediate needs. The characters do not have to include children like themselves; tales of familiar things in the outside world are very satisfactory. New situations arising from relationships between well-known objects, people and animals can be followed by most children and provide a wealth of imaginative experience. Action can be varied, but there must be action in every sentence, and the ideas expressed must belong to the world of the senses: sight, smells, sounds, movement, and direct conversation.

In collecting suitable stories for three-year-olds, or, better still, if they make them up themselves, teachers are wise if they keep in mind their own particular group. A little practice and due consideration for form is all that is required. The stories can be longer than for the two-year-olds and a more extensive vocabulary can be used, but the sentences and phrases must still be simple. Incidents must be put close together; one point must lead clearly to the next. They can stand any amount of repetition; the teller will be bored with the refrain long before the children. Just as children chant a phrase over and over again to themselves, so they love to hear sounds repeated continually.

There have been a number of excellent picture-books published during the last few years with the right kind of story for children with certain types of background. Three-year-olds in the country delight in Lois Lenski's *Little Farm.*

It is an account of Farmer Small's daily activities with his animals and at his wayside vegetable stall. There is no plot; it is unnecessary at this age. A recital of interesting events is still absorbing. Others in this series are *Little Train*, *Little Aeroplane*, *Little Sailing Boat*; each is just right for children with experience of the subjects. Marjorie Flack's *Angus Books* and Clare Newberry's *Cat Stories* are successful with most children. *Buttons* by Tom Robinson is another good cat story. *Little Black Sambo* is generally popular. There are some short, new stories about a dog called Sam by Marjorie Anderson (O.U.P.), which are excellent both to tell and as types of suitable tales for this age. *The Little Engine that Could*, retold by Watty Piper is an example of the story which combines the familiar with unusual situations which delight intelligent three-year-olds.

Many of the best stories are to be found in picture-books. Where the group is small, there is no better way of telling stories than to let the children cluster round and look at the pictures as the story is told. There will often be interruptions but the children do not mind. Questions and comments show that their interest is awake and their minds working. Although a special time can be devoted each day to story-telling, it is a very informal period when children wander off if they are not interested and when the story often tails off into conversation.

Verse

Their delight in simple words and design with plenty of repetition of sound and rhythm makes three-year-olds particularly sensitive to nursery rhymes, even when they but dimly understand their meaning. It is a good plan to introduce them during odd moments of rest or when a tranquillizing activity is needed. A few finger or face games command immediate attention, and then the teacher suggests, " Let's sing . . ." or " Shall we say . . ." Among the most suitable rhymes are:

Polly, put the kettle on.	*Jack and Jill.*
Hickety, Pickety, my black hen.	*Hot Cross Buns.*
Old Mother Hubbard.	*Little Jack Horner.*
Three Little Kittens.	*Hickory, dickory dock.*
Here we go up, up, up.	*Diddle, diddle dumpling, my son John.*
Sing, sing, what shall I sing?	*Diddledy, diddledy dumpty,*
To market, to market.	*The cat ran up the plum tree.*

Four- and Five-Year-Olds

With the next two years, comes a passion for naming everything and for verbal enquiry. The 'Why?' 'How?' and 'What's it called?' of the four-year-olds develop into 'Where do things come from?' 'Where do they go?' 'What are things for?' 'What do certain words mean?' of the fives. The younger children do not always appear to listen to the answers but they are busy trying to combine information with their own fantasies and experience. Very often one simple answer does not satisfy them; the questions multiply and lead from one to another. When answering a question put to himself, a four-year-old cannot stop with a few words but tells a long narrative, mixing up fact and fancy and unrelated nonsense. They are delighted with the odds-and-ends of word rubbish which they make up. The wild, senseless stories which they invent are the obvious expression of their urgent need to experiment with language. Their exchange of conversation with each other often takes the form of 'going one better.' " My mother has a blue jug like that," is the signal for exaggerated rejoinders such as " My mother has *hundreds* of blue jugs," followed by " My mother has *millions* of blue jugs."

The five-year-olds are rather more concerned to discover the connection between familiar things and the world outside which they are dimly beginning to realize. They discuss natural phenomena with each other and make suggestions about the origins of the sun, moon, and stars. Their minds run on death, killings, illness, operations, and accidents, but in a matter-of-fact way. When telling stories themselves, they are more accurate than four-year-olds, but if they sense approval they add more and more detail to the real facts until the story becomes quite fantastic.

Just as their constant questioning shows how deep is their interest in the ordinary life around them, their spontaneous activities show how tremendous is their need to understand and how little they still know.

At first they continue to play at being animals, people they see at home and others they meet in shops and streets. Being less concerned with their personal needs and able to watch with detachment, their observation is much keener. They differentiate more accurately, and because of their greater facility in talking, they use words more appropriately. When, therefore, they pretend to be workmen, they are foremen or conductors or electricians or gasmen. Twiddles with the fingers no longer give satisfaction as repair work; play-houses are wired for light in a concrete fashion. String is festooned round the walls, a box is set up for controls and a tintack here and there does duty as a switch. When they pretend to be grown-ups, they often mimic some characteristic which leaves no doubt as to which role they have assumed. They hold cardboard strips between their lips for cigarettes, pencils are tucked behind the ears and pipes are knocked out. Their capacity for closer observation is well illustrated in their play with bricks. Once they were used to build boats; now they make battleships, ferry boats, steamers, or rafts. Sleeping- and restaurant-cars are added to trains, and traffic lights are arranged along a street and are worked for the benefit of cars which are forced to take heed.

During their fifth year they reveal how their minds are concerned with the social life around them: the supply of food, its transportation, the duties of public servants like policemen, dustmen, and nurses. In their play they reflect their own social background much more than the four-year-olds. For instance, they play at parties according to the sort of functions they have at home. Some children are particular about having saucers to cups and the 'help' opens the front door. In some districts, 'pubs' and coffee stalls are made out of screens, but children from other parts of a town play at cafés and restaurants. Fathers go to the office or to the works but not just to work. There is great excitement when break-down gangs are doing repairs. Fire engines and fires are favourite interests; weddings and funerals are equally popular. Hospitals, nurses, and doctors provide constant material for dramatic play.

Stories

Those fairy tales that are characterized by a great deal of repetition and do not deal with children who find themselves in unreal situations are suitable for the four- and five-year-olds. Examples are:

Titty Mouse and Tatty Mouse.
The Cat and the Mouse.
The Gingerbread Boy.
Little Half-Chick.
The Three Billy Goats Gruff.
The Little Red Hen.
The Old Woman and her Pig.
Chicken Licken.
The Tale of the Turnip.
The Three Pigs.
The Cock, the Mouse, and the Little Red Hen.

Journeys, parties, picnics, holiday adventures, and a multitude of everyday events can be elaborated into fascinating stories to provide valuable imaginative experience for these ages, at the same time helping to clarify some of the problems they meet in their environment. Stories of people at work and of animal life, and others which personify mechanical things are especially well received. Towards the end of their fifth year, when children begin to think in terms of more complicated relationships, and when they realize the advantage and pleasure of friendly co-operation, adventures of groups of children which go beyond their immediate environment are appreciated. But while they are ready for considerably more imaginative experience, it must be of a kind which is closely allied to their own lives. It is a case of transferring the familiar to unfamiliar settings. Transport of all sorts, animal life, fairs and the circus, are among the suitable subjects.

These children can still enjoy a good deal of repetition and enumeration, but they are beginning to look for a slight plot and to appreciate a story which has a beginning, a middle, and an end. Their enjoyment of an interesting pattern shows an advance in literary appreciation. They love funny stories but they must be funny according to *their* ideas of humour. Events which result in the familiar routine becoming topsy-turvy, or which put adults in peculiar physical positions, particularly amuse them. How often they remark, " Wouldn't it be funny if so-and-so happened ? " The so-and-so is usually a jumble up of ordinary things. Examples of suitable stories are given in the Bibliography.

Verse

It is doubtful whether all *Mother Goose* can be considered as literature ; the rhymes are a hotch-potch from many sources, some not written for children at all. Yet it is the best source of verse for four- and five-year-olds and the discerning adult cannot go far wrong if she chooses some for sheer beauty, others for their delightful sound and rhythm, and still others because they can be associated with first-hand experience. For poetry, we might choose:

How many miles to Babylon?
I had a little nut tree.
Bell Horses.
Ride a Cock Horse.
Lavender's Blue.
Ladybird, ladybird, fly away home.
Wee Willie Winkie.
One misty, moisty morning.
There was an old woman tossed up in a basket.

—for sound and rhythm:

See-Saw, Marjory Daw.
Hey diddle diddle.
Gay go up and gay go down.
A farmer went trotting upon his grey mare.
Bobbie Shaftoe.
London Bridge is broken down.
I had a little pony.

When the winter winds blow round the school, we introduce the children to *The north wind doth blow.* When there is a bit of bother about a lost shoe, the skilful teacher cheers up a child by singing *Little Betty Blue. Daffy-down-dilly* will delight the children as they notice that the first bulbs are flowering. Short poems are best at this age and of course there is no need for 'teaching.' The adult sings and recites and the children join in. Rhymes occur during the day, whenever the time is suitable: before a story, while waiting for the milk to be distributed, after a noisy play period, and so on. The children learn without effort for they are immensely interested in words and rhythms. So long as the teacher enjoys the rhymes herself and uses a clear, sympathetic voice, the children will love their first experiences of poetry.

Six- and Seven-Year-Olds

Somewhere between six and eight years the children pass from a world dominated by immediate experience to a world in which the far-away can be understood. It is doubtful whether they appreciate the world of long ago until they are much older. But they begin to ask, " When you were little, did you do so and so ? " and they recall isolated incidents in their own histories; but long, long ago remains a difficult idea to understand. Most children during these years can make mental excursions into the distance without being confused. Of course, the ease with which they do this varies with the individual. This is well illustrated in classes which have adopted an activity curriculum. One group of six-year-olds had made a market stall and filled it with 'fruit' and they asked how oranges and apples got to the real market. After various expeditions, including one to a distributing depot and another to the docks, some of the group set about making the docks on the floor of the classroom. A large space was covered with blue cloth and their boats went to and fro from dock to dock, under swing bridges, carrying all sorts of cargoes for unloading or loading. Warehouses, yards, rows of little houses, a church, cinemas, etc. grew up round the docks. There was a good deal of discussion about the fuelling of the vessels. The teacher answered their enquiries with stories of coal production, and immediately several children began to construct a coal mine. " How do the oranges get to the ships which bring them ? " was another enquiry. The answer was given in stories of life in the orange groves and the ports of Egypt and South Africa. So another dock was built and the loaded vessels travelled across the ' ocean ' from country to country. For more than six weeks, this interest absorbed the group, but at the end of that time there were still some children who were content to play with the original fruit stall although they had heard the same stories and been on the same expeditions. They were simply not ready to accept the unfamiliar, and the fresh material aroused no response.

We can do no better than to choose stories which follow the characteristic interests of children of these ages. In progressive schools, teachers are able to select their stories at the moment when the interest of the majority of the class is at its highest. In more traditional schools, plans can be made for story-telling which is based on relationships which concern the fundamental needs of the children : food, houses, clothes, and transport. These universal interests of the six to eight group are wide enough to include people they have never met and things they have never seen. Something in their environment suggests a problem, for example, " Where does whale meat come from ? " Their minds can accept the strange, new information as the teacher tells, in the form of a story, how whaling is carried on and how the children live in countries where the men are engaged in the industry. Whale meat now has a wider significance than just food ; their first-hand experience has been enriched with a wealth of information, which is built into the pattern of their thinking.

Six-year-olds enjoy stories of wild creatures, even if they have met them only in the circus or in the zoo. Seven-year-olds respond enthusiastically to stories of the lives of children belonging to semi-primitive tribes. When H.M.S. *Vanguard* was taking the Royal Family to South Africa, many groups of children were making models of the ship in their activity period and many others were collecting pictures of the ceremonial displays of the natives in honour of the visit. Teachers used this opportunity to tell stories of the lives of children living amongst these semi-primitive tribes, describing their homes, their clothes and habits.

Thinking is more mature at this age. The children have ideas and discuss them with each other and with sympathetic adults. They are not only ideas connected with their practical lives ; they concern the reason why and because. Abstractions are still rather advanced for them but they are quite capable of generalization. As they make their toy towns with gasworks and pylons, garages and fire stations, they talk among themselves. One overhears such remarks as, "People have to pay first in case they have no money after," and, "Nobody can make anybody else do what they don't want to." They try to speak accurately, using similes to express exactly what they mean. They are also realizing the pleasures of friendship and the value of group co-operation; before they are eight, many of them have joined a gang. Their self-chosen activities become nearer to class projects and they begin to appreciate good workmanship. They observe the things which interest them very intently and try to construct with some reference to reality and with neatness, criticizing each other's work and asking for opinions independently.

The majority of children are now sure of the difference between magic and reality. It is the time when they sort out the Christmas myth of Santa Claus. There are, of course, exceptions. Some children are still upset at the very strange, and others are still nervous of the unknown and the dark. If possible, the more violent type of tale should be kept until these children are more sure of the familiar world.

Stories

As far as fairy tales are concerned, there are numbers of collections and it is the teacher's responsibility to choose the best possible rendering. While they all give immense enjoyment, many of them have, in their matchless form and imagery, great literary value.

For the rest, stories should be chosen in line with the interest of a particular group of children. This means some research and skill on the part of the teacher. No collection of stories could possibly supply the information particularly needed by one class during a year of creative, freely chosen activity. A good classroom library and membership of the local children's library are both essential. Teachers who are convinced of the value of an activity curriculum should begin at once to collect material which can be used as stories when the different interests emerge. Suggestions for suitable material are given in the Bibliography.

Verse

In some schools, there is a subtle difference between nursery rhymes for young children and poetry for the older Infants. The poetry lesson assumes more formality and there is stress on *learning* poems rather than *saying* nursery rhymes. There should be no such difference. The success of teaching depends on how much the children enjoy the verses they know and hear, not on how many they know.

Poetry in progressive schools is not a lesson; it is an informal activity in which both children and teacher take part. The teacher may begin by suggesting, "Let's say . . ." "Let me say one," "Now me," "I'll say one next," volunteers one after another of the group. A quiet child is encouraged: "Mary, will you say one now?"

Sometimes several children co-operate as voice and chorus or there may be several speaking parts and so the verse is shared. Perhaps the poem is dramatized as suggested in Chapter XI. Perhaps a longer poem has been made into a play with one child who is a narrator while others speak and act their parts as they occur. *Little Black Hen* and others by A. A. Milne are very suitable for this sort of treatment.

"Now here is one that you've not heard before," remarks the teacher. "It's about Mrs. Macqueen who kept a shop down on the cobbles," and she reads the first three verses of Walter de la Mare's *Mrs. Macqueen.* After one reading she says, "Now listen again and tell me, when I've finished, what time Mrs. Macqueen gets up and what colour her shutters are." There is a good deal of discussion after this reading, and children want to say something about cobble stones and 'glass like bulls' eyes' and 'candles which shone out.' The teacher does not attempt to explain difficulties; she allows the discussion and the sound of the poem to suggest the meaning. The new poem may be left till another day and then the two last verses are added, and gradually the poem becomes the children's own through listening, speaking and discussion of the words.

Partly-learned verses are often recalled and then the children are asked to join in if they remember the words, or someone is invited to try it alone. Sometimes children bring their rhyme books from home and they are used for reading aloud.

Occasionally the opinion is advanced that if we choose a poem because it fits in with another activity, we wrong the poem. It is true that we do not choose verses simply because they can be linked with interests, but we try to associate pleasurable, real experiences with appropriate and good verse, so stimulating more interest, both in the poem and the experience. When the children are discussing men who work for us and dramatizing postmen, policemen, firemen, etc., it is not out of place to read them Walter de la Mare's poem *Sooeep*. There could be no happier expression of this trade than:

> And once inside the house, he'll squat,
> And drive his rods on high,
> Till twirls his sudden sooty brush
> Against the morning sky.

The interest of the children in the sweeps of their real experience can only add to their appreciation of the poem.

Mother Goose is still a rich source of verse for these ages, but modern verse also provides suitable poems. Every teacher should keep her own anthology, for the right verses are found in the most unexpected collections. Eleanor Farjeon, Christina Rossetti, R. L. Stevenson, and Walter de la Mare are all children's poets. A very representative collection is found in *Collected Poems, Series I* (Methuen), where the poems quoted here can be found. The names of other suitable anthologies are given in the Bibliography.

* * * * *

We began by remarking that children have a natural interest in words. We cannot test the results of our efforts in story-telling or the wisdom of our choice, but if at the end of their Infant School lives the children retain that love of words and their natural gift for playing with language, we have done a great deal.

E. R. Boyce.

Chapter XIII

LEARNING TO READ

ABILITY to read must be regarded as an essential skill in the modern world. With its complementary skill, writing, it is almost as necessary to every man and woman as the strength of their hands and the use of their senses. It is important, therefore, that every child should learn to read and write just as soon as his abilities fit him for the task ; just as soon, but no sooner.

At what age, then, should children be taught to read ? There is little doubt that many children are introduced to formal reading at much too early an age.

Whilst some children wish to read at five-and-a-half years, there are others who betray neither the desire nor the ability to do so until much later. The conclusion must therefore be drawn that reading cannot be successfully taught at any particular age to large groups of children by using a rigidly graduated scheme or method which has no regard for the varying stages of development, natural capacity or tastes of the children.

Learning to Read through Activities

There is a widespread belief that it is extremely difficult to teach reading and that it is necessary to allot a large amount of time to the formal teaching of this subject. This is because, in the past, it was the custom to give instruction to children too soon, and to approach the subject by one of various highly conventionalized methods which obscured the real purpose of the teaching and directed the children's attention to the *form* rather than the *meaning* of words, while language, as a vehicle of expression, was ignored. The printed page was a collection of phrases and sentences which might or might not have any meaning for the little readers and which made little appeal to their interests.

The newer methods of teaching reading take cognizance of each child's stage of development and of his interest. In the school or classroom where free activities are encouraged, reading falls naturally into its place. " It's my birthday today," says John, staggering in with a large wooden engine in his arms, which he sets down and draws round the room to the envy of all. " We must put John's name in the birthday frame," says the teacher.

Most classrooms have some sort of birthday announcement board. A simple one consists of a skeleton wooden frame slotted at the sides. A permanent card bearing the words, 'It is . . . birthday today,' is kept in the frame. The name of the child whose anniversary occurs is slotted into the space. The card is made to fit tightly into the sides of the frame so that it will not slip to the bottom.

IT IS
JOHN'S
BIRTHDAY
TODAY.

This notice board is always in its place in the room. The children constantly hear the words, 'It is . . . birthday today' as the cards are put in. To sustain the interest, a card with the word 'Nobody's' is slipped in when no birthday is celebrated.

It is useful to keep a corner or space clear in the room as a depository for birthday gifts and other private possessions of the children. "This is my engine," says John aggressively, as another boy prepares to make free with it.

Habits of sharing the small pleasures of everyday life will be encouraged on all reasonable occasions; but it may also be necessary, occasionally, to underline the distinction between 'mine' and 'thine.' Many small children are acquisitive by nature and are liable to impose on the generosity of their friends. Labels showing the ownership of the toys brought to school may sometimes be used.

THIS IS JOHN'S ENGINE

THIS IS BETTY'S DOLL

THIS IS BILL'S BARROW

No effort is made to ensure that the children know what the words mean, but it is probably safe to say that few children in the class will be unable to read these words and even to pick them out in other contexts.

In general habit training, the children will learn to clear up and put away the materials and equipment they have used. Sand spilt about the floor will be swept up and put back in the tray or container; the clay will be put back in the bin; pieces of wood and tools will be replaced on the bench; objects used in water play will be gathered together and put in their places.

Put the sand back in this tray.
Put the clay back in this bin.
Put the tools on this bench.
Put the toys back in this box.

—are phrases which will be in use by children and teacher when clearing-up time comes.

A card printed with the words generally used can be placed near the spot which is indicated. There is no need to talk about it nor even to draw the children's attention to it; but after a short time practically all the children will know that the cards are telling them to do the little daily jobs which are carried out in their normal routine. There are other habits, such as closing the door, or wiping shoes on the mat which may have to be cultivated.

Please close the door.
Please wipe your shoes on this mat.

—are directions that will become familiar to the ear and may also become familiar to the eye if posted up in the appropriate places.

The foregoing instances indicate various ways in which children may be introduced to the idea that the printed word conveys the same meaning as the spoken word. It is possible that none of these suggestions is applicable to one particular group of children, but the underlying principles can be applied to the daily programme of any class, thus affording opportunities for the children to recognize, without any drudgery, certain printed sentences and their meaning. There should be no deliberate seeking after suitable sentences. If they do not present themselves naturally the occasion should be postponed until they do. Nor should large numbers of printed instructions be used. This would merely confuse the children. One or two cards printed with sentences in such common use that the children cannot fail to recognize them will at first be sufficient to arouse and sustain the interest.

Growth of Vocabulary with Widening Interests

As the children develop mentally and physically their range of activities widens. Interest is focused on some usual or unusual local event, such as the daily or weekly market or the annual fair or circus. Objects are made for the market stalls. Roundabouts, swings, booths for the fair are constructed by the more active children. Goods on the stalls must be labelled. Various notices are required for the amusements at the fair, and a class newspaper may be started.

These centres of interest are continually changing in scope and kind so that the number of words, phrases, and sentences which can be read at sight gradually grows. Many constantly recurring words and phrases will be recognized as they appear in a new context, for instance:

Here is . . .; There are . . .; This is . . .; Please . . .;

—likewise, verbs of action:

Put, shut, open, sweep, come;

—or common names, such as:

Sand, clay, water, toy, doll, aeroplane, barrow, train, engine;

—and connective words, such as:

And, or, on, in, by.

Some of the children, after a short time, will have acquired a reading vocabulary of several dozen words, though they may not be aware of it.

Introducing Pictures and Books

In providing the children's room and programme with opportunities for all kinds of free activities, the teacher will remember that vigorous muscular activity is not the only type in which children engage. There are, indeed, some young children who do not seek expression in physical movement. They prefer to go about quietly, observing the objects around them and the occupations of other children and, above all, to look at pictures and books. Provision must be made for such children. Pictures, both large and small, should be available as well as Nursery picture-books. The pictures should be such as to stimulate verbal expression, and if it seems desirable, stories should be told based on the subject-matter of the pictures.

Some of the children will make remarks about the pictures or ask questions about them. These remarks, or the answers to the questions, may be printed unobtrusively below the picture:

Mary says this is a circus.
The boy is carrying water in his pail.

The children will be pleased to know that the printed words are their own comments or the answers to their questions. They will probably look at the words and repeat them the next time they handle the picture and will become familiar with their form, associating it with their own spoken words.

The Use of Nursery Rhymes and Jingles

The singing and repetition of nursery rhymes and jingles is a source of pleasure to most children. The favourite rhymes may be printed on cards and shown occasionally when the words are sung or said. If the cards are left on view the children will examine them and repeat the words, thus adding further to the store of words whose look as well as sound has been remembered.

Some children will want to draw and paint their impressions. Equipment for this form of expression is a necessary part of the stock of the Infant School. The labelling of pictures drawn by themselves is many a child's introduction to the art of written expression.

"Look! I've drawn Jack and Jill," says the young artist. "Jack and Jill," repeats the teacher putting the names under the figures. The child may or may not be sufficiently interested to want to write the words himself under his next picture. If he is not, no comment is made, but if he wishes to do so, he should be encouraged and helped.

Writing and reading thus fit into the general programme of work. The motor activity involved in the writing of words and sentences serves to strengthen the visual impression of their form. Any child showing a wish to copy the words he sees about the room or as captions to pictures in his book should be encouraged to do so. At a later stage some of the children will make their own first reading book by clipping together papers on which they have drawn pictures with labelled figures or short descriptive sentences, or a group or class may make a class newspaper by dictating to the teacher items which she writes on large sheets of paper fastened together.

Formal Teaching Introduced

It will become evident to the practical teacher that, at some stage, it will be necessary to introduce formal teaching in order to supplement the knowledge gained during pre-reading activities.

It is usual to provide various types of matching exercises as a first step in the more formal instruction. Sentences that the children have seen frequently will be printed and shown. The children are asked to place the cards beside the objects to which they relate:

This is John's engine.
Please close the door.
Put the toys in this cupboard.

As each card is shown a child puts it in its accustomed place.

The next stage is the matching of the sentence cards themselves. Duplicate pairs are made and the children play a communal game of 'snap' by choosing one of the sentence cards and then watching for its duplicate to appear from a pile of cards. Success in the game shows that the children recognize the shape of the sentences themselves, a necessary first step in reading.

The recognition of individual words follows this stage. Many of the children will already be able to pick out words which frequently occur and recognize them as they appear in fresh sentences. This ability must be tested and recorded.

One of the duplicate pairs of several sentence cards should be cut up so that each smaller card bears one word. The children sort out the jumble of individual word-cards and arrange them so that the original sentences are formed. It may be necessary at first to reduce this to another matching game by leaving the complete sentences on view. No record, however, of individual word recognition should be made until the child re-arranges the words without this aid.

Individual Apparatus

It has been suggested that a first reading book may be made by the children themselves. Some teachers prefer to supply the children with hectographed copies of the children's own sentences to be used in the book, as they are easier to read. Such a book provides a very valuable piece of individual apparatus.

Another type useful at this stage is a reduced copy of the sentence cards already familiar to the children in their games and matching exercises. The whole sentence is read and then the smaller word-cards are sorted and placed in order by the individual child.

Children who are at the stage of word recognition may have pictures and word-cards to correspond. The words are placed beside the pictures which illustrate them.

The sentence with missing words is another familiar type of apparatus. A number of sentences, each with one or two missing words, are printed on cards :

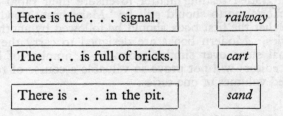

Here is the . . . signal.	*railway*
The . . . is full of bricks.	*cart*
There is . . . in the pit.	*sand*

The smaller cards bearing the missing words are placed by the children in the gaps.

The more advanced children using such apparatus are refreshing and confirming in their memory the vocabulary mastered in the more informal class and group activities.

It must be remembered that individual apparatus is only a poor substitute for direct teaching and is designed chiefly to occupy and interest children who are temporarily deprived of the immediate attention of the teacher. If the teacher has a very small class, or if the children are all approximately of similar age and attainments, individual apparatus may be unnecessary.

Later Stages of Teaching

The foregoing notes will suggest how the early, informal reading activities may be grouped round any centre of interest occupying the children's attention, and how these activities may pass into more formal instruction without any break or unnatural transition.

A group of children will begin to show that they are sufficiently interested in reading to carry the activities a stage further than those already described.

A story based on the narrative contained in the first few pages of the book which is to be the children's first reading-book should be told. Sentences taken verbatim from the book are introduced. For illustration, the books themselves may be used by the children. Most modern books have attractive pictures. The children will talk about the pictures and the story and, when the other groups are under instruction, write some of the sentences and use apparatus based upon them. Other sentences will follow quite quickly, for many of the common words will be familiar if the informal work has been carried on successfully.

If the books themselves are already in the hands of the children they will soon discover that they are able to read the early pages. Provided that the books give sufficient repetition of word and phrase and that the teacher supplies suitable informal occupation based on the material in the book, the first book will present no difficulty. Many of the children are now reading and require only well-graded reading matter to ensure their rapid progress. The teacher's motto should still be 'Make haste slowly.' It is desirable that the first book should be followed by another in the same series. Modern books are designed to carry the children by gradual steps over similar ground. A number of books by different editors will not prove so valuable a course of reading as the graded volumes of one series.

The Introduction of Phonic Analysis

Many teachers believe that at this stage children are assisted, both in reading and spelling, by a study of words as a collection of sounds. This study is most conveniently carried on side by side with the methods already described, when the children begin to read their first book. The sounds of the letters will already have been grasped by many of the children. To systematize this unrelated and rather vague knowledge, a more definite phonic analysis may be made as words occur belonging to similar sound families. The methods of pursuing this study are well known, and aids to teaching are given in many popular children's books, the words being collected in groups at the end of the volumes.

Children who have not made normal progress on a visual memory method may be assisted by the phonic approach. The progress of normal children in word recognition and spelling may also be hastened, after the initial difficulties have been overcome. It should be remembered, however, that many common words of the English language conform to no rules of spelling or pronunciation and must be learned by 'look and say.'

The Keeping of Records

Teachers whose classes have a wide range of attainment must keep progress records to ensure that all the children are receiving the teaching they require. Such records are unnecessary in the earlier stages of informal class and group activity. When, however, the children begin to pick out words and phrases and give indications that their interest has moved from the mere memorizing of sentences to the real business of reading, an individual record of their progress should be kept.

For convenience, the stages may be marked by the types of apparatus used. The simple matching exercises are followed by those demanding word recognition and then by the type requiring some discrimination in the use of individual words as parts of a sentence. Such apparatus has already been described.

When the children have made sufficient progress to use a book, the number of pages read by them may be recorded. Later still, the titles of books read by them may be noted. When this stage is reached, however, the need is for suitable reading-matter. Apparatus and step-by-step records may be dispensed with. The best apparatus is a good book. The progress subsequently made by the children and their interest in reading will depend on the number and quality of the books provided for them.

Kathleen Rich.

Chapter XIV

NUMBER CONCEPTS

Mathematical thinking is a tool. There is no point in acquiring t unless you mean to use it. (W. W. Sawyer)

IT may seem pretentious to apply the word 'mathematics' to anything which little children can do. Yet as teachers we should be aware that, from the earliest number teaching, we are not only laying the foundation for future work in arithmetic, but also in geometry and other branches of mathematics, and that the way in which we lay these foundations will largely determine the children's ability to cope with the numerical problems which will confront them both in their own affairs and in those of the community in which they live.

The development of mathematics has always been associated with something useful. It did not start because people with time to spare played with figures, but because it was needed to solve practical problems. (See Hogben, *Mathematics for the Million*, Allen & Unwin.) If mathematics is to be of value to the children, they should learn it in the same way. What they learn should be of immediate use to them, or at the least, they should see how it could be of use to them. In other words, it is not sums as such that are important, but the ability to *use* sums in dealing with the problems of everyday life. This is the attitude in which we approach number teaching.

The difficulties encountered when teaching number lie not so much in how to teach the various processes, as in how to teach them so that they become useful tools. There are two main difficulties involved. The first is that arithmetic is concerned with the abstract idea of number, so that "at the very beginning the child has to leave the world of concrete fascinating realities and concentrate on an abstraction, on a creation of the human intellect." —(Drummond, *Psychology and Teaching of Number*, Harrap.) On the other hand, there is the difficulty of preserving throughout the teaching the closest relations between what is taught and the child's own experience. At first sight these two aspects may appear to be opposed to one another, but if we consider how a child's earliest ideas of number develop, we see that with the same conditions both difficulties are avoided.

The Development of Number Ideas

The teaching of number does not start in school, and the first steps are taken without formal instruction. A child in his play, by doing what interests him, through contact with his environment and the people in it, gains quite definite ideas of number, size, and space. The extent of the knowledge which can be acquired in this way may be seen from an investigation carried out with more than a thousand Scottish children. (*The Early Development of Number Concepts*, Scottish Council for Research in Education.) It was found that when these children entered school at the age of five or thereabouts:

> Ninety-six per cent were capable of rote counting at least to 4, and more than a quarter of them could count to 20 or more. Almost all could tell the number of objects in a small group, more than half being able to count up to 10 or 15 objects.
>
> Many could match a group of objects by an equal group. Half were able to add and subtract to 4 and some could add and subtract higher numbers.
>
> A few could count backwards, knew the ordinals to 10 and could recognize a half.

These statistics will not necessarily apply to any other group of children, but they do indicate the extent of the number knowledge which may be acquired without any definite teaching.

Let us consider the difficulty of teaching an abstract idea in the light of this pre-school learning. Nearly all the children tested, when asked to give two beads, were able to do this correctly. That is, they had not only learnt to count two shoes or two buttons or two fingers, but by repeating this in their play, and by hearing the word ' two ' used, had been able to abstract the idea of ' two-ness.' On the other hand, some of these same children could count to three or more but were unable to give three beads; though they had learnt the word ' three ' as part of the series ' one, two, three,' they were not yet able to apply it to any group of three objects. This suggests how the abstract idea of number gradually develops. It is useless to try to explain it to the children. They must learn it in their own way and time. " It is mind growth that is necessary, not instruction."—(Drummond, *ibid.*) But this learning presupposes an environment in which the children are free to play and experiment with a variety of materials and where there are grown-ups or older children who will talk to them and allow them to share their activities. Under these conditions the other difficulty, that of relating the teaching to the children's experience, never arises. It is through their experience that the children are learning except, of course, where some physical, intellectual, or emotional factor retards learning, and neither the learning nor the experience can continue independently. Thus we see that where a child has freedom to experiment in a suitable environment, the development of number ideas occurs spontaneously without formal teaching and without difficulty. This learning of the fundamentals of number does, however, involve two factors: a suitable environment, and freedom to experiment within this environment.

In connection with number teaching, one is sometimes asked, "At what age does abstract thinking emerge?" From the above we see that some abstract thinking is inherent in the use of the smallest numbers and can be present at a very early age. But this is abstract thinking applied to real situations. Abstract thinking about abstract situations is certainly not the concern of the Nursery-Infant School.

It is important here to notice that not only is it *possible* for learning to take place informally under those conditions, but that if this opportunity for growth is not available in the early stage of number teaching, the subsequent learning is actually *hindered*. In *Diagnosis of Individual Difficulties in Arithmetic* (Oliver & Boyd), Schonell gives as one of the causes of backwardness in arithmetic among older children "paucity of pre-school experience": "lack of opportunity to acquire the requisite early number experiences through handling and dealing with the concrete"; "children who have had little chance of counting, comparing, contrasting, measuring, weighing, and sharing and who have had little opportunity of seeing number applied to real-life situations."

It would be a mistake to assume, however, that because the first steps in number knowledge can and should be taken without formal teaching, the later stages of learning would follow in a similar way, given time and a suitable environment. It is a question of distinguishing between two kinds of number knowledge; between ideas and techniques. The techniques (chiefly concerned with the writing of figures and the doing of sums) involve definite teaching and considerable practice. We shall consider these in connection with the Infant School stage. It is the ideas behind them that can develop only through activity and experience.

Number in the Nursery School

The teaching of number, as such, has no place in the Nursery School, but what we have already said about the early development of number concepts makes it quite clear that it cannot be ignored. One function of the Nursery School is to provide an environment in which these ideas can most readily develop. No special equipment is required. The environment described elsewhere as most suitable for promoting the all-round development of the children is obviously the one most suitable for the growth of their ideas regarding number and size.

The teacher herself, however, is part of this environment and the extent to which she uses number will have its effect on the children's ability to use number. Her part is chiefly concerned with number as language. Children learn the number names and counting by imitation, and they learn to attach meaning to these names and series of names by hearing them used in a variety of situations. There are endless opportunities for counting:

How many children present?
How many trucks in the train?
How many flowers?
How many places to set for lunch?
How many buttons to do up?

—and each time she can count aloud clearly so that the children can hear and gradually join in. Then there are number rhymes and stories—(*e.g.* Boyce and Bartlett, *Number Rhymes and Finger Plays*, Pitman), and many singing games and rhythmic activities which the children will enjoy for their own sakes, and which involve repetition of numbers. The older children may begin to recognize figures if these are used in the classroom; even wall-charts and apparatus may be designed to help the children to recognize figures. The children will turn to these when they are ready and will teach themselves, but the learning of figures is really the beginning of more formal teaching and nothing is gained by hastening this. " Figures themselves add nothing to the understanding of numbers and they should, therefore, not be taught until the children can make confident use of the sounded names corresponding to them."—(*Handbook of Suggestions for Teachers*, Board of Education.) This is the extent of the number teaching which is desirable in the Nursery School. As we saw with the Scottish five-year-olds about to enter school, many of the children will acquire considerable number knowledge. There is no danger that even the brightest children will not have enough scope. Given the right environment they will find their own ways of learning, and this kind of learning is more successful than anything which results from formal teaching can be at this stage.

Number in the Infant School

The aim of the Infant School should be to organize an environment in which the orderly development of children's early ideas of number and of their experiences of measurable quantities etc. can take place most easily.—(Handbook of Suggestions.)

It is in the Infant School that the child receives his first definite number teaching, but we still have to bear in mind that success in arithmetic depends on familiarity with the fundamental ideas of size, number, and counting before any formal teaching is attempted. The age at which this should start will obviously depend on the background and development of each individual child, but it is worth recalling the Board of Education pronouncement that " it is wisest with the majority of children to postpone formal instruction . . . until about the age of six."—(*Handbook of Suggestions.*) It is certainly desirable that at first the learning should proceed on similar lines to those which have obtained in the home or the Nursery School and that the more formal work should be introduced gradually.

Scope of the Infant School Course

The following indication of the number knowledge which can normally be expected of a seven-year-old leaving the Infant School should be compared with the *Handbook of Suggestions* (1937, pp. 523–525) :

COUNTING. Ability to count to 100 and probably to 1000, both in ones and in groups (*e.g.* 2's, 10's, 5's), and to count backwards.

NOTATION. Ability to read and write numbers at least to 100 and to have some understanding of decimal notation (*e.g.* to appreciate the difference between the 5 and the 2 in 52).

ADDITION AND SUBTRACTION. To be thoroughly familiar with the meaning of these processes in real situations and to be able to add and subtract units without the aid of counters. Most children will also be able to add and subtract tens and units.

MULTIPLICATION AND DIVISION. To have built up and learnt several multiplication tables and to be able to use multiplication and division of small numbers. The easiest tables to build up are 2 and 3 times because smaller numbers are involved, and 10 and 11 times are the easiest to learn ; these should therefore be taken first.

MEASUREMENT. To have some practical acquaintance with coins and giving change ; with measuring length, weight, and capacity ; to be able to tell the time and use a calendar.

Many Infant Schools cover far more ground than this. There is little doubt that some children can go much further, but we have to beware of progressing in the techniques of calculation when the children do not understand the practical applications of these techniques. It is much easier to teach the children to do sums than to show them how to use them. The ability of the children to do sums can easily be tested, but such a test is no criterion of the soundness of the arithmetic teaching. They should be able to use the skills they learn and see the point of using them.

The Environment

If the number work of the Infant School is to be continuous with that of the Nursery or home, a similar environment should be provided and the children should, for at least part of each day, be free and active within this environment. However limited the classroom space, the minimum requirements should be: a variety of counting materials—beads, bricks, counters, beans, etc.; opportunity for shopping play, scales and weights; measures of length and capacity, and a large wooden clock with clear figures and movable hands; and these can be supplemented by a variety of table games—jig-saws, dominoes, mosaics, playing-cards, lotto, snakes and ladders, ludo, etc.

Shopping play should be regarded as a definite part of the number work of the Infant School, since shopping is the real situation in which the children can see number being used most frequently and through which they can understand its use. The shopping need not be organized by the teacher, though she may find it advisable to choose the shopkeeper or to limit the number of purchases or the amount of money spent. The children may use the shop during a free activity period, or a group may play there during an ordinary arithmetic lesson. At first, they may merely hand over money and demand goods, irrespective of price, but they will soon begin to realize the use of money and check their change carefully. They may write out bills for their purchases or enter them in a shopping book. All this will gradually develop under the skilled handling of the teacher, and as they play the children will be learning to read and write figures, to know the value of different coins, to add the amounts of two purchases or subtract to give change. After play such as this they will be ready for definite teaching of addition and subtraction so that they can calculate bills or give change more rapidly, and for multiplication and division so that they can find quickly how much 2, 3, or $\frac{1}{2}$ will cost. When they have learnt these skills they will apply them in their further shopping play.

Scales, or measures of length, may be used in the shop. This depends on what kind of shop the children have chosen. But whether these are used in connection with the shop or not, they can be present in the classroom and arranged so that they are accessible to the children. There can be a weighing-table with scales and weights, and a chart can be pinned to the wall behind the table showing the relation between the various weights. The children will at first weigh anything—books, dolls, trains, marbles—and probably just balance them against each other or against the weights provided. Some child may give the weights in terms of ounces or pounds and others will follow suit, using the charts as guides. Similarly, a table may be provided with milk bottles and other receptacles and a bucket or bath of water. Again, the children will first compare sizes and finally measure in terms of cupfuls, or milk bottles, or pints. There can also be sticks of vraious lengths hanging from a hook on the wall and the children can take these down when they want to measure anything, or compare lengths with those of a foot, two feet, or a yard on the wall-chart. If a vertical strip of stiff paper, graduated in feet and inches, is attached to the wall, they will soon learn to use it to measure each other and to compare heights. When the children can read, question cards may be provided:

> How tall are you?
> How many cupfuls make a pint?
> Find something that weighs 1 pound.
> Make the clock say half-past three.

The cards can either be kept in boxes near the appropriate measures, or in a wall-pocket, using a different coloured card for each kind of measure. In this way the children learn by experimenting, by imitation and by teaching each other, until they are ready for definite instruction from the teacher, and written sums. The important thing is that they handle and experiment with various measures before oral teaching or written sums.

So far we have considered number work apart from the rest of the curriculum. Sometimes it has to be considered in this way, but we should be ready to take advantage of opportunities which arise for number training both from the ordinary classroom routine and from work in connection with other activities or centres of interest. Children may be responsible for ordering and checking milk for the class, for changing the calendar each day or for collecting the savings money; or they may need to measure or add in one of their activities. Chapter II, 1 in Activity Programmes shows how number may be required in connection with these. In all these cases there is a need for number knowledge and an occasion to use it. But number is a progressive subject, each stage depending on those which have gone before, and it is one in which a new process cannot be taught until the children have the necessary background knowledge. It is not reasonable to suppose that the children in their play, or other activities, will meet a demand for each individual process in the order in which, from the nature of arithmetic, it must be taught. As long as a sufficient proportion of their number teaching is in direct response to their immediate needs, we have to be satisfied. On the other hand there will always be aspects of their experience, in or out of school, to which the teacher can refer in showing them the use of what they are learning and which will provide problems which they can understand and to which they can apply their new knowledge. The skill of the teacher lies in preserving the feeling of reality and practical importance of a subject where the logical sequence of ideas must necessarily be followed, though these do not always coincide with the immediate interests of the children.

Teaching and Practice Work

The teaching of any arithmetical process involves three stages. First the children should understand the practical value of what they are going to learn in terms of their own experience. Discussion and simple oral problems often help here. Then there is the actual teaching and practice until the process is understood, and finally there is the practical application of what has been learnt to the situations which were discussed in the first stage of the teaching. We have already considered the importance of the initial and final stages and suggested methods of approach. The practice stage is also important because on the thoroughness with which the foundations are laid depends success in arithmetic at later stages. The number teaching of the Infant School should be judged, not by how *much* the children have learnt, but by how *thoroughly* they have learnt, and by the habits they have formed. Fortunately children enjoy the practice that is required for thorough learning, provided that it is accompanied by a progressive sense of achievement. It will be easier to consider how this mastery is obtained in terms of specific topics.

Addition and Subtraction of Units, and Multiplication Tables

There is no need to discuss the actual teaching of addition and subtraction, the stages into which this is graded, nor the individual apparatus which can be devised to help the children to learn. We shall merely consider methods of consolidating this teaching. There are 45 different pairs of units of the type $6+5$ (excluding 0 and the corresponding pair $5+6$) and the sums of all these pairs must be known before any rapid calculation is possible. It is not sufficient that children should be able to find the sum by counting; there must be an automatic and accurate response to each. The question arises, "Are we going to show the children how to find the sum of any pair using counters or groups of dots, give them a certain amount of practice, and then progress to something new and hope that the addition of pairs of units will gradually become automatic; or are we going to hold up the whole number teaching process until they are learnt?" Probably neither extreme is desirable, but there is a tendency to give too little practice in the first instance. This insufficiency of practice has two disadvantages: by leaving the children to depend on some prop (counters, dots or fingers) for a long time, we are allowing them to form a habit of using such a prop which may persist throughout life;

and secondly, we are making subsequent learning appear difficult because the children, while learning a new process, are still having to concentrate on the addition. To a certain extent the children will consolidate their knowledge of addition pairs as they use them, but for the sake of future speed and accuracy it is well worth spending more time on the learning in the first place. There can be plenty of written practice. The children enjoy this, especially if they are encouraged to watch their own progress from day to day. There can also be class or group games of various kinds. Even when the children have progressed to other work there should still be frequent practice of addition, possibly five minutes at the beginning of each lesson, so that the response becomes automatic as soon as possible.

The same applies to subtraction, but here there is less new learning once the children have grasped the relation between $6+5=11$; $11-5=6$; and $11-6=5$. In connection with subtraction it should be noticed that $11-5=6$ is a bond which should be known automatically, whereas $17-5=12$ need not be learnt, since once the tens and units notation is understood $17-5$ reduces to $7-5$ which is already known. Multiplication tables and the corresponding division bonds should be learnt with the same thoroughness and similar practice is required.

Subtraction of Hundreds, Tens, and Units

There are at least five recognized methods of working a subtraction sum and each of these is subject to modification. Details can be found in any text-book of arithmetic method, and though opinions differ as to the most successful, some form of equal additions or of complementary addition seems to give the best results in the long run and either can be satisfactorily taught to Infants. Whatever method is finally adopted, there are certain points to observe in the teaching :

(i) The practice of writing-in the carrying figure leads to slow and inaccurate subtraction, and should be avoided from the very beginning.

(ii) The practice of working through ten, *e.g.* in $64-29$ to say, "9 from 10 leaves 1 and 4 is 5," again leads to slow work. If the children have previously learnt thoroughly that $14-9=5$ this is quite unnecessary.

(iii) The method adopted should be identical throughout the Infant and Junior School, even to the rigmarole which the children recite to themselves as they work the subtraction ; otherwise confusion will result.

(iv) The method which is applied to subtraction of numbers should be continued with subtraction of quantities : shillings and pence, yards, feet, inches, etc.

Recording Individual Progress

Individual children learn at different rates. Occasionally class teaching is possible in number, but some group or individual teaching is inevitable. Usually the actual teaching takes place in groups, while the practice is individual. Even when a class has been arranged in groups, the grouping will not remain static. There are still variations of pace, and differences will be caused by absence or by some individual difficulty. With a large class it is almost impossible to be aware of all these differences unless some definite record is kept. Such a record facilitates re-grouping and makes it possible for the teacher to ensure the continuous progress of each child.

Summary

The fundamental principle on which all number teaching should be based is that number is a useful tool, and should be taught so that the children know how to use it, and see the point of using it in their everyday affairs. This involves:

(i) postponing all formal teaching until the children have acquired a familiarity with the fundamental concepts of number through free experiment in a suitable environment;

(ii) the teaching of any process in three stages:

- (*a*) presenting the need for the process in terms of the children's experience;
- (*b*) the actual teaching and consolidating;
- (*c*) the application of the new skill to real situations within the children's experience; and

(iii) arranging the work so that each child can progress at his own rate, and having some system of recording to ensure that this progress is continuous.

These conditions are best satisfied in an atmosphere of freedom and activity where much of the number work arises from the children's immediate interests, and is used in the solution of their real problems, but however difficult school conditions may be, there is no justification for attempting to teach number as a logical sequence of carefully graded sums without relating these to the actual experience of the children.

Jean Murray.

Chapter XV

NATURE STUDY

The world is so full of a number of things
I'm sure we should all be as happy as Kings

—applies particularly to the observance of the natural life of the countryside. The child who has learned to watch and appreciate the marvellous cycle of the unfolding year will have his life enriched by this observance. Surely anything that enriches life is much to be desired, and worth taking thought to achieve.

How can we cultivate the habit of observance in the child? The gods are on our side, for children are natural observers, and the bright wonder of their minds is not dulled by repetition, nor clogged by the artificial standards of adult life. To question and to watch is a natural joy to them, and they will most happily co-operate in any scheme for furthering so spontaneous a part of their own make-up.

True, very young children find the constant conscious assimilation of knowledge beyond their powers, but if we stimulate and feed their natural curiosity and encourage them to 'watch and know' they will learn happily and effortlessly the simple things we wish them to know.

Weather Observation

First, children enjoy weather of all kinds, not just the thrill of a snowfall or the sweet drowsiness of high summer. To the young mind, the rain which races down the window-pane or the bright drops that bounce and dance on the pavements have a magic beyond our appreciation. There are few teachers who will not recall some lesson that was completely interrupted by a heavy fall of rain. It is better not to try to regain the unwilling attention, but rather to stop the lesson for a moment, and let the children indulge the thrill they find in the torrent beating on the roof and racing through the gutters. They could talk about the things the rain is doing, the crops it is watering, and the puddles it is turning into pools. The children will think of many things, and will love to consider the creatures who enjoy the rain, and to be reminded of the tadpoles and eels who wriggle so joyously in the deluge of swollen waters. They feel a quick kinship with these small carefree things which brings an awareness more valuable than anything the memory of a lesson is likely to provide. I remember a day in late November when a small group gathered round a classroom fire to talk of their journey to school. The day was grey, with wreaths of mist on the hills, and not a twig stirred, nor a blade of grass. " It is a quiet day," said the children, " a sleeping day," and their fertile minds were touched for a moment by the mystery of the sleeping earth.

Nature News

It is a good plan for the children to talk about the things they saw as they came to school. The first daisy in the grass, or the bird which gathered hair and moss from the garden will provide a subject. Let only one child say that he saw a rabbit in a field and others will try to recall a similar experience. Often this will result in an embarrassment of riches, and one will hear some small child assuring everyone that he saw a lion or even an elephant in a garden. Children love to ' go one better ' and for them the dividing line between reality and make-believe is very slender. Since we do not wish to discourage imagination and inventiveness, it is best to deal gently with these exaggerations, and to pay particular attention to the child who really did see ' a rabbit with a bob-tail.' They will soon learn that the thing seen, watched, and carefully reported is the source of the greatest attention and appreciation.

Children genuinely want to *know* about other small living creatures. The thought of another world existing outside and beside their own is attractive to them, as is the idea of the shy, furtive creatures who live in it, and yet remain secret and hidden from them. They like to know that at certain times, prompted by their own laws, the migrants will gather and confer and plan before spreading their wings and going in search of another summer in warmer countries. They will take pleasure in the knowledge that, though wild creatures shun man and withdraw shyly and secretly from him, sometimes in an extremity of need they will turn to him for sympathy and aid. Perhaps they understand the shy and the fugitive better than we do. A small friend came to me one day to tell of a rather obviously placed nest, with two cold eggs, that he had found to be deserted. He spoke of the parent birds, " They're forsakers," he said, " but they wouldn't have been forsakers if people hadn't stared at them so much. They don't like you to stare and know everything."

Wild Life in the Classroom

The most helpful kind of observation is achieved when wild life can be brought to the classroom. A well-stocked aquarium is a great joy. Caterpillars and silk-worms can also be kept. Local museums will suggest the type of life suitable for your own district and if approached will prove helpful in many ways. Anything that lives or grows is of value in a town school, for children who spend their lives among bricks and mortar have no very true idea of the teeming mass of life which exists, for instance, in a pond.

If we give every opportunity for observation, and at the same time encourage the child's appreciation and reverence for all wild life, we shall have achieved much. This is a quest for understanding, and there is adventure in the satisfying of curiosity. It is a subject where teacher and children can work together on something approaching an equal footing, for the knowledge of both is, of necessity, limited. The discovery of an early wild flower, or the first sight of nesting swallows, is as likely to be made by the child as by the teacher. They love to watch and learn and match her observation, and will compete with energy and enthusiasm to the benefit of both.

Nature Activities for the Under-Fives

With very young children it is possible to mark only the broad outline of the changing year. Each new month can be greeted by a calendar, preferably coloured and topical, which should be hung prominently in the classroom and freely discussed. (Good Nature pictures are obtainable from *Child Education.*) Children will be happy to discover the outstanding characteristics of each month: for instance, January is a month of hard frosts, of hungry birds and snowmen and sleep; February is the month of beginnings, the time to look for the early snowdrop, and to see the first rooks visiting the rookeries; June is rich with flowers and full-leafed trees, the time of haymaking; in July the nesting season is mainly over, and the bird-chorus of dawn and evening dwindles; August and September are harvest months, the time of fulfilment, when there are apples and pears in the orchard, and the air is full of drowsy warmth. The year ends as it begins, in sleep and refreshment.

A Nature table can be both instructive and gay. Bulbs which flower when the year is very young and empty are special favourites. Lovely flowers can be grown in a mixture of peat and poultry manure, and in these days of backyard poultry this mixture is not difficult to procure. Nasturtiums and Virginia stock flower well in pots, and children enjoy watering them and watching them grow. In the autumn collect acorns and beech mast and plant them in a large flat bowl filled with a mixture of soil and leaf mould. Soon there will be a tiny forest growing in the classroom.

Even in industrial towns there is likely to be a park where the rooks are nesting. Take the children to the rookery in early spring and let them watch the birds house-building among the windy tree-tops, or see the martins making their neat mud houses under the eaves.

Keeping an Aquarium

It is possible to bring much of the beauty and interest of a pond into the classroom by keeping an aquarium. An excellent receptacle for this is one of the large glass accumulator tanks which can sometimes be obtained from electricians, or failing this, any receptacle which combines light and air with sufficient space for pond creatures to move freely will be adequate. First, scrub the tank thoroughly, and then place a layer of clean river sand or silver sand on the bottom to a depth of two inches. It is essential that the sand should be clean, and this can be achieved by putting it in a large bucket under a running tap and stirring it until the water is no longer cloudy. When the sand is spread evenly over the bottom of the tank, cover it with about six inches of water, and when this has cleared the aquarium is ready for the plants. These are absolutely essential, for they keep the water clean and provide oxygen and shade for the creatures who will live in the tank. If there is a pond near your school, you can collect your plants there, or failing this, secure them from a dealer in aquaria. Water starwort, Canadian pond weed, and Vallisneria are fairly easily obtained, being native and reasonably hardy. The Vallisneria should be planted in the sand with its roots well spread and its crown *above* the surface of the sand. The long grass-like leaves of this plant are very graceful and contribute greatly to the beauty of the aquarium. Gather the Canadian pond weed into bunches, tie each bunch to a small stone and drop them into the tank. Break off a few inches of each stem of starwort and drop into water. This is a floating plant and will open bright green, star-like whorls on the surface of the water. The tank may now be filled. It is advisable to use a watering-can with a fine ' rose ' so that the plants are not disturbed, and if possible allow them two or three days to settle in their new home before adding any live-stock. Water-snails are extremely useful in an aquarium for they eat the scum which forms on the glass and are altogether excellent caretakers. They can be found in most ponds if one hunts among the stones at the water's edge, and it is quite a simple matter to collect a few and take them to school in a jam jar. Many interesting creatures will live happily in an aquarium. The ever-fascinating tadpoles can be brought as eggs from the pond and each stage of their development watched and discussed. Since their diet is mainly greenstuff, it is important to have plenty of weeds growing in the tank. Watercress is enjoyed, and as the tadpoles grow larger, ant eggs should be provided. When it can be spared, a tiny piece of raw meat can be hung in the tank. The tadpoles will suck it white in a very short time. When the tadpoles become tiny frogs a platform should be placed on the surface of the water. A water-lily leaf or a thin strip of wood will serve, and this will permit the tiny creatures to clamber out of the water. At this stage it is advisable to cover the tank with a piece of muslin so that the frogs do not escape and meet an unhappy death on the classroom floor. (When this stage in their development is reached, the frogs should be taken back to the pond again.)

Caddis worms, sticklebacks, water-boatmen, water-spiders, and many other interesting creatures can be kept in the tank. The pupæ of water-beetles and dragonflies can be watched through their truly thrilling development. A class of children recently saw a dragonfly emerge from its case and dry its wings in the sun on the classroom window before flying away to search for a pond. Their wonder and delight were unforgettable. If pupæ are in the tank, they need to be provided with a twig up which they can crawl in search of air and sunshine. A good book on aquaria will tell which creatures live happily together and which are incompatible.

Do not place your aquarium in the direct sunlight. If the light is too strong, one or two sides should be shaded. Remove any debris lying on the sand. For this purpose use a dip tube. This is a length of glass tubing with a rubber bulb at one end. Squeeze the bulb before submerging the tube, place it over the debris and slowly release bulb. Keep the aquarium well stocked with water-plants. Should the fish rise frequently to the surface a lack of oxygen is indicated. If the tank is well stocked, the water should remain clean and pure for two or three months. Add pond water when possible, for it is rich in aquatic life. An aquarium offers such excellent opportunities for observation and is so rich in interest and beauty that it amply repays the effort made in stocking and upkeep.

Nature Stories

Much of the simple instruction appreciated by children can be given in Nature stories. It is a good idea to keep a scrap-book and collect as many as possible. They can be culled from magazines and newspapers as well as from periodicals which cater specifically for the educational needs of young children. It is almost impossible to have too many of these stories.

It is good, too, when possible, to fit the story to the season. Choose the short dark days of winter to tell of the otter babies which are born into a bitterly cold world at a time when the gales howl around their chilly ‘ hover ’ and the ice creeps over the river's edge, and of the snowdrop which strikes out from its 'sunripened, food-stored home,' to push its way through the frozen earth. When April comes, talk of the tiny blind fox cubs which are nursed so devotedly by the vixen in their cold 'earth' during the wet and stormy English spring. Let the children compare these chilly nurseries with their own comfortable beds and warm homes. Stress the difference, but emphasize the rightness of the environment of both. If interest is captured by some unusual or impressive fact about a wild creature, all other facts regarding it become of greater interest.

Then there is the migratory miracle of the homing birds. This may be more interesting to older children, but today many children even of Nursery School age are familiar with the names of the countries from which they come, for their fathers have served in these lands. They are aware that they are distant spots from which the homeward journey takes many days or even weeks, and that ships, trains, or aeroplanes are needed to cover these distances. Against the background of this knowledge they are moved to wonder by the performance of the tiny blackcap and swallow which cover these vast areas with the aid only of their wings and their homing instinct. Children will enjoy hearing of the empty spaces, the mountains, and the wide and lonely sea, which they must cross; of the great speed, approaching that of an express train, which the small wings can beat out in moments of special effort or great danger, as, for instance, when they fly before an approaching storm.

The strange behaviour of the cuckoo should not be overlooked since it provides an excellent opportunity for establishing the equal position shared in the study of nature by both children and teacher. We do not really understand the cuckoo's behaviour nor can we answer all the questions which arise concerning its habits. Children find this helpful and encouraging.

As high summer approaches, try to tell stories of the seashore and the strange and fascinating world of the rock-pools. Let the children bring shells to school and discuss the creatures whose homes they once were. Remind them to look for the crab which runs sideways and for the seagull fishing so beautifully and skilfully over the tossing water.

Autumn is as fruitful in story plots as it is in harvest treasure. Tell of the tiny mice seeking food and warmth in the stackyard, and of the squirrel, the dormouse, and the hedgehog searching for warm homes for their long, winter sleep. Children love the scatterbrain squirrel who hoards his nuts in many pantries, but is so forgetful that he has to search quite a long time before he discovers his treasures again.

Particularly fascinating are the stories of the airborne spiders which, on some misty September morning, set out in search of a new home on the end of a parachute. They have remarkable adventures; make lovely webs and strange tunnels; are mighty hunters, and lead secret and busy lives in the grass and the bushes, and even in corners of the classroom. Many lovely butterflies and moths are seen at this time of the year, and children will be pleased to remember their colours and be told their names.

Finally, the winter talks: the increasing shortage of natural food, the hungry birds, the fox who raids the poultry shed on a winter night; the cleansing frost and the blanketing snow all have interest. The gaily-coloured ducks and the brave little moorhen are clearly seen on park ponds at this time of the year. Children find interest in all these things, and even though they forget much of the detail they will, by the presence of life around them in the aquarium and on the nature table, and by the constant listening to and retelling of nature stories, develop that awareness of natural life on which detailed and accurate knowledge can be surely and soundly built.

Nature Activities in the Infant School

Any living thing, whether plant or animal, which can be introduced into the classroom, is of great value. Daffodils, hyacinths, and tulips flower excellently indoors and provide a constant Nature lesson, while giving colour and beauty to the rather empty months of the young year. September is the best time to buy bulbs, and the correct time to plant indoor bulbs for early flowering.

If possible, plant one bulb in one of the glass vases manufactured specially for bulb growing; it will prove very valuable, for by this method the children can see each stage of growth. Choose a large bulb for growing this way, and rest it on the curved neck of the vase, taking care that the bottom of the bulb is just clear of the water. The children will love to see the roots shooting from the bulb and growing longer and longer until they touch the bottom of the jar. If a piece of charcoal is kept in the vase it will not be necessary to change the water at all.

Autumn Activities

Let the children examine a bulb before planting; explain that it is really a well-stocked larder. At the end of the flowering season, try to find a tiny bulb which is forming on the parent plant. By these means one can emphasize the full cycle of natural life.

It is a good idea during the early autumn to walk in the nearest park or woodland to collect seeds, acorns, hips, and haws. Discuss the way seeds travel: those of the dandelion and thistle fly away on their own silken parachutes; the sycamore is winged and the wind carries it away from its parent tree; the hips and haws are eaten by the birds and their seeds scattered over the countryside. Try to find a poppy head—many suburban gardens grow poppies—and when it is quite ripe turn it upside down and pour out the tiny, dark seeds; explain how the wind, shaking the poppy, scatters the seeds over the ground; how the child, eating a sweet rosy apple, and dropping the core and seeds into some hedge bottom, is helping Nature to do her work.

When we eat cucumbers and French beans we are eating both seed boxes and seeds, and when we eat vegetable marrows we are eating a very large seed box indeed.

Plant some of the tiny seedlings in loam.

November is a good time to consider how wild creatures spend the winter. There is the choice of winter quarters and the long, deep sleep of hibernation: the hedgehog in the hole in the bank; the toad hidden deep under the big stones of the rockery; the squirrel which does not truly hibernate, but sleeps for long periods in the nest; the bat in the barn; the moth in some corner of the bedroom or attic; the snail which creeps into some sheltered spot in an old wall or rockery, before closing its shell with a cement door.

Cats, dogs, horses, and sheep grow thicker coats; the fox families break up, and each member hunts for itself; each robin chooses its own territory, and drives all other robins away.

If you have a good museum, and most large cities have, make constant use of it. Many wild creatures can be seen there, and the settings in which they are exhibited are a faithful and accurate presentation of their natural haunts.

Winter Activities

During December most schools can study evergreens. The holly, the mistletoe, and the Christmas tree are familiar to all. The holly demonstrates Nature's protective genius. The sharp spiked prickles stop the sheep and the deer from eating too many of the shiny leaves. The mistletoe is a very strange plant. It does not grow in the ground as others do, but the sticky seed in the pretty, pearl-like berry is usually 'planted' by some bird cleaning its beak on the branch of an apple, oak, or poplar tree. When the seed has found a home in a tiny crack in the tree it sends out roots or sinkers which grow until they reach the sap of the tree. The mistletoe feeds on this sap and soon shows green leaves and pearly berries. The lovely symmetrical Christmas tree is really the Spruce fir. When fully grown the tall straight trunks of this tree are used for telegraph poles.

Many delightful stories can be told about the evergreens.

During January consider the hard ground, and the bare trees. Let the children talk about their empty, sleeping gardens. How do wild creatures live in times so hard? The worm is safe, deep in the ground where the frosts cannot reach. In the stackyard —even town children are familiar with haystacks—many small creatures find warmth and safety. I think it is quite likely that most schools house willingly or otherwise a few mice. Their life history is not without interest. If the season is hard it is permissible to feed scraps and crumbs to the birds. This is wise as well as kind for the birds are controllers of insect pests. In the long frost of 1947, I saw a woodpecker in a tiny garden within a quarter of a mile of one of our largest industrial cities. Water and crumbs placed on a window-sill will attract bird visitors.

Frost, snow, and wind delight and interest children. Choose a morning of hard frost to talk about the mysterious magic of ice. When the mercury in the thermometer falls below 32° F., strange things happen to the puddle in the road, and to the water in the pond ; it ceases to be fluid and becomes solid and thick and strong. Then we can walk on the pond and play games on the lake. Ice needs more room than water, and that is why it bursts the pipes. Frost breaks down the large clods of earth by freezing and expanding the moisture within them, thus lightening and cleaning the ground at the same time. Snow is not frozen rain but frozen clouds. It acts as a blanket to the earth because it does not let the stored warmth escape from the soil.

Springtime Interests

During the high winds of March the children will enjoy making kites, windmills, weather-vanes, and darts. These are attractive toys for recording wind directions ; at the same time, the children may learn that the north-east wind brings bitter cold, the west wind rain, and so on.

Let the children measure their shadows in the sunlight. The difference in length of the shadows in the early morning and at noon helps to focus interest on the sun's daily journey across the sky.

If it is possible to have window-boxes fitted, they will prove very interesting. If not, use plant pots freely. Sow the seeds collected in the autumn, and let the children water them ; note the rate of growth, and see how the plants wilt when needing water.

Gather twigs in spring. Examine them and notice the way they are protected from winter cold and driving rain. There is the sticky gum, the waterproof jacket, and the soft warm lining. Keep the buds in the classroom until they open, and the children will discover that the leaves are folded in different and very fascinating ways.

Collect leaves, press and name them. Ask the children to collect wild flowers when visiting the country. Even the suburban park or woodland will yield a surprising number.

Many country schools have 'adopted' a town school and send boxes of wild flowers and twigs. If you are able to avail yourself of such a happy arrangement, hold periodical flower shows. Tell the children the country names for the flowers: Cuckoo-pint, Lords and Ladies, Kidney Vetch, Lady's Fingers, Ox-eye Daisy, Moon-penny. It is important, however, to show children how to pick wild flowers, always with care, and never greedily.

The worms that we see wriggling on the grass on damp mornings are firm friends of ours and allies of the farmers. These curious creatures have no eyes, yet can tell the difference between darkness and light. They feel vibrations and know when their enemies, the birds and moles, are hunting them. They feed on old roots, decaying vegetation, and the earth itself, later discarding the soil in the form of worm-casts which we find on our lawns. In the winter they burrow deep into the ground, closing the door of their tunnel homes by blocking them with dead leaves, roots, and bits of straw.

Keeping a Wormery

A wormery is easily made and simply kept. A large glass jar should be almost filled with moist soil and a few large worms collected and placed in it. If you wish to see the worms tunnelling along the sides of the glass, place black paper round the wormery. On removing the paper you should see the narrow tunnels made by the worms. You will also find worm-casts on the surface of the soil. If you place alternate layers of soil, sand, and gravel in the wormery you will see how the occupants mix the various soils by their tunnelling. The soil in the wormery must be moistened every few days.

Making a Vivarium

A simple vivarium can be made from a small, glass tank (or large jar) with a tightly-fitting, slightly-perforated lid. Soil should be placed on the bottom and grass seeds sown. Many insects are quite happy as temporary inhabitants of this 'small enclosed field.' Spiders are particularly interesting and will spin their lovely and intricate webs whilst resident in the vivarium. Their life history is full of interest. Do not keep your vivarium in strong sunlight, and always place dark screens round at least two sides. Keep it well watered.

Try to instil into the children respect for all life. Do not embroider or romanticize it. It follows a pattern more wonderful than imagination can suggest.

Muriel Green.

Chapter XVI

ART

Before considering the more practical aspect of art activities in the Nursery and Infant School, we need a clear understanding of the aims and principles determining our approach.

Much thought is given to providing a balanced education through which the child may gain the breadth of experience necessary for the integration and development of the whole personality.

Through art and craft the child enjoys some of the most satisfying and valuable forms of creative outlet. It is only in an atmosphere likely to encourage genuine creative activity that he can fulfil his need for self-expression in a purposeful way, gaining satisfaction through the experimental handling of varied materials, together with the emotional release resulting from his activities. A sympathetic and understanding relationship between children and teacher is of the utmost importance, as this will enable the children to work with confidence and a sense of security.

Today we realize that art cannot be taught, but that by sympathetic and wise handling we can hope to bring out and preserve qualities inherent in the natural spontaneous work of young children. We all enjoy the vigorous freedom, the strong feeling for colour and the rhythmical patterns characteristic of young children's work, as well as the rich imaginative content and the use of symbolism.

The Young Child's Picture-Making

In order to understand more fully these early forms of expression it is helpful to study the paintings themselves. Through them we can realize just how great is the difference between the child's way of seeing and that of the adult. We not only accept this fundamental difference but make it one of our guiding principles to encourage to the full the personal expression which is natural and right for the child. We need to discover and recognize the stages of visual development through which he will normally pass, so that we can offer the best stimulus and guidance as each stage is reached.

The child in the Nursery School enjoys spontaneous scribbling and delights in the adventurous use of colour and the feel of broad rhythmical movement with brush or crayon. From this early scribbling the first symbols gradually appear, for the young child draws in terms of symbols which he invents for himself and which vary according to his stage of mental and visual development. The child accentuates what is of greatest significance to him rather as the caricaturist emphasizes the main essentials of his idea. It is interesting to remind ourselves that this power of conveying ideas through symbols is used by the child considerably earlier than the written word ; it is therefore essential that he should have adequate opportunity for drawing and painting freely at this early stage.

Young children express their ideas in a completely logical way and here again we find marked differences between child and adult vision. For instance, the most important objects will usually be painted largest ; the child will emphasize in this way what is of special significance to him, the head frequently being the largest part of the human being. At the same time the eyes and mouth will probably be stressed, whereas the ears and nose may be omitted altogether, as playing a far less important part in his experience.

In fact the mature conceptions of realistic representation, with depth, recession, and the overlapping of forms, do not enter into the child's visual concept. Many of us must be familiar with the strip of sky, indicated by a band of paint at the top of the page, and the ground represented by another strip below, actually a perfectly reasonable way of painting at this stage. The child in fact paints what he knows ; the sky is above him and the ground below and for him the two do not meet. To point out to him that the sky and ground appear to meet at the horizon would be a mistake. Representational seeing simply does not exist for the very young child, and any attempt to teach it would mean the imposition of adult forms that are insincere and even meaningless to his natural way of expression.

With ' transparent ' drawing we have another interesting instance of the child painting what he knows, rather than attempting to copy what he actually sees. An example of this occurred with a boy painting a picture of a house on fire. The picture started with a symbol for the house ; two people were then shown inside it and this step was followed by a band of rhythmical circular scribbling around the outside of the roof, representing the idea of fire. The house was finally painted in solid colour, the paint covering the people entirely ; but since, as the child said, the people were inside, this was a logical way of treating the theme.

Decoration and Rhythmical Repetition

In addition to this interest in picture-making, the child has a natural feeling for decoration and rhythmical repetition.

Frequent experiments with varying forms of pattern work should be encouraged. Children in the Infant School enjoy very simple potato printing (individuals or small groups each working on fabric), writing patterns, all-over repeats for wall papers, cushions, play-houses, and puppet-theatres. Patterns combining torn or cut-out paper with soft crayon or paint may be introduced as well.

Through such a variety of pattern making, children, especially the more timid or tentative, readily gain confidence, discovering a language of brush strokes and textures through which their picture-making becomes all the richer and more complete. Pattern work and picture-making are in fact closely related, and many pictures painted by young children could well be regarded as picture-patterns.

The Young Child's Response to Colour

In the same way we find a strong response to colour. In some cases it may be used representationally, but on the other hand there are children who enjoy colour in a purely decorative sense.

Some of the most sensitive and personal qualities in a painting are conveyed through colour, so that the child should have real opportunity for mixing his own paints and discovering colours. (When making pictures in cut paper or stitched fabric it should be possible for him to experiment freely, and select from a wide variety of coloured papers and materials of different textures.) This need not mean an expensive outlay in paint, since the three primary colours, with black and white, give the child sufficient freedom of choice, provided he has a palette for mixing.

All the materials available should be of the kind likely to encourage breadth of approach and spontaneity. Timber or monster crayons, good-sized brushes, powder colour, fairly large sheets of kitchen paper or newspaper (say 18 in. by 24 in.), varying sizes and kinds of coloured paper, paste, a rag bag and modelling clay will provide a useful working basis.

Ideally, children should stand at easels, so that they can make large, easy arm movements. Even in the most crowded conditions it will sometimes be possible to improvise, arranging for at least a few children to work on a larger scale, by using blackboards, paper fixed to cardboard, or by letting some children work on the floor.

Wherever possible, group activities should be introduced, as through these the children gain experience in the actual handling of varied materials; and while themselves discovering the possibilities and qualities of any one medium, they are indirectly influenced and stimulated by the scope and variety of the work they see around them. All the children in a class may not want to do the same subject in the same medium, and for them the enjoyment and challenge of making their own selection provides excellent training in initiative and independence.

Art and Handwork Activities

Art and handwork activities should cover a wide range. Painting, finger painting, work in crayon, picture-making on coloured paper or fabric, puppets, weaving with rag, string, or rushes, and modelling in clay are suggested as some of the most valuable forms of creative work for young children. Even in difficult conditions where selection must necessarily be more limited, it should be possible to vary at least the size or colour of the paper, so that some freedom of choice is still left to the child, encouraging in him a thoughtful attitude to his work and keeping alive his enthusiasm and sense of adventure.

With regard to subjects for painting, young children usually have their own very definite ideas and little, if any, external stimulus and guidance will be needed. For the child the most ordinary scenes connected with his daily life are absorbing and full of wonder. Through his pictures he indicates clearly his main interests, and we find depicted in his paintings most of the things familiar to him through his own environment—trains, cars, ships, people, animals, trees, and houses being shown most frequently.

The child re-creates in his painting some of his most personal and vivid experiences. He may also feel the need for a more purely imaginative outlet, sometimes expressing ideas of sheer fantasy—strange, make-believe animals and giants or magic gardens—images reflecting something of the detached beauty of the child's world. As both subject and treatment vary so much with each child, any help or suggestion must be given individually, formal class teaching being ill-suited to these activities.

In the Nursery School all this work should be introduced as informal, spontaneous activity, the children being provided with suitable materials and ample opportunity to explore possibilities freely in their own way. When the children reach the Infant School stage some awareness of the interests and problems of the group as a whole may be encouraged. Brief informal discussions might be introduced at the beginning or end of activity periods. The children should contribute freely in these talks, experiencing increasing excitement about the pictures they are going to paint; or at the end enjoying the work that has been done by the whole group. The introduction, which should be very simple and brief, is valuable as it helps to arouse in the children the initial interest and urge to creative expression.

Once settled, children in the Infant School usually work

quickly and with intense absorption. They must be free to work at their own speed, and provision should be made for those who, at the end of quite a short period, may have spent their creative energy for the time being. When the classes are not too large the possibility of changing from one activity and material to another should be considered, for example, from paint to clay.

A good collection of mounted postcards or Puffin books for the children to look through as they finish is also helpful.

The Value of Art Activities

In the Nursery and Infant groups perhaps the main value of all these activities lies in the satisfaction and enjoyment gained by the children through the doing of the work. For what the child has himself felt and experienced in these varied forms of self-expression is of greater importance and significance than the actual results produced. Undue stress, therefore, should not be placed on the finished work. A readiness must be shown by the teacher to accept and appreciate the genuine in every child's effort.

Any element of competition tends to set up standards based on false values and to crush the sincerity and vitality of the children's approach. We can imagine how bewildering and frustrating it must be for children to see, week after week, a few selected 'best' paintings shown on the classroom walls; best, that is, according to the teacher's adult standards and personal taste. Provided it is the outcome of honest expression and effort, every child's work should receive approval and positive encouragement.

With sensitive guidance and in an atmosphere conducive to worth-while work, every child will quite naturally develop his potential possibilities to the full. He must be able to feel complete trust in the teacher's support and genuine interest. This alone will provide that basis of security through which real freedom and spontaneity can be experienced. These qualities will not only help the child to grow fully in the Nursery and Infant phases, but will establish a good foundation for the further development of aesthetic activities in the Junior and Secondary Schools.

Some Practical Aspects of Art Work with Young Children

Although it is almost impossible to describe what might be called a typical art lesson, yet it may be helpful to consider one or two practical aspects usually connected with the art period in the nursery and Infant School.

The actual form and content of the lessons will, of course,

depend on many individual factors and conditions. For instance, the qualifications, experience and personal enthusiasm of the teacher, the possibilities offered by the classroom, the equipment and materials available, all play a considerable part. Finally, understanding the children themselves, their background and environmental setting, together with their previous training, will provide the most important considerations of all. We are here considering the Nursery and Infant School stages ; the fully equipped art room and the specialist teacher are not, therefore, involved. In both the Nursery and Infant Schools most of the art and handwork will be taken in activity periods, when several media will be available, and a painting lesson, as such, will be a very rare occasion.

Ideally, creative activities should be introduced each day, the children being free to make their own choice. Once the decision has been made the teacher should endeavour to help the children sustain their interest for a reasonable length of time, so that they experience real satisfaction. For instance, it is likely that one group will be painting while another is working with clay ; others may be doing simple weaving, or using pastels or crayons. For a sound working basis with a large class, several groups of children, numbering six or less in each group, will be occupied with these various activities at the same time.

Whatever the individual conditions may be, it is always possible to have a fairly adequate supply of newspaper, kitchen paper, sugar paper, as well as brown wrapping-paper and pastel papers in various shades. Large hoghair brushes, some smaller ones, patty tins for dry powder colour, 'freart' crayons, chalk, pastels, paste, scissors, clay, string, and rag, with simple card-board looms for weaving, should also be available, as well as an interesting collection of all sorts of odd scraps of material, including cotton-reels, matchboxes, pipe-cleaners, wire, odd-ments of wood, etc., for experimental constructive activities. All these materials should have been previously prepared for use ; for instance, paper should have been cut to suitable sizes, and dry powder colours given out in small quantities in the bun tins (it is essential that each patty tin contains white, black, blue, red, and yellow) ; cold-water paste can be mixed and placed in small jars, with brushes nearby for pasting. A wide range of suitable materials (as already suggested) should be kept easily accessible on low shelves or tables. It is important that the children should be trained to set out and clear away their own materials, and be encouraged to look after, and take a pride in, the equipment in daily use. Thorough planning and careful thought in the organization of such activities can scarcely be over-emphasized, but we need also to remember that valuable opportunities for training in self-reliance are lost if the teacher attempts to do all the final preparations and more detailed setting out of materials herself.

The children, then, should be allowed to select the necessary materials for themselves, and should be able after a little training to prepare for the activity of their group. For instance, individual children in each group will be responsible for collecting and finally washing the brushes, emptying water pots, or storing the clay. It is also a good plan to have one set of tables or desks, or the corner of the room, always used for the same activity. The appropriate materials, for instance, clay, can then be kept conveniently near to that part of the room, fetching and carrying thus being reduced to a minimum, and the children being encouraged to form orderly habits in relation to their work.

As in most cases the room used will be the ordinary classroom, it will be necessary to protect desk or table tops with paper or cardboard, unless small easels or wall boards are available for painting. In very crowded rooms a group of three or four children might even have their paper on the floor for painting. When using colour, a group of four, or sometimes even six, children could share one patty tin of colour. It is, however, essential for each child to have his own mixing palette, a large tin lid or circular tin plate being the most suitable. If given a coat of white or cream enamel to prevent rusting, it will provide an ideal basis for colour mixing. One-pound jam jars are probably the most convenient for use as water containers, since they allow large brushes to be well rinsed, and stand more firmly than smaller jars.

For most work that is reasonably large in scale, a good-sized hoghair brush is needed, but a limited number of smaller hoghair brushes should be available for finer work or for paintings carried out on smaller sheets of paper.

A formal start for everyone would not be desirable and will not usually be necessary. Once the children have chosen their activity and have got their materials ready, they can begin work. The teacher may sometimes wish to give special help to one group or another, or perhaps will need to introduce some fresh aspect of work, such as a new type of pattern-making; or some fresh activity, such as finger painting, might need to be demonstrated. In this case the one group will have a short introductory talk, discussion or simple demonstration, while the other groups carry on. Sometimes it may be advisable to let the whole class listen and watch for some minutes, so that on another occasion they can each follow on with the new idea.

Any demonstration work should not be left on view, as young children are strongly influenced by what they see and may easily be over-dominated by adult conceptions. It is also helpful for the children to sit or move around freely, not necessarily always being in the same group or with the same people. A definite suggestion of subject-matter for painting or modelling may be welcomed by the children, who otherwise tend to repeat the same paintings again and again with little real creative enjoyment.

It is sometimes helpful to draw the attention of the class to a piece of work with especially attractive characteristics, not necessarily the best finished picture, for even the apparently less gifted painting will nevertheless have some good qualities.

Finally, we need to remember that the true value of the work lies in the children's actual doing and feeling, so that we must, in these creative activities, give them as much scope as possible for genuinely experimental work in a variety of suitable materials.

Kathleen Melzi.

Chapter XVII

MUSIC

In the Nursery School

MUSIC activities must, of course, be directed by the teacher. For the two- to five-year-olds it is helpful to think of the Nursery School as a seed-plot for music, a plot which we are privileged to tend and nurture for three years, during which time the children will assimilate many ideas at their most impressionable age, ideas which, if carefully planted and tended, will bear fruit in the children's future musical experiences.

Rhythmic Response

We start with rhythmic response because it is so instinctive in all young children who ' think ' through their muscles and try everything out in movement in order to sort out their impressions. We make use of familiar nursery occupations, particularly play of a repetitive order in which the two- to three-year-old exults.

For instance, dropping stones into a bucket could be used as a little rhythmic game. The teacher sets the movement going and if she can fit it into a spontaneous jingle so much the better.

Up and in, up and in,
Pick up the stones and drop them in.

This type of little rhythmic chant is of great value when playing with the children, many of whom enjoy making a sing-song about their doings.

Movement Songs

This type of rhythmic song helps the children very much in the early stages of movement. For the words tell them *exactly* what to do. The natural rhythmic movements upon which the songs are based are always connected with some occupation or action familiar to the children who should always be encouraged to play out the song *in their own rhythm* at first. The younger the children the more they need unaccompanied song and their teacher working with them in a friendly intimacy. But at this age, of course, no sustained interest will be expected, and the children will wander off to other pursuits when they wish.

Movement songs can be used advantageously right through the Nursery and Infant Schools. Older children can play them out with joyful assurance and enjoy the varying rhythmic movements upon which the songs are based. Real skill of movement can be developed through such rhythmic songs as these, from the early stage of free adventure to the more controlled movements with piano accompaniment.

Nursery Rhymes

It is never too early to sing traditional nursery airs to the children. Any good set will furnish copious examples of what might be termed ' movable ' rhythms, for these tunes walk, hop, run, gallop, and sway, just like little children do. Some simple ones for rhythmic response are :

Dance-a-baby, diddy	Hold child by both hands and let him jump up and down.
Polly put the kettle on	Run to the fire with the kettle, put it down at the end of the tune.
Dickory, dickory, dock	Swing arms loosely like the pendulum of a clock.

Be careful to use one basic movement only throughout the tune.

Use nursery airs, too, for free rhythmic expression, the children moving where they will. A large repertory exists, including songs from other lands, all so *exactly* fitting for rhythmic response. Children enjoy singing nursery rhymes in a group with their teacher. The song should be sung through as a mother sings to her child ; sung quietly, for young children have a tendency to sing loudly and will copy any harsh tone.

In addition to nursery rhymes, there are finger-play songs which strengthen finger and wrist muscles and awaken the child's imagination. These are very useful too for inducing a quiet mood.

Children love to hear nursery airs played on a pipe or recorder. A drum or tambourine is an invaluable ally, for with its aid the teacher can move with the children and set the ' tread ' of varying rhythms : ♩ walking, ♫ runnning, ♪♩ ♪♩ (gee-up gee-up, etc.) galloping ; a slower ♩ ♪♩ ♪ is necessary for swaying and rocking, and skipping may be taken to ♩.♬ or ♩ ♪ but this is not a natural step for young children who invariably respond by galloping.

Nursery rhymes with these rhythmic units predominating should be sung while the rhythm is tapped on a percussion instrument. When they are played on the piano, they should be taken rather quickly in order to suit the children's tempo.

Pulsation Exercises

Children in the Nursery School should be encouraged to feel the pulse or beat by stressing it through some simple play-movement : clapping, hopping, hammering, or pretending to clean a window are examples. Introduce as many occupational movements as possible for pulse response, for little children need plenty of practice in keeping the beat moving along. Nursery rhymes with the accompaniment stressing the pulse or beat are needed for this purpose. *Twice Twelve* (Cramer) has this rhythmic feature.

Listen, Children!

Very elementary aural observation can be embarked upon with the under-fives. Encourage the children to listen to familiar sounds: a bicycle bell, a spoon tapped upon a plate, beads rattled in a box, etc. The children should close their eyes and guess what the sound was.

From this starting-point we go on to pitch discrimination, using only broad contrasts of high and low pitched sounds. The melody of a nursery air can be used for pitch response, first phrase in the treble, second in the bass. One suitable response to this would be whitewashing the ceiling and scrubbing the floor. The children must not be standing where they can see the position of the teacher's hands. The children can also play ' up and down the stairs ' by the simple expedient of raising or lowering both hands in accordance with the direction of the notes of the scale.

Introduction to the Percussion Band

In the Nursery School we can embark upon an introduction to percussion band work by letting the children play bells. The bells are attached to wooden handles, used in pairs and shaken on the beat.

The children ' play with the music ' and so further deepen a feeling for pulsation that is already being encouraged through movement.

At this stage the children also enjoy a form of imitative play by pretending to play the drum or tambourine which they have frequently seen their teacher use as a rhythmic background for movement. A four-year-old with a strong and instinctive sense of pulse will enjoy being allowed actually to play a drum or tambourine to set a marching rhythm for his playmates.

Care should be taken that the strap supporting the drum is of correct length. The head of the drum should be just below the level of the child's waist and it would be easier for him to play with both hands. Tambourines are held vertically in the left hand and tapped with the fingers of the lightly clenched right hand. At the age of five, children have more muscular control, a longer span of concentration and are certainly more ready for the communal work of a percussion band. The outline of a progressive scheme of work is included in the Infant School scetion.

In the Infant School

In addition to music through movement we can now approach music through the percussion band, both activities very materially helping towards building up sound musicianship. It should be noted that in both activities (movement and band) the ear is always in advance of the eye ; that children never grapple with notational difficulties before they have had considerable rhythmical experience.

Before discussing band work, more ideas for movement are outlined.

Natural Movements

To those basic steps already familiar can now be added running very lightly and swiftly, taken to ♬♬ ; also a skipping step, frequently a stumbling block to the under-fives, taken to tunes in 6/8 time when ♩ ♪ predominates. Also to ♩.♬ which is more dynamic.

Then there are 𝅗𝅥, 𝅗𝅥. and 𝅝 all notes with sustained beats and frequently met at cadence-points where they mark the ends of phrases. If stepped, all these note-values require sustained and flowing movement for which young children lack the necessary muscular co-ordination. The inexperienced teacher would be well advised to let the children *clap* the actual sound and hold the sustained beat or beats :

𝅗𝅥 clap, hold. 𝅗𝅥. clap, hold, hold. 𝅝 clap, hold, hold, hold.

𝅗𝅥 can also be played out through an imaginative movement suggesting weight, such as the coalman with a heavy load on his back.

𝅗𝅥. and 𝅝 can also be treated as points of arrival or ' climax ' points. For instance, we can run to 𝅗𝅥. picking flowers on arrival, 3/4 ♫ ♫ ♫ | 𝅗𝅥. ; or skip up to 𝅝 and clash cymbals as a climax, 4/4 ♩.♬ ♩.♬ ♩.♬ ♩.♬ | 𝅝 . This illustrates onward movement or progression and is a very good way to instil it.

Phrasing

Children should be encouraged to feel how curves of melody make phrases and how these phrases in turn make complete tunes. *The phrase is the true rhythmic unit* and the child who early learns to think, and later to read, in phrases is already well advanced in musicianship.

Nursery airs having two well-defined phrases should be chosen. *Little Jack Horner* is an excellent example as each phrase moves towards a cadence or ' breathing-place ' very clearly marked *by a long sound occurring on the accented beat.* Make lists of similar tunes and compare them with *Jack and Jill* in which the cadences are not so obvious and therefore not so good for initial examples. Lists of such tunes will be found in *Twice Twelve*, with suggestions for rhythmic response and simple percussion. The main idea in movement is to change the movement response for each phrase, or merely to change direction. After considerable practice with tunes made up of two phrases, the children should have no difficulty in recognizing tunes with more phrases.

Accentuation

When the children can respond accurately to the pulse, encouraged by imaginative movements in the Nursery School, they are ready to recognize accent which determines the groupings of the pulse into sets of 2's, 3's, and 4's, resulting in 2/4, 3/4, and 4/4 time. Ear comes before eye, however, so, using the crotchet (♩) as the pulse unit, we illustrate each time-grouping by an imaginative movement:

2/4 Bounce and catch a ball.
3/4 Pick, flowers, put them into a basket.
4/4 Drive horse, crack whip on accented beat.

Improvisation in crotchets is necessary at this stage. Melodic improvisation would do if accompanied by a percussion instrument to show accent. After considerable rhythmical experiences on these lines write up a series of twelve crotchets on the blackboard putting an accent over the first of every four.

Children clap as the teacher points. Then explain that a line is drawn before the accented note, and the accent is rubbed out. The music between is called a bar of music. Do the same with groups of two's and three's. Counting can then be introduced and also time signatures.

Note Values

When ♩, ♫ and 𝅗𝅥 are recognized aurally, introduce the symbols. We call them by their rhythm names:

♩ Ta (pronounced Tah) ♫ Ta-té (pronounced Tah-tay) 𝅗𝅥 Ta-a (pronounced Tah-ah)

Children clap and say rhythm names (not *all* notes in one lesson). Then combine these into rhythm-patterns for children to clap (and also to play on percussion instruments):

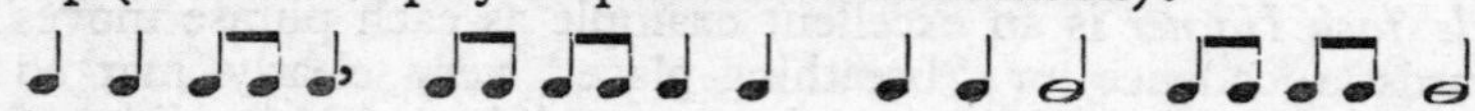

etc.

Percussion Bands

The inexperienced teacher would do well to divide the work into two parts of which the broader aspects are outlined. But, as in movement, the approach will be more alive if the teacher has had actual experience of playing in a percussion band.

PART I. In the first part, the feeling for pulsation and phrasing is developed. Begin with two groups of instruments: bells (soon replaced by triangles) and drums. To these are added tambourines, making a third group of instruments. The children play pulse. The conductor or leader of the band uses a temporary conducting movement, responding to the beat *unit* as the children have not as yet been taught to recognize accent. This should run parallel to occupational movement for pulse response and the realization of phrasing through movement. Games and exercises are included for quick response and pitch discrimination.

PART II. The children's response is now more conscious. Pattern-playing and recognition of accent and time are added to pulsation and phrasing. The metrical beat is used for conducting, in 2/4, 3/4, and 4/4 time. Note values ♩, ♫ and 𝅗𝅥 are written on the blackboard and combined into patterns which the children play on their instruments. *Rhythm names should be used all the time.* Four groups of instruments are now in use: triangles, tambourines, cymbals, and drums. Percussion band work should run parallel with movement in which children show accent through imaginative movement, and note values through clapping and rhythmic games.

INITIAL EXPERIENCES. As a starting-point (Part I), songs with two phrases, having the melody in pulse notes (♩), should be chosen. 'Question and Answer' type of songs are good. Bells might suggest the question, drums the answer; the children will suggest which instrument should be used and should always be encouraged to do so. Proceed to songs having the accompaniment in the bass in pulse notes and use three instrumental groups. The children are taught to take leadership of the band by using a temporary 'knocking' movement, and as each beat is indicated in the same manner it is obvious that any time can be conducted.

Instruments should be grouped in a semicircle with tambourines in the middle. The conductor must be ready to turn towards the group which is going to play the next phrase in good time. Gradually, the children will learn to keep accurately and steadily together and to watch the conductor. Exercises for quick response, pitch, discrimination and variety of tone and speed are added.

WIDENING EXPERIENCES. When four instrumental groups are

in use (Part II), the scope of the work is broader and the children work with increasing awareness. They are encouraged to recognize the number of phrases in a tune (still playing pulse). Generally speaking, *each* phrase is played by a different group of instruments according to the conductor's indication.

The metrical beat is now used to indicate 2/4, 3/4, 4/4, and 6/8 time. Children play rhythm patterns from notes on the blackboard and should now be ready for large coloured charts which are used for elementary sight-reading in percussion band work. (Rhythm patterns, by the way, are much more suitable for band than for movement. In the Infant School a flowing nursery air is frequently mutilated by unco-ordinated stepping. Moreover it is frequently taken at too slow a tempo in order to let the children step . . . every . . . word. This is not music! Clapping or band work is much better.)

Rhythm names must be used exclusively and continuously.

Instruments are expensive. Only good ones should be used and there is a *correct technique* for playing them. A good text-book on percussion bands should be available for reference, in which all matters pertaining to this most valuable aspect of rhythmic training will be discussed in detail.

The children in the Infant School should get as far as learning to do without words, that is, imitating the pattern of short piano pieces. Part-playing comes in here, as very often drums take the bass parts. (The conductor, however, always indicates the *beat*, not the pattern.) Eventually the children will go on to read from individual parts. Pipes and recorders will be introduced and there are also arrangements for band and optional string parts.

If continuously developed through the Junior School all this excellent groundwork should ultimately lead on to orchestral playing.

Pitch Training

The children assimilate many of the broader aspects of pitch through rhythmic training. The use of pitch games is also advisable, for through them the five-year-old can learn much about the mental effects of the notes of the scale and their relation to each other. Singing from hand signs to sol-fa syllables is also recommended.

The children should be encouraged to sing all the notes of the scale to sol-fa syllables when written vertically and horizontally on the blackboard. This *step-wise method* is very extensively used now.

The children should also be able to sing to sol-fa small groups of notes arranged step-wise: for example, ***d r m r d*** and ***s f m r d***.

There should be no delay in transferring *doh, me, soh* to the staff:

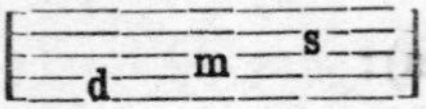

followed by

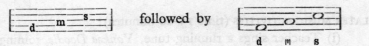

Show a picture of *doh, me, soh* on lines too:

followed by

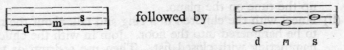

—thus early demonstrating the principle of the movable *doh.* We want the children to realize that *doh* may be on a line or in a space and that, wherever it is, *me* and *soh* are there too.

The teacher should sing little sol-fa phrases for the children to imitate.

Children must be trained to listen quietly to the teacher's singing, to her playing and to suitable gramophone records, and the teacher should enjoy singing and playing to the children. To quote Dr. Percy Young (*Child Education*, Spring 1944): " Every piece of music should be performed for children as though it were the most-loved piece in the performer's repertoire."

Specimen Activities

The following specimen music activities are included in illustration of the foregoing.

For Under-Fives

INTRODUCTORY ACTIVITIES (time approximately 10 minutes):

(i) Set a familiar movement going to incite rhythmic response. Birds hop and fly about looking for food. While moving with the children, sing a little song about it. *Birdies' Tea Time* (from *Clipperty Clop*, Kathleen Blocksidge.)
(ii) Sit in a ring and sing a quiet nursery air. *Hush-a-bye-baby.* All the children rock their dollies to sleep. Repeat the tune *ad lib.*
(iii) Suggest putting dolly to bed. Everyone walks quietly round the room and puts dolly into an imaginary cradle.

The teacher will encourage the children to move purposefully if she works with them. It is absolutely essential that each child moves freely and at his own pace. For this reason the little songs are much better taken unaccompanied. The children ' catch ' them as they play them out. At any other time during the day when opportunity offers, the teacher should play the tunes they have moved to on piano or pipe. Finger plays, too, should be utilized freely.

LATER MUSIC ACTIVITIES (time 15–20 minutes):

(i) Teacher sings a running tune, *Yankee Doodle,* joining in with the children who run freely anywhere. When the movement is going well the teacher drops out and takes up the tune on the piano.

(ii) Kneel with the children in a ring and talk about the nails to be hammered into the floor. Join in with the children hammering with closed fist. Then use a drum or tambourine to set a steady beat or pulse. Children should be free to hammer anywhere. Suggest hammering a few nails into the wall for the pictures to hang on. (Later, this pulsation game could be developed, making it a pitch game, too. ♩ ♩ ♩ ♩ played in Treble for nails in the wall. ♩ ♩ ♩ ♩ in Bass for nails in the floor. Change from one pitch to another.)

(iii) Play a nursery air on the piano, pipe, or recorder for free rhythmic response. (If it is not possible to provide such variety, sing the tune and tap the rhythm lightly on a tambourine.) Children dance freely to it. French nursery air, *Il était une bergère.*

(iv) Sit in a ring and sing *Yankee doodle* played at the beginning of the lesson. The children should tap the running rhythm quietly on the floor while they sing. Take care not to pitch the song too low; little children should not sing below D.

For Fives to Sevens

EARLY ACTIVITIES (time 20 minutes):

(i) The children are given two contrasting tunes for rhythmic response: *Paul's steeple* (running); *A hunting we will go* (galloping).

(ii) Set an easy rhythm-pattern on drum or tambourine and teach by rote: ♫ ♫ ♩ ♩. Children clap it back and realize it through movement by running and walking to it. (In percussion band work they can play it on their instruments.) Improvise on the pattern; melodic improvisation is quite effective if the rhythm is tapped on a tambourine.

(iii) All sing *Little Jack Horner.* Then divide the class into two groups. One group claps the pulse of the tune to the teacher's piano accompaniment. The second group shows the tune's phrase-plan through movement. During the first phrase they skip off to market to buy plums for the pie, arriving there at the first cadence point.

During the balancing phrase they skip home again putting the plums carefully down on the kitchen table on the final chord. (In the percussion band period, easy two-phrase tunes will be played.)

(iv) Teacher sings *Here's a Squirrel* (from *Playing with Sounds*, Elizabeth Barnard). She repeats it, moving her hands up and down to show the rise and fall of the melody. The children join in, too, and then try to sing it with their eyes shut. The teacher can check the results.

MORE ADVANCED ACTIVITIES (time 30 minutes):

(i) All skip freely to *The Miller of Dee*, utilizing all the floor space. Repeat tune. Children sit down quietly when the music stops. Play the tune again and ask them to clap at the cadences or 'stations' as they are sometimes called. Pause slightly on the cadences in order to help the children. All skip to the tune again, stopping at each phrase-end.

(ii) Play a note-value game using ♩, ♫ and 𝅗𝅥. *Snowballs* (from *Rhythmic Training*, Marion Anderson.)

(iii) Write up easy patterns on the blackboard, using ♩, ♫ and 𝅗𝅥. We can use ♩ ♩ 𝅗𝅥, ♩ ♫ 𝅗𝅥 and ♫ ♫ 𝅗𝅥 all clearly written one under the other. Children clap the patterns as they are pointed to, saying the rhythm names at the same time. (Use same patterns for band work.)

(iv) Accentuation game for realization of 4/4 time. Pretend to drive horses, holding imaginary reins in left hand and cracking a whip high overhead on accented beat of every bar. Improvise or use a drum stressing the accent well. Then write up:

The children clap it back, stressing the accented beats, and finally march to it, pretending to clash cymbals on the accented beats.

(v) The teacher sings *The bugle calls us out to play* (from *Playing with Sounds*). Children join in. All make sol-fa hand-signs as the song is sung again.

The tune is made up of *d. m. s. d'*. and can be used as an ear-test. The teacher plays any of these notes, the children singing the correct sol-fa name back.

The recommended text-books in the Bibliography will help the teacher to draw up her own programme. It is important to work all the activities concurrently, so that each illuminates the others.

Marion Anderson.

APPENDICES

I. INTELLIGENCE AND INTELLIGENCE TESTING

THE wide individual differences in intelligence among children are early apparent in Nursery and Infant groups, for example, as one watches the children engaging in free construction activities. It is necessary to appreciate that in a large *unselected* group of children 50 to 60 per cent are average in intelligence, their mental age corresponding with their chronological age. Approximately 21 to 24 per cent are above and 21 to 24 per cent are below the average. Tests have been devised which enable us to make a reasonably accurate assessment of the child's mental age.

The most commonly used term of measurement is the INTELLIGENCE QUOTIENT which gives us in the form of a percentage the ratio or relationship between the mental age and the chronological age of the individual tested.

Thus a child of 7 with a mental age of 7 has an I.Q. of 100 found by the formula:

$$\frac{\text{Mental Age}}{\text{Chronological Age}} \times \frac{100}{1} = \frac{7}{7} \times \frac{100}{1} = 100 \text{ I.Q.}$$

A child of 7 with a mental age of 5 years 9 months has an I.Q. of 82:

$$\frac{\text{Mental Age}}{\text{Chronological Age}} \times \frac{100}{1} = \frac{5\cdot75}{7} \times \frac{100}{1} = 82 \text{ I.Q.}$$

To ensure accuracy the mental age must be assessed by the careful use of a standardized test. For testing young children an individual test must be used, such as the 1937 Terman–Merrill scale or Cattell's Dartington Scale O. For making serious decisions, *e.g.* certification of a child as M.D., the tests should be administered by a trained and skilled tester, either doctor or psychologist. For ordinary school purposes, however, teachers who have been trained in testing may efficiently assess the mental age of their pupils by use of tests such as the above. Training courses in the study of intelligence and its measurement are given regularly by the National Association for Mental Health (39 Queen Anne Street, London, S.W.1).

The whole purpose of knowing the relationship between the child's mental age and his chronological age is that we may be able to cater for him accordingly, especially when helping him to acquire knowledge of the tool subjects. Too often levels of performance are expected from children who by reason of their low mental age are incapable of reaching these standards. But there is always the danger that in the hands of unskilled testers results may be erroneous or false interpretations may be made. For this reason, children who are found to be exceptionally high or exceptionally low in intelligence should be re-tested by a specialist at the earliest opportunity. The services of the school educational psychologist or of the local child guidance clinic may be sought in cases presenting special problems.

Attainment Tests

In the case of children at the top Infant class stage who are ready to pass into the Junior department, attainment tests in reading and number may be given and the results interpreted in the light of their mental age (without knowledge of his mental age the child's arithmetic and reading age does not tell us much). It is important to remember that intellectual ability, or the lack of it, is by no means the sole factor in determining the child's school progress or his retardation. The attainment test measures the child's ability in a specific school subject in relation to the attainment of normal children of the same age. There are a number of such tests on the market (see list below), but there is an urgent need for further research and standardization of a large number of reading and number tests suitable for children at the top Infant and lower Junior stages.

INTELLIGENCE TESTS

1937 *Terman–Merrill Revision on the Binet Scale*	(Harrap)
Cattell's Dartington Scale O (ages 4 to 8 years)	(Harrap)

ATTAINMENT TESTS

SCHONELL, F.	*Graded Vocabulary Test*	(Oliver & Boyd)
SCHONELL, F.	*Simple Prose Reading Test*	(Oliver & Boyd)
SCHONELL, F.	*Diagnostic Arithmetic Test*	(Oliver & Boyd)

(Test 5 gives arithmetic age for simple rules.)

An Administration Booklet for the three tests is available.

Dorothea Fleming.

II. KEEPING RECORDS

In planning an environment which will cater for children's all-round growth it is most necessary that we should keep careful records of all aspects of development throughout each child's school career. Record-keeping has always been a characteristic feature of Nursery Schools, and for the full realization of the

Education Act, 1944, it becomes vital that every school department should adopt a scientific attitude to systematic study of the child's growth and progress. There is no reason why keeping records should prove difficult to any teacher, even when they have not previously been kept. There are various types of records and they serve a number of purposes. The main record-card should give a concise but comprehensive picture of the child's physical, mental, social, and emotional development from year to year. The information on these cards should aid the teacher in planning the working programme for the benefit of each individual in the group. As the final stage of each school department is reached the record-card should pass on with the child to the head of the next department. It forms a cumulative history of his performance, advancement, and effort at each stage and the information should be used in planning his further activities.

Parents, too, should have regular opportunities of knowing how their children are developing, and this will become a matter of real significance when the time comes to decide to which type of Secondary School the child will proceed. While it is probably undesirable and impracticable to show the record-card to the parent, main items of the record can be passed on by the head.

Too often, progress is thought of only in terms of knowledge acquired, whereas development of new interests, growth of independence, self-control, reliability, inventiveness, ability to persist and concentrate are qualities too often overlooked.

Many Education Authorities are planning their own record-cards to be used by all schools in their area ; there is much to be said for this plan, as it makes for continuity and will facilitate the transfer of the child from one school to another as the need arises.

While space should be provided for verbal comments where necessary, the aim throughout should be for simplicity in recording. Recent research has shown that rating scales, preferably the five-point scale, are very simple to understand and in most cases the information thus given is adequate. Thus for any quality or subject the child may be rated a, b, c, d, or e. Average would be designated by ' c,' above average by ' b,' very much above average by ' a.' Similarly ' d ' stands for below average, and ' e,' very much below average.

Ratings in the case of a particular child would refer to his placing in relation to other children in his group or of his own age level. A brief verbal description of the rating term might be of use in instructions at the head of the card.

In the case of reading, etc. :

a	b	c	d	e
very much above average	above average	average	below average	very much below average

In the case of persistence and similar qualities:

a	b	c	d	e
very high	high	average	low	very low

It is important to note that a child who was rated 'd' or 'e' for performance in most school subjects, like reading or number, might yet be marked 'a' for effort, showing that he does try to do well to the best of his ability, and that reasons other than lack of effort must be sought to explain his poor performance.

Teachers' Records

In addition to the main record-card, class teachers will no doubt want to keep their own record-books where they may record in greater detail each child's attitudes, progress and accomplishments of specific work units and his development from day to day and week to week. Some teachers may wish to keep a page for each subject with the children's names down the side and appropriate ratings and comments opposite. Others may prefer to devote one or two pages to each child and record accordingly. These more detailed records will undoubtedly be of assistance in making final decisions or literal ratings to be used on the main record-card.

Classroom Records and Charts

In a different category come the personal records of the children which help each child to appreciate his own rate of progress and which aim at spurring individuals to further effort. These may be large wall-charts bearing all the children's names, with records, for example, of 'Books We have read this Term' done in attractive pictorial set-out and neatly lettered. Again, the names of children who have satisfactorily accomplished various steps in arithmetic may be indicated by coloured cut-out designs, the children mounting their own. While charts of this type are used by many teachers who will testify to their value, there are strong psychological reasons why they should be discontinued and the individual type of record substituted where each child's efforts are pitted against his own previous efforts instead of against those of other children in the class. In any class, however carefully graded or selected, children do vary one from another in intelligence and in specific ability. While it may dubiously be urged that the majority revel in the zest of competition, there will always be the small group of more sensitive children who are seriously penalized by such competition, who would thrive in personality development, as well as in the acquirement of knowledge, if the main incentive was that of *Self-Competition*. For the superior child, too, the arguments are all in favour of self-competition. Most attractive and colourful individual cards can be prepared (older children will design their own) and children will delight in seeing their progress from week to week. In the case of the tool subjects, such as reading and number, if we are to make practical application of our knowledge of individual differences in intelligence, in rates of progress and in traits such as persistence, memory, concentration and the like, there can be no question of which is the most desirable type of classroom record from the psychological standpoint. Apart from verbal comments relating to ability, effort, interest, etc., in the teacher's own record-book, it seems undesirable to rate the children for drawing, handwork and other creative work.

It should finally be noted with emphasis that the whole modern approach is towards group and community effort in centre of interest activities and projective work (apart from the necessary drill work in the tool subjects which must always be individual), and this surely sounds the death knell for individual competition where the odds are so uneven.

Dorothea Fleming.

III. BACKWARDNESS

It seems appropriate to include here a brief note on the psychological treatment of backwardness.

Basic is the recognition that backwardness may be due to poor innate mental endowment, or to other causes of a removable type, *e.g.* bad teaching, poor health, long absences from school, emotional difficulties, unfortunate home background, etc. The former group of children we term *dull* and they fall in the I.Q. range 70–85. The latter group may have I.Q.'s of 90 and upwards, yet they are backward in school work. In the case of dull children, we must be prepared to accept them as such, and with patient interest attempt to help them to reach the full height of their limited capacity. In the case of retarded children, where backwardness is due to causes other than dullness, we must seek first to discover the cause, if possible to remove it, and then proceed with remedial treatment and coaching.

In the Nursery School the backward child is happily accepted as is any other member of the Nursery community. He does not stand out from his fellows in obvious and hurtful ways. True, he is slower, he is less capable of concentration, can attend for only short periods, shows less enterprise and initiative, has a poor memory, and in general his all-round development probably proceeds more slowly. But he is allowed to go at his own pace and receives due credit and encouragement for every effort he makes.

It has been noted that opportunity for effort and achievement are basic needs of the child, but too often, shortly after he enters the Infant School, the backward child finds that, however much effort he puts into the daily activities, he is not able to taste the joy of success and achievement, and by the time he reaches the top of the Infant School he has already begun to regard himself as a failure. This attitude is detrimental to future learning. It produces feelings of anxiety and insecurity and tends to make the child lose his self-respect, so that in addition to being backward in acquiring knowledge, emotional problems may begin to develop as the child attempts to compensate for his own felt inadequacies.

Having ascertained the cause, the first step in the remedial treatment of backwardness is to build up the child's self-respect and to try to encourage a willing readiness to learn. Often it takes considerable patience and time to bring about this change in emotional attitude, especially if after a long period of failure the child has already built up an antipathy to learning.

It is difficult to offer general rules for working with backward children, as each child in this group requires special individual consideration and guidance. The above suggestions are, however, basic, and should determine the teacher's attitude in all remedial work.

In recent years a number of schools have instituted a special class for backward children at the top of the Infant School. The maximum number in such a class should not exceed twenty, and the teacher in charge of it should be chosen for her experience and, perhaps more important, for her interest in this special type of work. Great care should be exercised in the matter of attaching a ' label ' to such a class ; it is perhaps wise that it should be known as the class of the teacher in charge, *e.g.* ' Miss Brown's class.' Work should proceed at a slow pace in line with the children's needs and abilities, and there should be adequate periods for free play and informal activities in the daily programme. On proceeding to the Junior School it is imperative that detailed advice relating to each child's needs, stage, and difficulties, be passed on to the new headmistress and class teacher, if all the ground gained is not to be irrevocably lost.

These sections are intended simply as an outline introduction to some aspects of the very wide subject of child psychology. It is recommended that all teachers should make full use of the many new books available on the subject. The more the teacher knows of the children she teaches, the more does she add to her efficiency, and the daily round takes on a new significance.

It may be added that every well-informed teacher is a potential research worker in a field which has as yet acres unexplored. The first practical step in taking part in such work is to join a local branch of one of the recognized educational associations, *e.g.* The Nursery School Association, the National Froebel Foundation, or the New Education Fellowship.

Dorothea Fleming.

IV. PARENT-TEACHER CO-OPERATION

There is a saying that the teacher who walks to school teaches more than the teacher who rides. This is a vivid way of suggesting that a teacher needs to know more about her children than she can find out in the classroom. Knowing and understanding our children is more important than knowing and understanding the subjects we teach, especially with younger children.

A good way of getting to know the children better is to get to know the parents, to know their homes and the games they play, the shopping and holiday expeditions they make when they are not at school. This background knowledge helps both in behaviour problems and in understanding and supplementing the children's activities. The boy who is always demanding attention may turn out to be an orphan living with grandparents who show no affection. The unhappy looking child who seems so backward may be suffering from continual comparison with a brighter brother or sister. The cheery, confident boy, a leader in the class, will probably come from a happy home where the mother is longing to know what she can do to help the school in its work. These are actual examples from a single class, every one of which will be treated in a more suitable way by an understanding teacher than would have been possible without knowledge of the home environment.

It is hard work visiting all the homes, though the teacher who does so will never regret finding time for it. The chapter on ' Home and School ' in the Ministry of Education's Report, *School and Life*, recommends that the staff should be increased to allow for further co-operation with the parents. Some schools make the most of medical inspections, open days, end-of-term plays, and other occasions when the parents come to the school, but a well-run parent-teacher association is a very valuable aid to parent-teacher co-operation.

These bodies serve a number of different ends and vary enormously in what they do. From the teacher's point of view the most effective are those which provide opportunities for parents and teachers to meet. A talk in the school hall on teaching methods, for instance, may be followed by a visit to the different classrooms where the parents may see activities in progress.

Similarly, a talk on behaviour problems may be followed by small group discussions over a cup of tea, in place of the usual abrupt departure after a formal lecture. In each case the emphasis is laid on the opportunity for parents and teachers to meet. In schools where the parents are less keen, and there is much variation in this respect, a different approach must be made. Performances by the children are a great attraction (though not late at night !) and in some schools every meeting is partly a social. If approached the right way, parents become so keen that they are willing to do all in their power to help the teacher.

A good Parent-Teacher Association will not merely help the teachers and increase the parents' loyalty to the school, but it will provide opportunities for the parents to help each other in learning to bring up their children. Domestic science omits the most important side of home life, namely, child management, the choosing of books and toys, the creation of an atmosphere of ordered activity based on the wise dictum that busy children are happy children. So Parent-Teacher Associations can be centres of adult education : vocational, in that parents learn how to do their job ; cultural, in that for many parents it is a fresh approach to art and literature.

So far, teachers and parents have been mentioned. Where do the children come in ? In parent-teacher work the children come first and last. They gain in class because their teachers know them better. They gain at home, too, but they gain most of all because they feel that parents and teachers, the two partners in education, are pulling together ; they can talk about school at home and be understood ; they live in one world, not two.

Teachers who are starting associations need to find out which is the most suitable kind for their particular school. It may be best to hold meetings in the afternoon ; sometimes it is necessary to begin with socials until the parents know each other and make a habit of attending. On new housing estates, where there is no community centre, the association may serve a double purpose. There are now local federations of associations springing up in many parts of the country. New associations are well advised to write for help to those who have already found what great opportunities open up to those who undertake this work.

A. N. Gillett.

V. HANDWORK ACTIVITIES AND WASTE MATERIALS

Some years ago the Ministry of Education issued a report on Infant and Nursery Schools containing this statement : " Manual and aesthetic development are better secured when the child is left to make what he likes, how he likes, and within reason, when he likes, than by any set lessons."

To pursue this policy of activity in an Infant School needs a much wider selection of play material than was used in the old handwork periods. The shortage of equipment during the last war led teachers to explore sources of waste, and parents and shopkeepers are always willing to help.

The following description of what the staff in a large school, situated on a city housing estate, collected for use in free activity periods is rich in suggestion.

Improvised Outdoor Equipment for Nurseries

Old motor tyres, grape-barrels, apple-boxes, large tin jam containers, orange-boxes, logs, and old planks; tents made from cotton parachutes, and hammocks from small army tarpaulins. A couple of light forms used in air-raid trenches made a bus and a lorry, with boxes for seats, and tyres for wheels. An old metal drip tray from under a motor car was fixed on a light wooden frame and made into a sand and water-play centre. It was raised a foot from the ground and fixed on castors. Rubber tubing, brightly painted tins, funnels, bottles, corks, and wooden toys, gave great joy to young children.

After the war, sand-bags were bought very cheaply. Two bags stitched together and bound with a bright braid made a mat for floor play. Others were used to make a wigwam, on which the children painted Indian scenes. The same source produced clothes for the Red Indians. These were decorated with waste snippings of felt bordered with dyed parachute braid. Sacks of bricks from the waste wood of a heel factory gave lots of building material. Chimneys and towers were made from the cardboard spools given by a hosiery warehouse. Small pieces of brightly coloured woven fabric from the same factory supplied the children with material for their dolls. The fluffy woollen sweepings from the machines were used for stuffing dolls and animals. Black-out felt in neutral shades made elephants, cats, dogs, teddy bears, monkeys, and giraffes. A box with a movable roof provided a Noah's ark for the animals. Skewers, bobbins and clothes pegs made the people of the ark.

All children love shops. An apple-box was sand-papered and painted green. Old splints from air-raid equipment were used for the shelves. Fruit and vegetables were modelled from papier mâché. The scales were made from small sandwich tins and inch strip wood. 1-lb., ½-lb. and ¼-lb. weights were made from finely woven bags filled with sand. Lengths of white tape, marked off in inches, were used for measuring. A toy telephone, made from two tin lids and a length of cord, was a great asset to the shopkeeper. Old linoleum was cut into pieces 24 in. × 12 in., and the plain side was surfaced with ripolin paint and used for drawing. Black-out material was made into hats for postman, porter, and bus conductor. Outfits for baker, nurse, and doctor came from cotton and linen waste. Cheese boxes were used for the doctor's case and a Red Cross supply box. His stethoscope was a piece of rubber tubing. The 'dispensary' of the 'hospital' was stocked with insulin bottles filled with coloured water. Swan matchboxes were used to make the medicine trolley and the patients' bed-trays. The beds were made from inch strip wood and small lengths of chair webbing. The rag-bag furnished material for mattresses, sheets, pillows, blankets, and bed-covers. Pipe-cleaners were used to make the nurses who were dressed in grey with white aprons. Coarse seed-bags made a suit for the ambulance attendant.

A sack of waste wood from a picture frame works started a centre of interest in a street scene. With the aid of small cartons and an old broom handle, the children made Belisha beacons, a pillar-box, lamp-posts, houses, shops, church, school, and various street vehicles.

N. Clarke.

BIBLIOGRAPHY

Some Books of Reference for the Teacher

General

Chesters, Gwen — *The Mothering of Young Children* (Faber)
Buhler, Charlotte — *From Birth to Maturity* (Kegan Paul)
Watts, A. F. — *The Language and Mental Development of Children* (Harrap)
Isaacs, Susan — *Intellectual Growth in Young Children* (Routledge)
Social Development in Young Children (Routledge)
De Lissa, Lillian — *Life in the Nursery School* (Longmans)
*Boyce, E. R. — *Play in the Infants' School* (Methuen)
Infant School Activities (Nesbit)
Gardner, D. E. M. — *Testing Results in the Infant School* (Methuen)
Gesell, Arnold — *The First Five Years of Life* (Methuen)
Gesell, A. and Ilg, F. L. — *The Child From Five to Ten* (Hamish Hamilton)
Hollamby, Lilian — *The Young Child Living and Learning* (Longmans)
Mellor, Edna — *Education through Experience in the Infant School Years* (Blackwell)
Bowley, Agatha — *The Natural Development of the Child* (E. & S. Livingstone)
Griffiths, Ruth — *Imagination in Early Childhood* (Routledge)
Primary Education (H.M.S.O.)
Wheeler, O., Phillips, W., and Spillane, J. P. — *Mental Health and Education* (Univ. of London Press)
Bowlby, John — *Child Care and the Growth of Love* (Pelican)

Reading

Fleming, C. M. — *Individual Reading in the Primary School* (Harrap)
Harris, A. J. — *How to Increase Reading Ability* (Longmans)
Harrison, M. L. — *Reading Readiness* (Houghton Mifflin)
Schonell, F. J. — *The Psychology of the Teaching of Reading* (Oliver & Boyd)
Vernon, A. D. — *Experimental Study of Reading* (Cambridge Univ. Press)
Morris, J. — *Reading in the Primary School* (Newnes)
Gagg, J. C. and M. F. — *Teaching Children to Read* (Newnes)
Downing, John — *The Initial Teaching Alphabet Explained and Illustrated* (Cassell)

Arithmetic

Brideoake, E., and Groves, I. D. — *Arithmetic in Action* (Univ. of London Press)
Monteith, A. — *Counting and All That* (Harrap)
Mott, E. M. — *First Steps in Practical Number Work* (Evans)
Stern, C. — *Children Discover Arithmetic* (Harrap)

CHAMBERS, C. E. *The Cuisenaire-Gattegno Method of Teaching Mathematics* (Educational Explorers, Reading)
GAGG, J. C. *Beginning the Three R's* (Evans)
CHURCHILL, E. M. *Counting and Measuring* (Routledge)
DIENES, Z. P. *Building Up Mathematics* (Hutchinson Educational)

Religious Education

CASTLE, E. B. *Moral Education in Christian Times* (Allen & Unwin)
HOYLAND, G. *The Great Outlaw* (S.C.M. Press)
MATTHEWS, BASIL *A Life of Jesus* (Oxford Univ. Press)
MONTEFIORE, C. G. *The Bible for Home Reading* (Macmillan)
HASTINGS, J. *Dictionary of the Bible* (Clark)
STUDENT CHRISTIAN MOVEMENT *The Teacher's Commentary* (S.C.M. Press)
MCCREA, M. *Bible Stories Retold* (Evans)
New Testament Stories (Evans)
BIRD *A Hundred Bible Stories* (Nelson)
Jesus of Nazareth Stories (Nelson)

For Assembly

BREMNER, V. *Growing Up* (Muller)
OXFORD UNIV. PRESS *Songs of Praise for Little Children* (Oxford Univ. Press)
EVANS *The School Hymn Book* (Evans)
RUSSELL, DR. LESLIE (ed.) *Kingsway Carol Book* (Evans)

Stories

STUDENT CHRISTIAN MOVEMENT *The Little Bible Books* (S.C.M. Press)

Pictures

SOCIETY FOR THE PROPAGATION OF THE GOSPEL, 15 Tufton Street, London, S.W.1.
CHILDREN'S SPECIAL SERVICE MISSION, 5 Wigmore Street, London, W.1.
NATIONAL SOCIETY OF RELIGIOUS EDUCATION, 69 Great Peter Street, London, S.W.1.

Nature Study

JEFFERIES, RICHARD *Field and Hedgerow* (Longmans)
PITT, FRANCES *Waterside Creatures* (Allen & Unwin)
Woodland Creatures (Allen & Unwin)
Wild Creatures of Garden and Hedgerow (Allen & Unwin)
MAETERLINCK, M. *Life of the Bee* (Allen & Unwin)
TEALE, EDWIN MAY *The Golden Throng* (Hale)
HODGE, A. E. *Vivarium and Aquarium Keeping for Amateurs* (Witherby)
BATEMAN, G. C. *Fresh Water Aquaria* (Link)
FURNEAUX, W. S. *Life in Ponds and Streams* (Longmans)

Speech Training

SANSOM, CLIVE *Speech Rhymes. Introductory Book* (Blackie)

KING, HILDA	*Speech Training for Infants*	(Nelson)
SWANN, MONA	*Playway of Speech Training*	(Oxford Univ. Press)
HAIG-BROWN, H., and WALTHOW, Z.	*Speech Training Rhymes and Jingles*	(Oxford Univ. Press)
BENNETT, RODNEY	*First Steps in Speech Training*	(Evans)
GULLAN and GURREY	*Poetry Speaking for Children. Part I*	(Methuen)
COLLINS, FREDA	*Acting Games and How To Play Them*	(Pearson)
GULLAN, M.	*Speech Training in the School*	(Evans)

Art

ENG, HELGA	*Psychology of Children's Drawings*	(Kegan Paul)
VIOLA, W.	*Child Art*	(Univ. of London Press)
TOMLINSON, H. R.	*Children as Artists*	(King Penguin)
	Picture Making by Children	(Studio Pbns.)
GIBBS, EVELYN	*Teaching of Art in Schools*	(Williams & Norgate)
LOWENFELD, VIKTOR	*The Nature of Creative Activity*	(Kegan Paul)
BLAND, DOREEN (ed.)	*Songs and Pictures of a Child*	(Williams & Norgate)
MINISTRY OF EDUC.	*Art Education*	(H.M.S.O.)

Handwork

NURSERY SCHOOL ASSOCIATION	*Repairing Toys*	
	Wheels for Toys	
	Toys from Tins	

Physical Training

Books

BILBOROUGH, A. and JONES, P.	*Physical Education in the Primary School*	(Univ. of London Press)
	Moving and Growing	(H.M.S.O.)
SHARPE, J.	*P.E. Teacher's Handbook for Infant Schools*	(Evans)

Apparatus

Essex Agility Apparatus
Oldham Agility Apparatus
Manchester Agility Apparatus
} *Agility Apparatus for Primary Schools* (Evans)

Southampton Agility Apparatus
Somerset Agility Apparatus
Bristol Climbing Apparatus
} *Simple Climbing Apparatus* (Obtainable from Messrs. Tretman & Lowther Ltd., 20–21 Broad Quay, Bristol, 1)

Stories

4- and 5-Year-Olds

POTTER, BEATRIX	*Stories*	(Warne)
HALE, K.	*Orlando Books*	(Transatlantic Arts)
ROSS, DIANA	*The Story of Louisa*	(Transatlantic Arts)
	The Story of the Little Red Engine	(Faber)
	Whoo, Whoo, the Wind Blew	(Faber)
JOHNSTON, ARNRID	*Pigwiggen*	(Transatlantic Arts)
UTTLEY, ALISON	*Animal Stories*	(Faber)
BANNERMAN, HELEN	*Sambo and the Twins*	(Nisbet)
ENGLEFIELD, CICELY	*Bert the Sparrow*	(Muller)
GRAMATKY, HARDIE	*Little Toot*	(Dent)
SHILLABEER, MARY	*At First*	(Museum Press)

6- *and 7-Year-Olds*

Collections of Fairy Tales

De la Mare, Walter	*Told Again*	(Blackwell)
Jacobs, Joseph	*English Fairy Tales*	(Muller)
Steel, Flora	*English Fairy Tales*	(Macmillan)
Ross, Diana	*Nursery Tales*	(Faber)
Lang, Andrew	*Fairy Tale Books*	(Longmans)
Andersen, Hans	*Fairy Tales*	
Grimm, Jacob and W. K.	*Fairy Tales*	

Other Collections

Harris, Joel Chandler	*Uncle Remus*	(Routledge)
Kipling, Rudyard	*Just-So-Stories*	(Macmillan)
Collodi, Carlo	*Adventures of Pinocchio*	(Dent)
Petersham, Maud and Miska	*Story Book of Real Things*	(Dent)
Carrick, Valerie	*Picture Tales from the Russian.* 4 parts	(Blackwell)
Bryant, S. C.	*Stories to Tell to Children*	(Harrap)
	How to Tell Stories to Children	(Harrap)
Milne, A. A.	*Winnie the Pooh*	(Methuen)
	The House at Pooh Corner	(Methuen)
Clark, Elizabeth	*Stories to Tell and How to Tell Them*	(Univ. of London Press)
Guterman, Robert	*Russian Fairy Tales*	

Other Stories

Ardizzone (ed.)	*Nicholas and the Fast Moving Diesel*	(Eyre & Spottiswoode)
	Little Tim and the Brave Sea Captain	(Oxford Univ. Press)
Denes, G.	*John and Jennifer* Books	(Nelson)
Lida (trans. by Rose Fyleman)	*Frou*	(Allen & Unwin)
	Scaf	(Allen & Unwin)
	Cuckoo	(Allen & Unwin)
Tolstoy	*Russian Tales for Children*	(Routledge)
Barr, Enid	*From Story into Drama*	(Heinemann Educational Books)

Verse

6- *and 7-Year-Olds*

Williams, Michael (ed.)	*Modern Verse for Little Children*	(Oxford Univ. Press)
Arr. by The English Section of the Assoc. of Training Colleges	*Collected Poems.* (Series I)	(Methuen)
De la Mare, Walter (Introduction by)	*Nursery Rhymes for Certain Times*	(Faber)
De la Mare, Walter	*Collected Rhymes and Verses*	(Constable)
	Peacock Pie	(Constable)
Boyce and Bartlett	*Number Rhymes and Finger Plays*	(Pitman)

EVERYMAN'S LIBRARY	*Mother Goose's Book of Nursery Rhymes and Songs*	(Dent)
GULLAN and GURREY	*Poetry Speaking for Children. Part I*	(Methuen)
MILNE, A. A.	*When We Were Very Young*	(Methuen)
	Now We are Six	(Methuen)
FYLEMAN, ROSE	*Widdy-Widdy-Wurky*	(Blackwell)
FARJEON, ELEANOR	*Nursery Rhymes of London Town*	(Oxford Univ. Press)

Poems from Collections by :

John Masefield	Edith Sitwell	R. Bridges	Christina Rossetti
Humbert Wolfe	W. H. Davies	R. L. Stevenson	etc.

Music

For Movement

POULSSON, EMILE	*Finger Plays*	(Curwen)
ELLIOTT, ANN	*Fingers and Thumbs*	(Stainer & Bell)
BARNARD, ELIZABETH	*Nursery School Music Activities*	(Curwen)
ANDERSON, MARION	*Playtime Tunes.* Bks. I and II	(Cramer)
MACBAIN, J. MURRAY	*Movement and Song for the Little Ones*	(Evans)
	Movement and Song for the Fives to Sevens	(Evans)
HOLT, GWENDOLINE	*Movement and Song for Infant Classes*	(Boosey)
ADAIR, YVONNE	*Rhythmic Dances and Singing Games*	(Boosey)
SHAW, MARTIN	*Left ! Right !* (Marches)	(Cramer)
ANDERSON, MARION	*Twice Twelve.* (Pulse response)	(Cramer)
	Rhythmic Games for Infants	(Cramer)
	Rhythmic Training	(Cramer)
	Note-value Exercises	(Cramer)
	Bounce and Catch. (Easy ball games)	(Cramer)
	Musical Ball Games	(Cramer)
	The Rhythmic Road. (Guide-book to the above)	(Cramer)
	Hop, Skip and Jump	(Novello)
	German Folk Tunes	(Novello)
	Ratapataplan. (French Nursery Airs)	(Augener)
	Ten Dutch Nursery Rhymes	(Augener)
	Carolare. (Folk Carols)	(Oxford Univ. Press)
	Ten Tunes from the Appalachian Mountains. (Arr. for movement)	(Leonard, Gould & Bolttler)

For Pipes or Recorders (useful for movement)

ANDERSON, MARION	*Nursery Rhymes for Pipers*	(Cramer)
	National Airs for Pipers	(Cramer)
JAMES, MARGARET	*Country Dance Tunes*	(Novello)

Songs (can also be used for movement)

DEARMER, PERCY, and SHAW, MARTIN	*Songtime*	(Curwen)
MOFFAT, ALFRED	*Fifty Traditional Scottish Nursery Rhymes*	(Augener)
BARNARD, ELIZABETH	*New Nursery Jingles*	(Curwen)
	Echo and Refrain Songs	(Stainer & Bell)
ELLIOTT, ANN	*Singing Babies*	(Stainer & Bell)

Houghton, Winifred	*Thirty Songs for the Nursery School*	(Boosey)
Anderson, Marion	*Nursery Songs.* 2 Sets	(Boosey)
	All About Arabella. (With percussion)	(Cramer)
De Rusette, Louie E.	*Seven Day Songs*	(Novello)
Driver, Ann	*Animal Songs for Young Children*	(Oxford Univ. Press)
Driver, Ann (words by Trevor Blakemore)	*New Songs for Old*	(Oxford Univ. Press)
Farjeon, Eleanor	*Nursery Rhymes of London Town*	(Oxford Univ. Press)
Whittaker, W., Wiseman, H., and Wishart, J.	*Sixty Songs for Little Children.* (Bks. I, II and III)	(Oxford Univ. Press)
Tegner, Alice	*Sing-Song from Sweden.* Books I and II	(Augener)

For the Percussion Band

Blocksidge, Kathleen	*Clipperty Clop.* (With percussion)	(Cramer)
Adair, Yvonne	*Jingle Songs.* (Pulse)	(Boosey)
	Ducks and Drakes	(Boosey)
	Rote Training in the Percussion Band	(Boosey)
	A Little Anthology of Folk Tunes	(Boosey)
	Folk Tunes from All Nations. Series I (Sets I, II, III, IV)	(Boosey)
Greenfield, Marjorie	*Sixteen Percussion Songs for Little Children*	(J. Williams)
	Folk Rhymes and Rhythms	(Curwen)
Blocksidge, Kathleen	*Children's Percussion Band Book*	(Cramer)
	Animals	(Cramer)
Bavin, C.	*Percussion Band from A to Z*	(Evans)

Teachers' Books

Nelson's Music Practice	*Infants' Teachers' Book*	(Nelson)
Adair, Yvonne	*Music Through the Percussion Band*	(Boosey)
Driver, Ann	*Music and Movement*	(Oxford Univ. Press)
Pfaff, P.	*Music Handbook for Infant Schools*	(Evans)

SOME USEFUL ADDRESSES

UNIVERSITY OF LONDON DEPARTMENT OF CHILD DEVELOPMENT,
University of London Institute of Education,
57 Gordon Square, London, W.C.1.

BIRMINGHAM UNIVERSITY DEPARTMENT OF CHILD DEVELOPMENT,
Edmund Street, Birmingham, 3.

THE NURSERY SCHOOL ASSOCIATION OF GREAT BRITAIN AND NORTHERN IRELAND,
89 Stamford Street, London, S.E.1.

THE NATIONAL FROEBEL FOUNDATION,
2 Manchester Square, London, W.1.

H.M.S.O.,
York House, Kingsway, London, W.C.2.

THE CENTRAL COUNCIL FOR HEALTH EDUCATION,
Tavistock House, Tavistock Square, London, W.C.1.

THE NATIONAL ASSOCIATION FOR MENTAL HEALTH,
39 Queen Anne Street, London, W.1.

THE ENQUIRY BUREAU OF "CHILD EDUCATION,"
Montague House, Russell Square, London, W.C.1.

Answers to enquiries on professional problems will be forwarded if a Bureau Coupon from the magazine and a stamped addressed envelope are included with the enquiry.